AF326625

Dark Seduction 5-in-1

The Complete Guide to Covert Persuasion, Magnetic Charisma, NLP Mind Control, Irresistible Charm and Instant Influence

SEBASTIAN NOCTURNE

TABLE OF CONTENTS

INTRODUCTION

Do you ever watch someone walk into a room and instantly command attention? They get the contract. They secure the commitment. They leave others feeling energized and ready to follow. This ability is not simply a natural gift. It is a practiced skill. It rests on specific, verifiable knowledge of how the human brain works.

What if you could consistently predict the reactions of the people around you? What if you knew exactly what to say to move a choice from "maybe" to "yes"? This book answers those questions with concrete, actionable methods.

We cut through the confusion. We reject vague theory and juvenile tactics. This is an instruction manual for psychological leverage, built entirely on documented science. You will find proof and detailed methods, not just weak philosophy. Studies in behavioral economics confirm our approach. Research in social psychology shows why our tactics work. This structure ensures true value, moving beyond surface-level advice and simplistic generalizations.

This guide works for you, whether you are a man or a woman. Successful influence depends on aligning with how a person processes information. We show you how to shift your approach for a male listener versus a female listener, maintaining maturity and nuance throughout the exchange. The focus remains on psychological alignment, not simple gender typing.

This five-part collection teaches you complete control across every social interaction.

First, **Covert Persuasion** gives you the blueprint for controlling the decision environment. You learn to stage information so people rely on mental shortcuts, known as cognitive biases, which favor your desired outcome. We show you how small requests now create large commitments later.

Second, **Magnetic Charisma** focuses entirely on your silent presence. You will learn to use non-verbal cues to plant perceptions of competence and authority, all below conscious awareness. We detail how controlled, appropriate touch builds rapid trust, as haptics are the first form of communication established in infancy.

Third, we approach Linguistic Influence as a verifiable, practiced skill. We honor the core principles of **Neuro-Linguistic Programming (NLP)** while providing an advanced framework rooted in **cognitive science** and **Behavioral Economics**. This book replaces vague, subjective interpretations with **specific, evidence-based methods**. You will learn validated **framing techniques**, based on the science of how the brain structures choice, that allow you to accurately **predict reactions** and guide any decision from "maybe" to a firm "yes" in real-time.

Fourth, **Irresistible Charm** shows you how to build rapid, deep connections. We show you how strategic self-disclosure creates intimacy, provided the disclosures are frequent and perceived as appropriate. We also examine how shared laughter acts as a powerful social resource, confirming alignment on core values and building group cohesion.

Fifth, **Instant Influence** forces immediate action. This is the art of creating urgency. We show you how to exploit the brain's strong preference for immediate gains over larger future rewards, a concept called Temporal Discounting. You will learn to activate the powerful motivation of loss aversion and scarcity, which compels immediate compliance.

The time for wishing for connection or opportunity is finished. This collection offers specific steps and the psychological context necessary to implement them. It is time to acquire the specific skills that dictate the outcome of any interaction.

BOOK ONE

COVERT PERSUASION:
PSYCHOLOGICAL LEVERAGE

INTRODUCTION

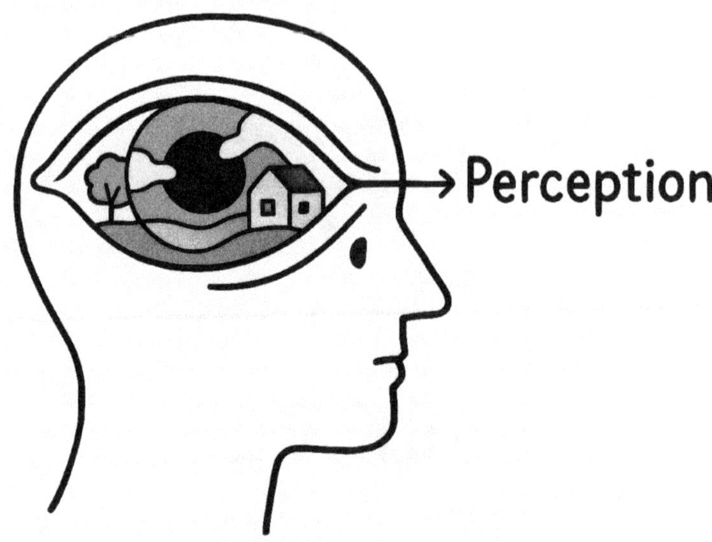

Influence is the act of securing a preferred action without resorting to force. It is not about manipulation that harms others. It is a precise method for guiding people toward a decision that benefits both them and you. This book provides a detailed map of how human beings make choices. It moves past vague theory and emotional guesswork. It relies instead on the documented principles of social psychology and behavioral economics. We seek to understand the levers of the mind, not just the surface of conversation.

The ability to move others rests on one fundamental truth: reality is not objective. Every individual constructs a **subjective reality** based on their perception of information inputs. This personally built reality dictates behavior in the world, not the actual facts of the situation. If you change a person's perception of reality, you change their behavior. Covert persuasion is the intentional structuring of information to manage that subjective reality.

The Predictable Error in Human Judgment

Systematic errors occur continually in human judgment. These errors are known as **cognitive biases**. These biases cause deviations from a rational norm, leading to inaccurate judgments and irrational behavior. For the persuader, these errors are not flaws; they are precise, repeatable openings.

Why do these biases exist? The brain uses shortcuts. These shortcuts, or heuristics, allow for faster decisions. In many situations, speed is more valuable than perfect accuracy. When you meet someone new, you must make a fast social assessment. You use mental shortcuts rather than waiting for years of data collection. This need for quick assessment creates the conditions where biases thrive.

Other biases happen because of human processing limits, a concept known as **bounded rationality**. The brain cannot process everything. When faced with too much data or too little time, the mind defaults to these established cognitive paths. Covert persuasion capitalizes on this limitation. The persuader designs the interaction to overwhelm the target's capacity for slow, rational thought. The target is then forced to use their fast, heuristic system, leading to predictable decision errors.

The goal is to provide claims that require less evidence for acceptance. This happens when the claims confirm the target's existing beliefs or preconceptions. This is the function of **Confirmation Bias**. People naturally seek or interpret information that validates what they already believe. The persuader does not fight existing beliefs. They simply frame the request as a logical confirmation of the target's current values. This significantly distorts perception and makes acceptance feel like a conclusion, not a new choice.

The Six Drivers of Compliance

Covert persuasion employs established psychological principles that act as mental shortcuts for agreement. These are known as the core compliance drivers. They operate across all aspects of social interaction and decision-making. These drivers include Reciprocity, Commitment and Consistency, Social Proof, Liking, Authority, and Scarcity. They are universal mechanisms that allow others to influence our choices.

One of the most potent drivers is **Commitment and Consistency**. People feel internal pressure to align their future actions with their past decisions. Once a person makes a commitment, they naturally want to stay consistent with that choice. For a commitment to genuinely change a person's self-image and future behavior, it must possess three qualities: it must be **active, public, and effortful**.

A commitment must be active, meaning the person performs a distinct action. It must be public, visible to others, which increases the external pressure to maintain the image of consistency. It must be effortful, meaning the person had to overcome a perceived hurdle to complete the action. Fraternities, for example, often use effortful steps to increase commitment to the group.

The persuader's objective is to minimize the appearance of external control. If a person acts under a large reward or strong external pressure, they will not accept inner responsibility for the action. Once the reward or pressure is gone, they will revert to their old way of thinking. The persuader must secure the target's personal responsibility. This is achieved by having the target agree to small, internally justifiable steps first. These small, voluntary efforts create a self-sustaining commitment that originates from the target's own will.

Social Proof is another critical mechanism. When people are unsure about how to act, they look to the actions of others to guide their own behavior. The tendency to see an action as more appropriate because others are doing it is incredibly strong. This principle explains why testimonials, reviews, and popularity metrics are so influential in consumer behavior. People assume that if a lot of others are doing something, they must possess information the target lacks.

The effective persuader controls the group conditions to allow social proof to work maximally. No leader can control every single person at once. But they can influence the most receptive or devoted members. Once a certain, visible portion of the group is convinced, their adoption naturally persuades the rest. In fact, the strength of the social bond can be twice as likely to determine a product purchase as the buyer's preference for the product itself.

Managing Psychological States and Social Judgments

Social activities are often prone to irrational, biased decisions, known as **social biases**. These include social conformity and judgments based on superficial attributes, such as the halo effect. The halo effect causes a general impression to be inferred from a single trait, such as attractiveness or a calm demeanor.

The persuader must understand the role of emotional states, or negative affects. Anxiety and other negative affects play important roles in social judgments and conformity. When a target is anxious, they are more likely to rely on quick, biased assessments. By projecting extreme calm and competence, the persuader reduces the target's need for impulsive social judgment. They also capitalize on the halo effect. The target, experiencing anxiety, seeks stability and guidance from the composed figure. This immediate, positive social judgment facilitates the acceptance of later, substantive proposals.

The concept of Theory of Mind (ToM), the ability to attribute mental states to others, is also mutually associated with social judgments and conformity. A persuader who can accurately gauge the target's cognitive and affective state possesses a clear advantage. The persuader anticipates resistance, emotional instability, or uncertainty. This anticipation allows for pre-emptive framing to ensure the message lands correctly.

The Requirement for Gender-Specific Communication

A single, one-size-fits-all approach to persuasion will fail. Persuasion strategies must account for documented differences in how men and women process persuasive messages. This is not about stereotyping. It is about aligning the message with established psychological tendencies.

The **Elaboration Likelihood Model (ELM)** suggests different processing routes for genders. Women are often more likely to engage in **central route processing**. This means they focus intensely on message content, message quality, and the critical analysis of arguments. They may find detailed product reviews or verifiable data more persuasive. Conversely, men may be more susceptible to **authority influence**. They may find assertive statistical evidence or endorsement by a recognized expert more compelling.

Linguistic resonance greatly enhances message effectiveness. Masculine language, which is direct and assertive, resonates strongly with male audiences. Feminine language, which is collaborative and empathetic, appeals more to female audiences. The successful persuader must master a broad range of communication styles. They must be able to switch between **push energy** (assertive, direct expression) and **pull energy** (collaborative, seeking opinions).

Men often exhibit more assertive, push energy. Women often tend toward seeking collaboration and ideas, using pull energy. Success requires the ability to switch flexibly between these influence styles at the appropriate moment. The persuader must diagnose the conversational environment. A pull strategy is essential for establishing rapport and gathering information. Once rapport is secure, the persuader can strategically switch to a push strategy to drive compliance.

Furthermore, research confirms that men are generally more influential than women. Women are particularly less influential when using dominant forms of communication. Males specifically tend to resist influence attempted by women who employ highly competent or assertive communication styles. This highlights a specific requirement for female persuaders.

Resistance to competent women can be reduced when women intentionally temper their competence with displays of warmth and communality. This strategic requirement is the **communality buffer**. It involves displaying empathy and collaborative language immediately before or during the assertion of a competent position. This softens the delivery and neutralizes the tendency for resistance. We must balance addressing these known processing differences with avoiding harmful or simplistic stereotypes. The goal remains thoughtful, empathetic framing, not caricature.

Exposure to social gender role information also affects persuasion. When the female gender role is made prominent, women demonstrate weaker attitudes and become more susceptible to change. Conversely, when male gender role information is prominent, both men and women process messages more thoughtfully and carefully. The framing of the environment, not just the words, is crucial. A high-stakes, analytical environment (aligned with the male role prime) encourages thoughtful processing in both genders. A collaborative, non-critical environment (aligned with the female role prime) can reduce cognitive processing effort for both genders. The persuader must set the environmental context to align with the desired depth of thought.

The Technical Manual for Influence

This first book is a technical manual for understanding and applying these psychological facts. We avoid mimicking others. We provide specific, verifiable mechanics. Our content is not vague; it provides step-by-step strategy. We focus on true value and the mature exploration of these themes.

We must always remember that persuasion is achieved through structuring the target's subjective reality. It is never about brute-forcing facts or overwhelming with raw data. It is about understanding the brain's predictable path of least resistance. The following chapters detail how to control the environment around a decision, frame arguments to exploit biases, and activate the core psychological drivers that guarantee compliance. We turn influence from an abstract concept into a reliable, repeatable process.

This process starts with precision. It requires the accurate diagnosis of the target's existing biases and psychological state. Only then can the persuader select the appropriate driver, be it commitment, social proof, or authority, to ensure the outcome. The covert persuader is an architect of choice. They guide the target through a series of small, justifiable steps that lead logically to the final, desired agreement. The target believes the final decision originated entirely from their own will and logic. This self-attribution is the ultimate mark of successful covert persuasion.

The next chapters will expand on each of these tools. We begin with a deep exploration of cognitive biases, detailing how to **Frame Reality** so that the target's innate mental shortcuts always point to your proposal. This is where we learn how to make the necessary, complex decisions easy for the target by forcing them to rely on their fast, heuristic-based system. The objective is to make agreement the path of least cognitive resistance. This ensures that the target moves past critical thought and accepts the proposal as an unquestioned reality.

Then we move to **Secure Action** by activating the core compliance drivers. We will detail the exact timing and sequencing required to deploy Reciprocity, Liking, and Authority. You will learn how to engineer effortful public commitments and how to leverage social information to influence non-conforming members. Securing action means ensuring the target feels inner responsibility for the choice, making the change permanent.

We will then learn to **Control Narrative** by staging information for acceptance. This involves using the Contrast Principle effectively. You will learn how to present ambitious requests first, making the actual desired request seem disproportionately small and acceptable. This staging controls the target's perception of value and cost.

Finally, we discuss how to **Map Influence** and **Mitigate Resistance**. Mapping influence requires diagnosing the target's preferred processing route and adapting the communication style accordingly, shifting between push and pull energy or adjusting the reliance on statistical versus empathetic evidence. Mitigating resistance involves learning how to use the communality buffer and ensuring that the proposal confirms, rather than challenges, the target's existing subjective reality. These elements combined create a comprehensive, scientifically grounded strategy for covert persuasion.

CHAPTER 1

FRAME REALITY: DIRECTING CHOICE WITH COGNITIVE BIAS

STEP 1

STEP 2

Every single person you talk to lives inside a reality they have built just for themselves.

Think about it this way: You are not seeing objective facts. You are seeing facts filtered through your own fears, hopes, and shortcuts. This private version of truth, this **subjective reality**, is what actually drives behavior and choices. People act based on their perception of the input, not the input itself. Covert persuasion is not about fighting the facts. It is about restructuring the presentation of facts so they fit perfectly into the target's existing subjective reality.

How do we do this? We use the brain's own predictable errors.

These errors are called **cognitive biases**. A cognitive bias is a systematic pattern where a person's judgment constantly deviates from rational thinking. These patterns often lead to inaccurate judgment, illogical interpretation, and irrational actions. For the person interested in influence, these errors are not flaws. They are consistent, documented patterns that create repeatable access points.

The Speed of Thought: Bounded Rationality

The reason these biases even exist is simple: the brain cannot handle everything. We have a limited capacity for processing information. This is known as **bounded rationality**. The mind must constantly look for ways to cut corners. It sacrifices thoughtful depth for processing speed. This reliance on shortcuts is called using heuristics.

Sometimes, these shortcuts are helpful. A fast decision is often better than a perfectly accurate but delayed one, especially in social or urgent situations. But often, they just lead to mistakes.

The persuader's task is to force the target's brain into this quick-thinking mode. When a subject is overloaded with data, distracted, or simply hurried, the slow, analytical part of the brain steps back. The fast, intuitive system takes over, and that fast system relies heavily on biases. By subtly increasing the mental load or rushing the conversation, you ensure the target defaults to the biased path you set up earlier.

Anchoring: Setting the Value Baseline

The **Anchoring Effect** is one of the most reliable cognitive biases you can use. It describes how much people depend on the very first piece of information they receive when they make a decision about value. Even if that first number is random or irrelevant, it becomes the anchor. That anchor then sets the range for what is considered acceptable or fair for the rest of the conversation.

If you are negotiating a service, you must introduce the highest justified number early. Say you know the final, profitable price is $\$5,000$. Instead of starting there, you should set a confident anchor at $\$8,000$. The initial anchor frames the entire discussion. If the negotiation brings the price down to $\$5,500$, the target feels they successfully moved the value down by $\$2,500$. They feel a sense of winning. If you had started at $\$5,000$, a final agreement at $\$5,500$ would feel like a loss.

The initial number dictates the perceived context. Every subsequent offer is judged relative to that first, high anchor. This makes moderate offers seem immediately more reasonable. You must state the anchor early, with certainty, and with some concrete reference point to make it slick.

The Contrast Principle: Managing Sequential Perception

Humans are terrible at evaluating things in isolation. We constantly exaggerate the difference between two things presented in sequence. This is the **Contrast Principle**. If the second item is quite different from the first, we perceive the difference as even larger than it is.

This principle is constantly used in sales environments. When a man goes into a store to buy a new suit, he will almost always pay more for the accessories, the belt, the tie, the cuff links, if he buys them *after* he buys the expensive suit. Why? Because compared to the thousand-dollar suit, the hundred-dollar tie seems cheap. The expensive purchase set a high reference point.

In persuasion, this means you must use **proposal staging**. You present the largest, most ambitious request first. This is the setup. Then, you follow it immediately with the request you actually want approved. By contrast, the true, desired request seems disproportionately small, acceptable, or easy. This sequencing guides the target's perception of cost and effort, making the desired action feel like minimal resistance.

Confirmation Bias: The Need for Self-Validation

People possess a powerful desire to believe things that match what they already think. This is **Confirmation Bias**. This tendency is psychological armor. It keeps an individual's internal security and worldview intact.

If you try to directly challenge a target's established belief, you activate their strongest defenses. They will resist the new evidence. The smart way to persuade is to frame your request as a logical conclusion or necessary validation of something they already value.

If a business leader values innovation above all else, you do not sell the idea as risky. You frame it as "the one necessary action for a true innovation-focused company." This framing drastically reduces the amount of proof they need to accept the claim. The target perceives the agreement as confirming their existing identity and path, making the choice feel secure and logical instead of risky or novel. This systematic selection of supporting information is what leads to inaccurate judgments.

Social Biases and the Halo Effect

Social interactions are rife with their own type of bias, known as **social biases**. These include things like conformity and making judgments based on superficial attributes.

The **Halo Effect** is the most significant of these. It causes others to infer a general positive impression from one single trait. This trait could be confidence, composure, or physical attractiveness. You control the single trait, and the target grants you all the associated positive qualities, competence, trustworthiness, and honesty.

Research shows that negative affects, such as anxiety, are strongly linked to social judgments and conformity. A target who feels anxious or uncertain is much more likely to seek stability and make a quick, biased social assessment. They look for an authority figure who seems calm and in control.

The effective persuader projects **extreme composure** and **stillness** at all times. This projection capitalizes on the halo effect. The target feels their own anxiety subside in the presence of this composure and is more likely to accept guidance from the calm authority figure. By strictly managing presentation, environment, and demeanor, you dictate the target's initial positive evaluation. This favorable social judgment accelerates trust and makes later proposals easier to accept.

Strategic Deployment of Framing

Covert persuasion requires moving past simply recognizing these biases. It demands deliberate deployment. You must create the environment where the target's own mental shortcuts point them straight to your desired outcome.

1. Diagnosing the Subjective Path: You must first find the target's established values, their constant justifications, and their core assumptions. These are the bricks of their subjective reality. You find them by listening for their habitual language and noting where they consistently choose speed over thoroughness. If they repeatedly talk about "efficiency," you frame your request as "the most efficient path."

2. Increasing Cognitive Demand: To force the brain into the fast, intuitive system, you must subtly increase the cognitive load. This is a delicate process. You can present information in fast succession. You can introduce a minor, easily resolved technical issue. You can give them a simple but necessary mental task to focus on during the setup phase. The objective is to keep the slow, analytical part of the mind occupied, ensuring the key decision relies on the fast, shortcut-based system.

3. Framing Loss Over Gain: While the detailed mechanics of loss aversion are covered later, the concept is essential here. People are driven more strongly by the fear of losing something than by the desire to gain something of equivalent value. When framing a choice, present compliance as **necessary risk mitigation**, preventing a specific, guaranteed loss. Avoid framing it only as a potential benefit. The emotional pressure of avoiding a loss is a much stronger driver for immediate action.

4. Controlling the Processing Context: The social environment contributes to how carefully the target processes your message. Research suggests that when cues associated with the male gender role are prominent, both men and women tend to process persuasive messages more thoughtfully and carefully. Also, when cues associated with the female gender role are prominent, both genders process messages less carefully.

If you need a deeply considered, long-term commitment, you set a context that is analytical, high-stakes, and rational. If you need immediate, non-critical acceptance, you can frame the environment using cues that favor the less critical processing style. The key is setting the context, not just the words, to align with the required depth of thought.

The Architect of Choice

The person skilled in covert persuasion is an architect of choice. They do not rely on brute force or aggressive argument. They quietly build a set of ramps, anchors, and shortcuts that lead the target directly to the desired outcome. The target believes they arrived at the conclusion through their own superior logic. This internal attribution is what makes the decision stick.

We have established how to set the stage by directing the target's perception. The next crucial step is securing their commitment. The following chapter moves from managing perception to actively activating the six core behavioral rules that guarantee human compliance. We will show you how to use these innate drivers, Reciprocity, Commitment, Social Proof, and others, to secure an action that feels like the target's own idea. This combination of framing reality and activating compliance drivers ensures that the path of least resistance is always the path you want them to take.

CHAPTER 2
SECURE ACTION: ACTIVATING CORE HUMAN COMPLIANCE DRIVERS

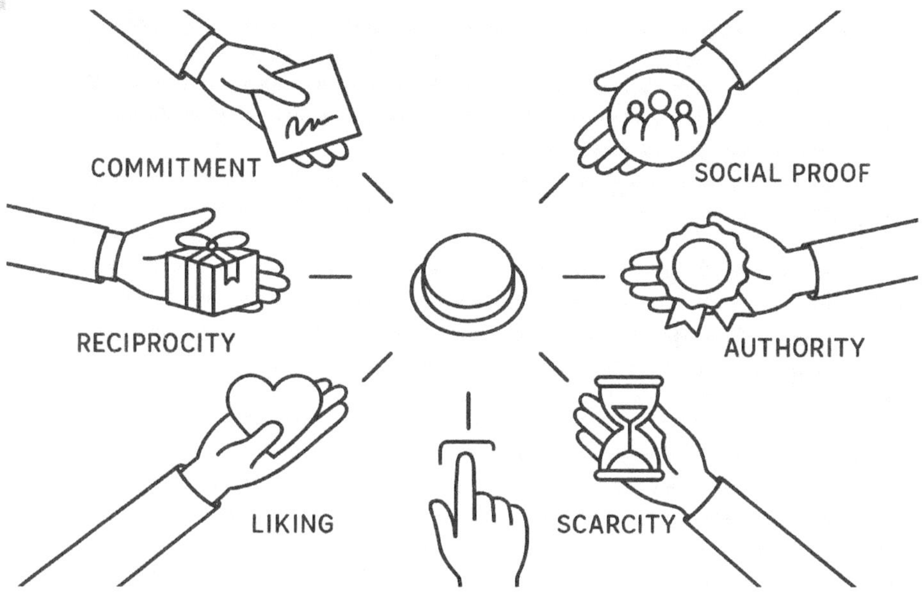

Securing action is the final step of influence. It moves beyond simply setting the stage for a decision. It involves activating the six foundational rules that guide human compliance. These rules function as universal psychological shortcuts. They provide systematic, repeatable mechanisms for increasing agreement. If you understand these drivers, you can guide a person toward a decision they will later believe they chose independently.

This chapter breaks down each driver. We explain how to activate them precisely. This creates a secure, long-term commitment.

1. Commitment and Consistency: The Anchor of Self-Image

People possess a powerful, innate need to appear **consistent** in their behavior. Once a person makes a commitment, they feel immense internal pressure to align their future actions with that initial decision. This desire for consistency simplifies life. It allows us to avoid thinking deeply about every new choice.

The secret to using this driver is forcing the target to accept **inner responsibility** for an action. If you apply too much external pressure, the commitment will not last. A massive reward, or an aggressive demand, makes the target think, "I did this for the money," or "I did this because I had to." Once the external pressure is removed, the target will immediately revert to their old desires or behaviors.

To build lasting commitment, the initial action must possess three key qualities:

It Must Be Active: The commitment requires a physical, distinct act. A mental agreement is weak. A written statement, a signed document, or a public statement is a physical marker. This act ties the decision to the target's sense of self-image.

It Must Be Public: When others witness the commitment, the target feels social pressure. They must maintain an image of consistency for the group. This public accountability reinforces the internal drive for alignment.

It Must Be Effortful: The person must perceive that they overcame a small hurdle to complete the action. The effort makes the commitment stick. Think of groups, like fraternities, that use effortful steps to increase loyalty. The process makes members take inner responsibility for the group's rules and identity.

The Foot-in-the-Door Technique: This approach is the most common application of Commitment and Consistency. You ask for a small, easily justifiable favor first. This small agreement establishes a beachhead of commitment. Once the target agrees to the small request, their self-image shifts slightly. They now see themselves as the type of person who helps, or the type of person who supports the cause. The large, desired request that follows is then perceived as a logical, consistent extension of their new, self-attributed identity.

Example Application: Do not ask a potential investor for a major capital commitment first. Ask them to write a one-paragraph email detailing their core investment philosophy. They are making an active, effortful commitment to a principle. You then show them how your proposal is the **only consistent** financial action that honors their written philosophy. They are no longer deciding on your proposal. They are simply fulfilling their own commitment. The decision becomes their idea.

This is the art of engineering a self-sustaining adherence. You want the target to believe the choice originated from their own personal will. You remove the appearance of strong outside pressure. You maximize their personal responsibility for the small initial step. This psychological structure ensures the final, large action is secure and long-lasting.

2. Social Proof: The Crowd's Silent Guide

When people feel uncertain, they naturally look to the actions of others to guide their own behavior. This tendency is known as **Social Proof**. The strength of this principle is immense. It drives consumer decisions, social conformity, and large-scale behavioral shifts.

The power of Social Proof is magnified by uncertainty. When a target is unsure about the correct action, they assume that if many other people are doing something, those people must possess information the target lacks. This assumption makes the action seem more appropriate or correct.

The Role of Group Conditions: Effective influence requires controlling the social environment to ensure Social Proof works optimally. A leader cannot control every individual in a large group. However, a leader can control the most dedicated members. By influencing a certain, respected portion of the group first, their adoption then persuades the rest.

Example Application: Testimonials are a form of Social Proof. But they are strongest when the source is someone the target identifies with. A testimonial from a highly successful person may not work as well as one from a person who shares the target's exact profession, geographical location, or struggle.

The **Social Bond Multiplier** is also critical. Social scientists have found that the strength of the social bond between individuals can be twice as likely to determine a purchase as the preference for the product itself. If the target feels a strong connection to the person recommending the action, the resistance disappears.

The Strategy of Modeling: Do not tell a target what to do. Show them others succeeding through the desired action. The proof must be visible, relevant, and perceived as genuine. This makes the target feel safe. They are following the established, successful path. This reduces the risk in their subjective reality.

3. Reciprocity: The Weight of Obligation

The **Reciprocity Principle** states that we feel obligated to return a favor or a concession that another person has provided to us. This rule is ingrained in human society. It creates a network of mutual assistance that benefits the group.

The key to activating Reciprocity is to give something **first** and to ensure the gift is perceived as **personal and unexpected**. The gift does not need to be expensive or elaborate. It must be meaningful to the target. An uninvited gift creates a sense of immediate, unsolicited obligation. This pressure often feels uncomfortable. The target wants to relieve the psychological burden by returning the favor, often with a much larger one.

The Strategy of Initial Concession (Door-in-the-Face): This technique uses the Contrast Principle alongside Reciprocity. You first present a large, ambitious request that you fully expect the target to reject. This is the "door-in-the-face" part.

Immediately after the rejection, you present the smaller, actual desired request. This second request is framed as a **concession** on your part. The target feels two powerful forces working on them: first, the actual request seems much smaller by contrast to the initial huge request (Contrast Principle). Second, they feel obligated to reciprocate your perceived concession by agreeing to the smaller request (Reciprocity). This is a highly effective sequence for moving from denial to compliance.

Example Application: Do not ask a manager for a three-month extended deadline immediately. Ask for a six-month delay and a full restructuring of the project's scope. When they reasonably reject this large request, immediately follow up with the actual desired request: "Okay, I understand. If six months is too much, can we agree to just the three-month delay? I'll personally handle the restructuring without team input." The three-month delay suddenly seems like a small, reasonable request, and the manager feels obligated to agree since you "retreated" from the six-month request.

4. Liking: The Foundation of Effortless Agreement

We are significantly more likely to agree to a request from a person we like. The emotion of liking often supersedes rational thought. The goal is to cultivate genuine rapport quickly. This involves focusing on three core components:

Similarity: We like people who are similar to us. Finding common ground, in hobbies, background, or opinions, builds rapport quickly. Even small, irrelevant similarities increase the feeling of connection. The persuader should subtly mirror the target's posture, language style, and emotional state. This behavioral synchrony makes the target feel an instant, subconscious bond.

Compliments and Approval: We enjoy being praised. Genuine, specific compliments increase liking. The compliment must be tailored to the target's efforts or abilities, not just superficial appearance. Approval is a powerful psychological currency.

Cooperation and Shared Goals: Working together toward a shared, common objective generates connection. The persuader should frame the request not as a sales pitch, but as a joint effort to overcome an external obstacle. "It sounds like we both agree on the goal of cutting costs. How can we work together to implement this solution?" This technique transforms the persuader from an antagonist into a helpful partner.

The **Halo Effect**, discussed earlier, also feeds into Liking. When a person projects competence and controlled composure, they gain an immediate, favorable social judgment. This initial positive impression makes the target want to like the persuader, as they are perceived as a safe, successful connection. Liking is the emotional lubricant that makes every request easier to accept.

5. Authority: The Deference to Expertise

We possess an ingrained tendency to defer to legitimate authority figures. This deference simplifies decision-making. We assume that authority figures, such as doctors, police, or experts, possess a higher level of specialized knowledge.

The persuader does not necessarily need a formal title. They must use the **symbols of authority**. These symbols include titles, tailored clothing, and the controlled environment.

Symbols of Authority: A person introduced with a title like "Dr." or "Director" is perceived as more knowledgeable and influential, regardless of the actual content of their message. The persuader must ensure their credentials and titles are presented to the target before the interaction begins. The environment also projects authority. A clean, organized, and professionally decorated office conveys status and expertise.

Composure and Certainty: Composure is a powerful non-verbal symbol of authority. A person who speaks slowly, uses precise language, and shows no sign of emotional distress projects competence and control. When the target is uncertain or anxious, they look to the composure of the authority figure for guidance. The composed figure seems to possess the illusion of informed certainty. The target trusts this certainty and follows the recommendation.

Scientific Grounding: Authority is why this collection emphasizes scientific evidence. By grounding every claim in verifiable research, the persuader uses the ultimate symbol of Authority: documented, accepted knowledge. The facts are not just opinions; they are validated truths.

6. Scarcity and Urgency: The Drive for Immediate Action

The final and perhaps most potent driver for instant action is **Scarcity**. We value things more when they are rare or limited.

Rarity Equals Value: This is a basic psychological truth. A famous 1975 experiment showed that people rated identical cookies from an almost empty jar as more desirable than the same cookies from a full jar. The desire was determined by the perception of limited availability, not by the cookie's actual quality. The persuader must engineer scarcity by visibly reducing perceived availability, limited time offers, limited quantities, or exclusive access barriers.

Loss Aversion: The power of Scarcity is rooted in **Loss Aversion**. The psychological pain of losing something is generally more powerful than the pleasure of gaining an item of equivalent value. People are highly motivated to avoid loss. Scarcity triggers the **Fear of Missing Out (FOMO)**.

The persuader should frame the decision as necessary to **prevent a loss**. If you do not act now, you will lose the opportunity, the discount, or the advantage. This triggers an impulsive decision to avoid the powerful psychological pain of regret associated with missing out.

Psychological Reactance: When a person's freedom to choose or acquire something is threatened by limited availability, they experience **Psychological Reactance**. This is an innate desire to reassert that threatened freedom, often by pursuing the restricted item even more intensely.

By introducing a temporary, slight barrier to access, a deadline, a quantity limit, or an exclusive qualification, the persuader increases the target's desire for the restricted option. Combining this reactance with loss aversion creates an urgent, high-stakes scenario that compels immediate compliance.

Temporal Discounting (The Time Trap): Scarcity is amplified by time pressure, a behavioral economic concept known as **Temporal Discounting**. This is the cognitive process of preferring immediate rewards over greater future benefits.

People are impatient by nature. They often choose a smaller reward today over a slightly larger reward tomorrow. To compel immediate action, the persuader must associate the action *now* with an immediate, tangible psychological or material reward, even if the main payoff is delayed. This small, present payment counteracts the hyperbolic devaluation of the long-term benefit.

Example Application: Do not frame a decision as "invest now for a big future profit." Frame it as: "Agree to this now to **secure immediate access** to the exclusive community and avoid the fee increase that happens at midnight." You are offering immediate access (a present reward) and preventing an immediate loss (the fee increase). This combination makes the decision impulsive and highly effective.

Synthesis: The Combined Compliance System

The six drivers are rarely used in isolation. They are most potent when deployed in combination, creating a system of compliance:

1. **Commitment** secures the target's initial self-attribution.
2. **Liking** provides the necessary emotional rapport.
3. **Reciprocity** creates the immediate obligation to agree.
4. **Authority** provides the necessary psychological justification for the decision.
5. **Social Proof** guarantees safety by showing others have gone first.
6. **Scarcity and Urgency** collapse the decision window, forcing immediate compliance before rational analysis can interfere.

By consciously activating these core drivers, the persuader moves the process from vague discussion to secure, immediate action. This is the difference between hoping for agreement and engineering it. The following chapters detail how to control the narrative, map the target's decision process, and neutralize resistance before it even appears. We ensure that every interaction is structured for maximum leverage.

CHAPTER 3

CONTROL NARRATIVE: STAGING INFORMATION FOR ACCEPTANCE

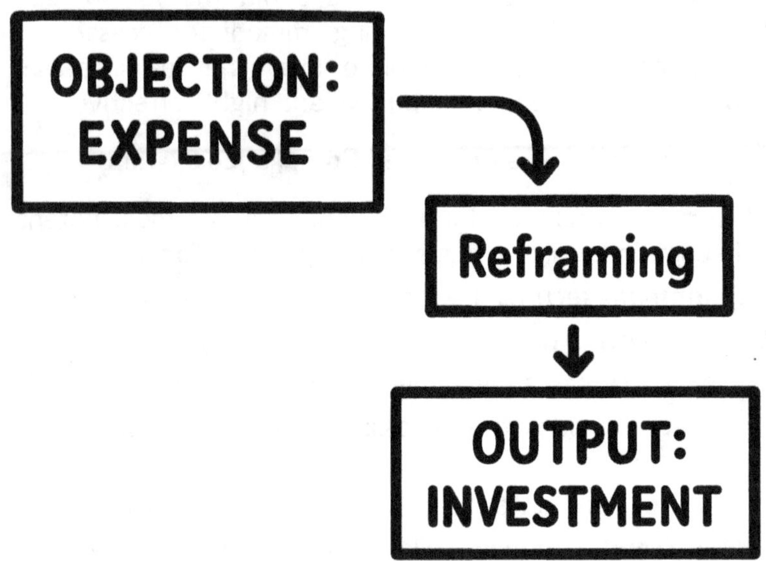

Influence depends less on the argument itself and more on the way you present the argument. This is the difference between facts and narrative. You must be the editor of the story that plays out in the target's mind. Controlling the narrative means staging every piece of information to guide acceptance. You manage the context around the proposal.

The power of narrative control is simple. It ensures that when the target finally makes a choice, the agreement feels like the only logical conclusion to the story you built. This chapter shows you how to structure information so that the target's natural biases move them toward your desired outcome. This approach uses validated cognitive science, moving beyond unproven methodologies that lack verifiable academic support.

The Scientific Foundation of Framing

While some historical theories used the term "reframing" in a way that lacks scientific basis, the underlying concept of **framing** is deeply validated by behavioral science. Framing is the core act of structuring the decision environment. It dictates the context of a choice.

Pioneering research demonstrated that simply presenting the same outcome in two different ways, as a potential loss versus an assured gain, drastically changes the choice subjects make. For instance, a medical treatment framed as "90% chance of survival" is accepted far more readily than the same treatment framed as "10% chance of death." The facts are identical. The psychological response is entirely different.

The persuader's objective is to understand that the architecture of the choice matters more than the content itself. You use controlled language and strategic sequencing to structure choices that exploit predictable cognitive biases. This ensures the target makes a decision based on the emotional charge of your description, rather than a dispassionate, rational calculation. You are editing the story before the target reads it.

Mastering the Contrast Principle Through Sequencing

Human perception uses comparison as a primary tool for evaluating value and effort. We are not good at judging things in isolation. This is why the **Contrast Principle** is so effective. This principle states that the difference between two items presented one after the other will be exaggerated if the second item differs significantly from the first.

If you stage your request correctly, you control the relative perception of value.

The Strategy of the High Anchor: In any discussion about price, time, or required effort, the expensive or ambitious request must come first. This sets the initial, high reference point, the anchor. For example, if you are attempting to secure two hours of a person's time, you might first ask for an entire day of their schedule, alongside an urgent commitment of resources. The person will likely reject the large, initial request.

The Concession Follow-Up: Immediately following the rejection, you present the actual, desired request: the two-hour commitment. Because the second request is immediately preceded by the much larger, more ambitious request, the two-hour demand appears disproportionately small and acceptable.

This sequencing technique is highly effective because it manages two psychological factors simultaneously:

1. **Value Distortion:** The Contrast Principle distorts the perceived cost of the second item. The target thinks, "Compared to the previous demand, this is easy and cheap."

2. **Reciprocity Activation:** The target often perceives your shift from the high demand to the low demand as a concession on your part. They feel compelled to reciprocate this perceived "retreat" by accepting the smaller request, even if they would have rejected the smaller request if it had been presented first.

This staging allows you to control the target's perception of cost and effort. You set the stage with a high-effort reference, making the low-effort, desired action seem almost effortless. You use sequential presentation to guide the perception of value and cost, all through managed narrative flow.

The Art of Reframing Objections

Reframing is the advanced skill of narrative control. It is the act of shifting the context around a specific fact or objection, rather than arguing against the fact itself. When a target resists a request, they are usually doing so based on a perceived negative context they have applied to a neutral fact.

For instance, a neutral fact is: "This solution costs $\$20,000$." A negative context is: "That is an excessive cost." The target is resisting the **context** (excessive cost), not the **fact** ($\$20,000$).

The unsophisticated persuader argues the number. The covert persuader argues the context.

The Strategy of Contextual Shift: You must identify the target's negative frame and immediately redefine the objection's category. You shift the reference point until the original objection becomes irrelevant.

- If the target says, "This is **risky**," they are framing the decision as a potential source of loss. You must reframe the decision as a necessary form of **risk mitigation** against a larger, guaranteed future loss. "It is not risky; it is the necessary premium for guaranteed security against market volatility."

- If the target says, "This is **expensive**," they are framing the cost as expenditure. You must reframe the cost as a necessary **investment** in future capacity. "It is not expensive; it is a fixed, necessary investment that guarantees a five-year capacity increase."

This contextual shift invalidates the target's initial resistance by changing the very category of the objection. The target's initial resistance is based on their subjective reality. By reframing, you make the decision fit their positive self-view, satisfying the Confirmation Bias. They now see the decision not as an act of risk, but as an act of calculated security, which aligns with their existing desire to be secure.

Linguistic Precision: Moving from Abstraction to Detail

The specific words you use directly affect the psychological distance between the target and your proposal. Abstract language creates cognitive distance. Common, concrete words trigger immediate, specific emotional responses.

Language is deeply connected with personality, intention, and psychological state. The goal is to be an intuitive emotional mapper, selecting words that trigger the precise affective response you want.

Unpacking NLP: The acronym NLP stands at a fascinating crossroads, pointing to both the foundational human influence field of Neuro-Linguistic Programming and the computational discipline of Natural Language Processing.

This book is dedicated to the former, positioning it as the master blueprint for human influence. The pioneers of NLP gave us a brilliant, early map for understanding how language, neurology, and behavior interconnect. This foundational work is what allowed millions to begin improving communication, but the time has come for a verifiable, advanced evolution of the practice.

This book delivers that evolution. We leverage the core genius of traditional NLP, concepts like Modeling, Anchoring, and Reframing, and seamlessly integrate them with the latest verified findings from cognitive science and behavioral economics.

The precision in linguistic patterns that the technical field of Natural Language Processing confirms is now brought to you as a practiced, measurable skill. This allows you to move beyond outdated theory to proven methods that reliably structure choices, reshape arguments, and give you the verifiable knowledge to consistently predict reactions and secure commitment.

The effective persuader adheres to the *scientific* insight: word patterns matter greatly.

Actionable Linguistic Principles:

- **Substitute Abstract Nouns:** Never use general, abstract terms where a specific verb or noun exists. Do not talk about "success." Talk about "a signed contract on Thursday" or "a 15% reduction in expenditure." Concrete details are always more compelling.

- **Use Sensory Language:** Describe the future outcome with immediate sensory detail. Make the target *feel* the comfort, *see* the result, or *hear* the client's approval. This sensory detail minimizes the perceived time gap between the present decision and the future result.

- **Minimize Jargon:** Technical jargon or overly complicated language increases cognitive friction. It forces the target to slow down and use their rational processing system, increasing the chance of resistance. Use common, concrete vocabulary to ensure the emotional and intellectual impact is delivered directly.

When faced with resistance, the persuader must perform internal sentiment analysis. Which keywords is the target using? Are they using words like "unfair," "worried," or "risky"? These words reveal the precise emotional state that must be addressed or reframed before the narrative can proceed positively.

Building the Narrative Anchor: Pre-Suasion

Controlling the narrative begins before you even present the proposal. **Pre-suasion** is the act of directing the target's attention to an idea or concept that will make them receptive to your actual message later.

The narrative anchor is established by controlling the target's environment and their focus.

Environmental Control: The physical setting dictates much of the target's pre-conceived narrative. A messy, chaotic environment suggests disorganization and lack of control. A controlled, organized, and professional environment suggests competence and authority. This external narrative reinforces the perception of your professional capability.

Focus Control: Before you introduce the solution, you must ensure the target is thinking about the problem in the right way.

- If you want them to focus on *quality*, ask them to spend five minutes describing the highest-quality product they ever owned.

- If you want them to focus on *security*, ask them to recount a time they felt exposed or vulnerable.

By directing their focus, you are activating a specific cognitive framework that makes them more receptive to your message when it arrives. If the target is thinking about security, your security-focused solution will be perceived as highly relevant and necessary. This pre-framing makes the eventual agreement feel like a natural progression of their current thoughts.

Narrative Control and Gender Processing

Effective narrative control means knowing which type of evidence to present to which audience. Since men and women often process persuasive messages through different cognitive routes, the content of your narrative must be tailored.

1. **Central Route (Detailed Evidence):** Women show a stronger tendency toward central route processing. This means they are likely to analyze arguments critically and focus on message quality. When your target favors this route, your narrative must be dense with verifiable data, detailed case studies, and critical analysis. The story must be logical and withstand deep scrutiny.

2. **Peripheral Route (Authority/Emotion):** Some individuals, particularly men, may be more susceptible to authority influence or assertive evidence. In these cases, your narrative can rely more heavily on the endorsement of recognized experts or powerful, assertively stated statistical evidence.

The persuader must map the target's decision profile and select the appropriate narrative evidence. The goal is to achieve **linguistic resonance**, a sense of effortless understanding, by aligning the language and the evidence with the target's preferred processing style. This practice avoids cognitive friction, making the persuader appear trustworthy and familiar. The careful adjustment of the narrative ensures maximum acceptance without triggering unnecessary conscious evaluation of the influence attempt.

The Narrative System

Controlling the narrative is the system of sequencing and framing that makes the decision path obvious and desirable. You move from the high anchor to the smaller request, exploiting the Contrast Principle. You dismantle resistance by reframing objections into confirmations of the target's positive self-view. You use concrete, sensory language to ensure the emotional message is delivered without cognitive friction.

This complex system of strategic staging ensures that the target's mind, operating on its own internal logic and biases, arrives at your desired conclusion naturally. They walk through the doors you built for them, believing they found the path themselves.

The next step is to diagnose the target with precision. The following chapter details how to **Map Influence**: using observation, questioning, and analysis to uncover the target's internal decision profile and personalize your strategy instantly. This provides the intelligence needed to apply these narrative controls with surgical accuracy.

CHAPTER 4

MAP INFLUENCE: DIAGNOSING THE TARGET'S DECISION PROFILE

Covert persuasion is not a monologue. It is a highly responsive engagement built on accurate diagnosis. Before you speak, you must gather intelligence. You need to know the target's specific emotional pressures, their typical processing route, and the underlying beliefs that structure their subjective reality. This process of intelligence gathering is called **Mapping the Influence Profile**.

A generalized approach fails quickly. If you rely too heavily on social proof for a person who trusts only internal data, you fail. If you use slow, analytical arguments on someone driven by immediate anxiety, you fail. Success requires personalizing the strategy instantly, which only happens if you accurately diagnose the target's decision path.

1. Diagnosing the Default Processing Route

The mind uses two primary systems for processing persuasive messages. The first step in mapping is figuring out which one the target uses most often.

The Central Route: This path involves careful, critical analysis of the message content and quality. The target focuses on logic, facts, and verifiable data. If they use this route, they are looking for logical consistency and proof that can withstand scrutiny.

The Peripheral Route: This path involves relying on quick, emotional, or external cues. The target focuses on the speaker's authority, their composure, social proof (what others are doing), or simple emotional appeals. This is the path of least resistance, often driven by heuristics and cognitive bias.

Reading the Route: How do you quickly determine the default route?

- **Listen to Justification:** When the target talks about past major decisions, listen to how they justify the choice. Did they cite detailed research and long-term analysis (Central)? Or did they reference a respected expert, a popular consensus, or a gut feeling (Peripheral)?

- **Observe Questioning Style:** A Central Route processor asks technical, detailed, and specific questions about mechanics and evidence: "What is the margin of error?" or "Show me the data set." A Peripheral Route processor asks questions about safety, popularity, and ease: "Who else is doing this?" or "How quickly can we start?"

- **Factor in Context:** When men and women are exposed to cues associated with the **male gender role**, they both tend to process messages more carefully and thoughtfully. This happens because the context emphasizes a thoughtful, high-stakes environment. Conversely, when cues associated with the **female gender role** are prominent, both men and women tend to process messages less carefully. By observing how the target responds to the current social context, you gauge their level of active, critical thought.

Understanding this route determines the content of your narrative. If the target is a Central processor, you must dedicate the majority of your time to detailed, statistical evidence, knowing that emotional appeals will be ignored.

2. Mapping Emotional Pressures and Affective States

Decisions are rarely made in an emotional vacuum. The target's current psychological state, especially negative affects like anxiety, dictates their readiness to agree and the type of information they seek.

The Role of Anxiety: Studies show that feelings of anxiety are mutually associated with both social judgments and conformity. When a target is anxious, they are more likely to seek stability and make quick, biased social assessments. They are looking for an authority figure to guide them.

- **Diagnosis:** Look for non-verbal cues associated with anxiety: fidgeting, nervous vocal delivery, or rapid-fire questions. Verbally, listen for expressions of risk, worry, or uncertainty.

- **Action:** If you diagnose anxiety, you must prioritize projecting **extreme calm and competence**. Your controlled demeanor activates the **Halo Effect**, causing the target to infer positive traits (trust, safety) from your composure alone. This favorable social judgment accelerates trust. Your first priority becomes addressing their emotional stability, not their rational objection. Reducing anxiety removes the impulsive requirement for a quick, defensive, biased assessment.

Intuitive vs. Deliberative Styles: Anxiety and negative affects are often associated with an intuitive, non-analytical decision style. If the target is displaying negative affects, they are likely defaulting to their fast, shortcut-based system. Conversely, a calm, analytical approach suggests they are using their slow, deliberative system. Your map must include this insight. If they are intuitive, you must immediately frame the decision using strong emotional anchors like loss aversion or scarcity, which speak directly to their intuitive system.

3. Uncovering Core Cognitive Biases and Assumptions

Every individual has a preferred set of cognitive biases they rely on habitually. These revealed preferences form the exact structure of their subjective reality. Your map must identify these foundational errors.

The Anchoring Bias Habit: Does the target consistently refer back to historical performance, initial budget proposals, or early-stage ideas when making final decisions? This indicates a strong **Anchoring Bias**. If this is their habit, you know that the initial high value you set at the beginning of the discussion will retain disproportionate influence over their final valuation.

Confirmation Bias Structure: What are the target's deeply held, non-negotiable beliefs about their identity, their company, or the market? If they believe they are "forward-thinking," any proposal that confirms that self-view will be accepted with minimal evidence. This reveals the structure of their **Confirmation Bias**. The map tells you *which* identity you need to confirm: innovator, security-focused manager, or efficiency expert.

The Social Proof Threshold: How does the target respond to peer influence? Some individuals are highly susceptible to social proof; others are not.

- **Low Self-Monitor:** This individual is less focused on adapting their behavior to social cues. They may be slower to adopt a charismatic persona or new idea. Once they internalize a commitment, however, it is stable and long-lasting. For this individual, you need detailed, verifiable proof, and strong consistency arguments.

- **High Self-Monitor:** This individual is highly susceptible to emotional and behavioral cues. They rapidly absorb and reflect the charismatic state (enthusiasm, confidence). They are excellent for creating immediate group fervor. For this target, social proof, charismatic delivery, and emotional contagion are highly effective.

Your map should include a quick assessment of their self-monitoring trait. This determines whether you lead with group consensus (for high self-monitors) or with deep, logical commitment (for low self-monitors).

4. Mapping Communication Style and Gender Primes

Successful persuasion requires the ability to switch influence styles based on the target's preference, regardless of their actual gender. This skill, often called **flexible influence**, requires diagnosing whether the target prefers **push** or **pull** energy.

Push Energy (Assertive): This style involves direct expression, assertion, and leading the conversation. Men often exhibit this style more frequently.

Pull Energy (Collaborative): This style involves seeking opinions, using inquiry, and giving space to others. Women often tend toward this style.

Flexible Influence: Your map must determine which style builds rapport faster. A pull strategy (collaboration, questions) is essential for gathering information and establishing initial trust. Once you have the necessary information and trust is secured, you can strategically switch to a push strategy (assertion, directness) to drive compliance and finalize the action. The ability to switch prevents you from getting stuck in one ineffective style.

Linguistic Resonance: Your map must also include the target's preferred language style. Using language that is **gender-congruent**, direct and assertive for those who prefer "masculine" language, or collaborative and empathetic for those who prefer "feminine" language, enhances message effectiveness. This practice builds **linguistic resonance**, a sense of effortless, familiar understanding, which increases message acceptance without triggering conscious evaluation.

5. Strategic Deployment: The Diagnostic Funnel

Mapping the profile is not an abstract exercise. It is a funnel that dictates the exact sequencing of your six compliance drivers and framing techniques:

1. **Initial Scan (First 30 Seconds):** Diagnose the processing route (Central/Peripheral) and the current affective state (Anxious/Calm). This determines your initial delivery style (Analytical vs. Composed/Emotional).

2. **Rapport Building (Next 3 Minutes):** Use a Pull strategy to uncover core assumptions (Confirmation Bias structure) and collect surface similarities (for Liking). If the target is female or resists authority, begin applying the **communality buffer** (displaying warmth alongside competence) to mitigate resistance from the start.

3. **Anchoring and Concession (Next 5 Minutes):** Deploy the high anchor (Anchoring Bias) and prepare the Contrast Principle by presenting a large request followed immediately by the smaller, desired request (Reciprocity/Contrast).

4. **Closing Sequence:** If the target is highly anxious or peripheral, close quickly using **Scarcity and Loss Aversion** (impulsive drivers). If the target is calm and central, use **Commitment and Consistency** (secure the active, public, effortful step) and **Authority** (present final, verifiable evidence) to ensure long-term adherence.

This layered approach ensures that every step of your influence strategy is personalized and aligns with the target's unique psychological structure. You are not guessing. You are executing based on a verified map of their decision profile. This precision is the essence of covert persuasion.

The next critical step is ensuring this carefully constructed profile and strategy does not collapse. The following chapter details how to **Mitigate Resistance**: neutralizing defenses before they can form and managing objections by reframing them as confirmations of the target's own logic.

CHAPTER 5

MITIGATE RESISTANCE: NEUTRALIZING DEFENSES BEFORE THEY FORM

Resistance is not a personal attack. It is simply a defense mechanism. It means the target's subjective reality has encountered information that conflicts with their core beliefs, social image, or self-view. The target is protecting themselves from internal inconsistency or perceived external threat. The skilled persuader does not argue with this defense. They neutralize it before it is fully formed.

This chapter details the specific, scientifically verified methods for mitigating resistance. We move past confrontation and focus entirely on pre-emption. By anticipating the exact nature of the target's objection and addressing it first, you eliminate the mental energy the target needed to deploy their defense. This process ensures the meticulously crafted influence profile, built in Chapter 5, does not collapse at the moment of decision.

1. Pre-Emption: Addressing the Unspoken Objection (The Firebreak)

The most effective way to neutralize resistance is to state the objection yourself before the target gets the chance. When you voice the target's primary reservation, three crucial psychological shifts occur:

A. Cognitive Release: You remove the target's mental burden. They were preparing to interrupt you with their objection. By stating it first, you remove the need for them to think about it. This allows their brain to process the rest of your message with less effort. The mind naturally seeks paths of least cognitive resistance.

B. Increased Credibility: By accurately predicting and stating the counter-argument, you project supreme confidence. You show the target that you have thoroughly considered their perspective. This transparency increases perceived trustworthiness, making the target less guarded.

C. Framing Control: Most importantly, when you voice the objection, you control the **framing**. You dictate the context of the problem and its limits. This allows you to immediately follow the objection with your reframed solution. The target is denied the opportunity to frame the problem using their own negatively charged language.

The Strategy of the Firebreak:

The process requires identifying the strongest, most likely objection during the Mapping stage (Chapter 5). Do not choose a trivial objection; choose the central one (cost, time, or risk).

1. **Acknowledge the Pain Point (The Objection):** Introduce the objection using precise, neutral language. For example: "Before we proceed, let me address the single largest factor people consider here: the upfront investment required to implement this solution."

2. **Validate the Concern (The Empathy):** Briefly confirm that the concern is legitimate. "It is a significant commitment, and anyone who is financially responsible must think carefully about this number." This validates their self-image as a responsible decision-maker.

3. **Refactor the Context (The Pivot):** Immediately change the category of the objection. If the objection is cost, pivot to future security. If the objection is time, pivot to long-term efficiency. "However, the more critical question is not the amount of the upfront investment, but the guaranteed long-term cost of *not* securing this protection."

By deploying this **firebreak**, stating, validating, and refactoring the objection, you prevent the target from setting their own internal narrative. You position yourself as a collaborator who anticipated their needs, not a salesperson pushing a product.

2. The Art of Contextual Reframing

Reframing is the advanced technique of narrative control. It involves shifting the context around a neutral fact so that the target's subjective reality changes. Resistance is fundamentally a contextual problem. The target is applying a negative meaning to a neutral piece of information.

The critical insight, confirmed by behavioral economics, is that framing significantly alters decision-making. By presenting an outcome as a guaranteed loss versus a potential gain, you change the subject's choice, even if the objective facts are identical.

The Strategy of Category Change:

When a target expresses an objection, they are giving you a gift: the negative frame they are using. Do not argue the frame. Change the category entirely.

- **Resistance Frame:** "I cannot accept this kind of **risk**."
    - **Reframed Category: Security and Insurance.**
    - **Response:** "I understand you see risk here. But let us view this differently. This is not risk; this is purchasing guaranteed protection. The true risk is maintaining your current, exposed position. We are buying security."
- **Resistance Frame:** "This is too much **expense**."
    - **Reframed Category: Investment and Capacity.**
    - **Response:** "You are right, it is an expense in the short term. However, the correct way to assess this is as a fixed investment that triples your processing capacity. We are not spending money; we are purchasing future growth."
- **Resistance Frame:** "This takes too much **time**."
    - **Reframed Category: Efficiency and Future Savings.**
    - **Response:** "The time required today is significant. But we must frame this as a one-time process to guarantee future efficiency. The time you spend today saves you ten times that amount in management time over the next year."

This strategy ensures that the target's initial resistance is rendered irrelevant. They cannot logically argue that an "investment" is too expensive if they agree on the principle of necessary investment. The negative frame is nullified by placing the fact into an entirely different, positive category that aligns with their self-view (Confirmation Bias).

3. Neutralizing Resistance from Social Pressure (The Communality Buffer)

Resistance is often influenced by social dynamics, particularly those related to gender and competence. Research confirms that men generally possess more influence than women in professional and group settings. Women are particularly less influential when using overtly dominant communication styles.

A core finding is that males specifically tend to resist influence attempted by women who use highly competent or assertive communication styles. This resistance is not always about the idea; it is often about the perceived challenge to status or social expectation.

The Strategy of the Communality Buffer:

The specific tactic for female persuaders to mitigate this resistance is to intentionally **temper competence with displays of warmth and communality**. This is the **Communality Buffer**.

- **Actionable Implementation:** Before or during the assertion of a highly competent or assertive position, the female persuader must use deliberate language that emphasizes shared goals, empathy, and cooperation.
    - *Instead of:* "My analysis dictates we must proceed with Solution A."
    - *Try:* "I agree with the team's objective, and based on the analysis we ran together, I believe we share the understanding that the best path forward is Solution A. Let us collaborate on how to roll this out."

The display of empathy and collaborative language softens the delivery of competence, neutralizing the target's tendency for resistance. This strategy ensures that competence is perceived as a shared resource, not a unilateral challenge to the target's position.

Managing Social Processing Primes:

Furthermore, the external social environment influences the target's decision-making process. Exposing men and women to cues associated with the **male gender role** causes both genders to process persuasive messages more thoughtfully and carefully. Also, cues associated with the **female gender role** cause both genders to process messages less carefully.

- **If you need critical buy-in (long-term secure agreement):** Maintain a setting and language style (e.g., highly analytical, data-driven, assertive discussion structure) that primes for careful, thoughtful processing, regardless of the target's gender.
- **If you need rapid, low-scrutiny agreement (peripheral agreement):** The environment and language style should favor a less critical processing style.

Understanding how to control these **social primes** allows the persuader to pre-emptively manage the depth of thought the target applies to the proposal, mitigating the resistance that comes from either too much scrutiny or misplaced deference.

4. The Linguistic Shield: Reducing Cognitive Friction

Language that is overly complicated, abstract, or filled with jargon creates cognitive friction. This friction forces the target to slow down and exert effort, increasing the probability of resistance. The brain seeks to avoid unnecessary work.

The Strategy of Concrete Vocabulary:

Effective mitigation uses simple, concrete vocabulary and direct verbs.

- **Abstract words** require the target to perform translation. They must connect the general term ("optimization," "synergy") to a specific action. This work creates resistance.
- **Concrete words** (names, dates, numbers, facts) require no translation. They deliver the emotional and intellectual impact directly.

Research in language processing confirms that specific word patterns correlate reliably with psychological states. The persuader must act as a precise linguist, ensuring every word choice is functional, not decorative.

When writing or speaking, focus on the immediate effect:

- **Avoid:** "We need to operationalize the new structure."
- **Use:** "We need to sign this contract by 3 PM Thursday."

Sentiment Mapping in Resistance: When the target begins to resist, use the research principles of **sentiment analysis** (as used in computer science) instinctively. Listen for their negative keywords: *unfair, risky, unnecessary, worried.* These keywords reveal the target's current emotional state and the precise objection that must be reframed. If they use "risky," you know their resistance is rooted in anxiety and loss aversion. You must immediately respond with a frame of security, not a frame of profit.

5. Using Loss Aversion as a Counter-Weapon

Resistance mitigation is powerfully achieved by leveraging **Loss Aversion**. The pain of losing something is measurably stronger than the pleasure of gaining an equivalent item. Humans are overwhelmingly motivated to avoid loss.

The Strategy of Guaranteed Loss:

If the target is resisting your proposal (compliance), you must frame non-compliance as a guaranteed, immediate, and quantifiable loss.

- **Do not frame:** "If you agree, you will gain X." (Potential gain)
- **Frame:** "If you *do not* agree right now, you guarantee the loss of Y." (Guaranteed loss)

The "loss" must be specific and immediate. It could be the loss of the current discount, the loss of an exclusive opportunity (Scarcity), or the loss of their current perceived status.

Example Application: When a target hesitates at the final signature, you use loss aversion: "I respect the need to deliberate. But let me be absolutely clear about the cost of that deliberation. If we do not execute this document today, the materials cost increases by 7%, which means you immediately lose $\$3,500$ from your budget. That is a guaranteed, immediate loss you accept by simply waiting."

This technique collapses the decision window, activating the **Fear of Missing Out (FOMO)**. The psychological pain of accepting that immediate loss, the regret of non-action, compels the target to make a rapid, impulsive decision to avoid the cost. This immediate action bypasses further rational analysis.

Mitigating resistance is the final layer of control in the persuasion process. It ensures that the target's psychological defenses are either lowered by empathy and transparency (Pre-Emption) or bypassed entirely by the emotional force of loss aversion and strategic reframing.

The last chapter of this book is a final resource list. It provides the full compendium of sources for all the verified principles, studies, and concepts used throughout this book. This ensures that every technique presented is grounded in documented science, providing true value and the maturity necessary for secure, repeatable influence.

CONCLUSION
THE ARCHITECTURE OF GUIDED CHOICE

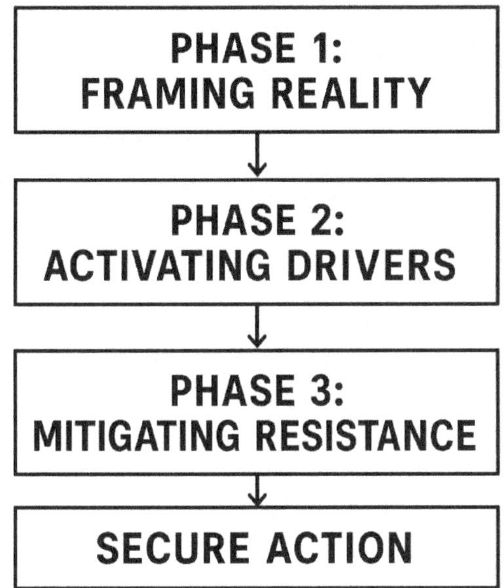

We have covered the foundational mechanics of influence. This first book establishes that persuasion is not a mystical talent or a natural gift. It is an act of engineering. It relies on precise, verifiable knowledge of the human decision structure. We learned how to move past chance and into the realm of consistent, repeatable outcomes. The core lesson is this: success depends on controlling the environment, not arguing with the target's opinion.

Every principle detailed across the last six chapters builds toward a single, unified system. This conclusion synthesizes those concepts. It provides a complete map of how to apply the techniques of Framing, Activating, and Mitigating in a fluid, real-world sequence. We confirm that every successful persuasive action begins with two non-negotiable prerequisites: an understanding of **Subjective Reality** and the ability to diagnose the target's **Decision Profile**.

The entire system rests on a single truth, often overlooked: people do not act on facts. They act on their unique version of reality, which they build themselves. This **subjective reality** is the core belief system that dictates their behavior in the world.

A persuader's objective is never to destroy this subjective reality. That creates resistance. Instead, we must simply modify the information inputs so that the target's reality naturally leads to our desired outcome. This is possible because the mind uses **cognitive biases**: systematic, predictable errors in judgment.

These biases are the levers of influence. They exist because the brain needs shortcuts, or heuristics, to make faster decisions. The brain possesses only a limited capacity for information processing, leading to the condition known as **bounded rationality**. When you subtly increase the pressure on the target, by limiting time or introducing a minor distraction, you force their mind to bypass slow, analytical thought. They default to the fast, intuitive, biased system, making them highly susceptible to our framing techniques.

Synthesis of Framing (Chapter 2):

The goal of framing is to make the decision seem inevitable and rational within the target's subjective world.

1. **Anchoring and Contrast:** You must always set the initial high reference point first. The **Anchoring Effect** ensures that this first number dictates the acceptable range for subsequent negotiations. You then exploit the **Contrast Principle** by immediately following the high anchor with the desired request. The desired request seems disproportionately small and acceptable, making the decision easy.

2. **Confirmation Bias as Alignment:** Never fight a target's beliefs. Instead, ensure your request validates their existing self-image. If the target believes they are a responsible planner, you frame the decision as "the responsible, logical extension of sound planning." This alignment requires less evidence for acceptance and avoids triggering their internal defenses.

This foundational stage ensures the target sees the decision not as a new risk, but as a logical, easy step consistent with who they already are.

II. The Activation Sequence: Using the Six Drivers

Once the decision environment is correctly framed, you must activate the target's innate behavioral rules. These are the six core compliance drivers. They are highly effective because they tap into deeply ingrained societal expectations and psychological needs. They are most powerful when used in sequence.

1. Secure Long-Term Commitment (Consistency):

Commitment is secured by engineering inner responsibility. The act must be **active, public, and effortful**. If the target takes a small, initial step that requires effort, they attribute the action to their own will, not to your pressure or a large reward. This self-attribution makes the change permanent.

- **Application:** Ask for a written opinion, a small task, or a public verbal agreement on a principle, not the final contract. This small step changes their self-image. The final action then becomes an act of consistency, which is psychologically easy to sustain.

2. Build Rapport (Liking and Reciprocity):

Liking provides the emotional foundation for agreement. Use genuine compliments and find genuine, subtle similarities to build immediate connection. Simultaneously, you activate **Reciprocity** by giving a concession or a small, unexpected gift first.

- **Application:** The "Door-in-the-Face" technique perfectly integrates these. You offer a large, expectedly rejected request first. When you concede and ask for the small, desired request, the target feels obligated to reciprocate your perceived concession by agreeing to the smaller demand. This psychological weight of obligation is difficult to ignore.

3. Provide Safety (Social Proof and Authority):

Humans seek safety in numbers and expertise. **Social Proof** is activated when the target is uncertain. They look to the actions of others to guide their own behavior. **Authority** provides the justification for deference.

- **Application:** Show the target that others, especially others they identify with (a strong social bond), have already taken the action. This reduces the perceived risk. Simultaneously, use the symbols of **Authority**, composure, titles, an organized environment, to ensure the target sees you as a safe, knowledgeable source of guidance. Controlled composure is a powerful, non-verbal symbol of competence that triggers automatic deference.

4. Force Immediate Action (Scarcity and Urgency):

This is the final, powerful trigger for instant compliance. You must collapse the decision window to prevent rational analysis from interfering.

- **Application:** Use **Scarcity** by visibly limiting availability (time or quantity). This rarity increases the perceived value, regardless of actual worth. Crucially, you couple this with **Loss Aversion**. The pain of losing an item or opportunity is stronger than the pleasure of gaining it. You must frame non-compliance as a guaranteed, immediate, quantifiable loss (losing the current price, losing the exclusive slot). This triggers the **Fear of Missing Out (FOMO)** and compels the target to act impulsively to avoid regret.

III. The Strategy of Precision: Mapping and Mitigating

The greatest risk to this system is resistance. Resistance is neutralized through precision, which requires correctly diagnosing the target's decision profile.

1. Diagnosing the Processing Route (Mapping):

You must know if the target prefers the **Central Route** (critical analysis of facts) or the **Peripheral Route** (reliance on authority, emotion, or social cues).

- **Application:** Observe their justification style and the nature of their questions. If they are Central processors, your narrative must be dense with specific, verifiable evidence. If they are Peripheral processors, your narrative should emphasize Social Proof and the symbols of Authority. Remember that **gender role primes** influence processing depth: cues emphasizing careful, high-stakes thought lead both men and women to process messages more thoroughly.

2. Contextual Reframing (Controlling Narrative):

Resistance provides a gift: the target's negative frame (e.g., "This is risky"). You neutralize this by immediately changing the frame's category. If they say "risk," you reframe it as "security." If they say "expense," you reframe it as "necessary investment." This instantly aligns the decision with their Confirmation Bias, making their objection irrelevant.

3. Neutralizing Social Resistance (The Communality Buffer):

If you are a woman asserting high competence, you may encounter predictable resistance, particularly from male targets.

- **Application:** Deploy the **Communality Buffer**. This involves intentionally tempering the assertive communication with displays of warmth, empathy, and collaboration. This language of shared goals neutralizes resistance by ensuring competence is perceived as a shared resource, not a challenge to their status.

The Shift in Perspective

This book has provided a verified, systematic methodology. You now understand that you do not need to be the loudest or the most aggressive person in the room. You need to be the most precise. You are the architect who frames reality, sets the anchors, and activates the internal drivers. The entire process is built on making the desired choice the path of least cognitive resistance.

The techniques covered here, from Anchoring to Loss Aversion, are powerful tools for securing action and commitment. But they are only half the battle. They focus on *what you say* and *how you structure the presentation*.

The next book, **Magnetic Charisma**, shifts the focus entirely to *who you are* and *how you exist* in the room. We move from the conscious management of language to the non-verbal control of perception. We explore how charisma creates effortless influence through the silent transfer of emotion, the strategic use of touch (haptics), and the control of micro-behaviors that establish authority before you speak. The systems of Covert Persuasion rely on accurate diagnosis; the systems of Magnetic Charisma rely on accurate projection. We move now to master the silent signals that dictate trust, authority, and attraction.

REFLECTION QUESTIONS

We have reached the end of the first book. Before moving on to the skills of charisma and non-verbal projection, we must pause. The lessons of Covert Persuasion, that choice is manufactured through predictable biases and structured compliance drivers, must move from simple information to ingrained habit.

True mastery of influence is not just knowing these concepts. It is integrating them into your natural, daily interactions. Use the following questions to reflect on the systems we have discussed. The objective is to personalize the material, mapping it onto your own past experiences and preparing for your next interactions.

Section 1: Diagnosing Reality and Cognitive Bias

The foundation of persuasion is understanding that everyone lives in a **subjective reality** built on their own perceptions, not objective facts. Every decision is filtered through this personal lens.

1. Think about a recent time you failed to convince someone of an idea. Did you fight their **subjective reality**? If you could rewind, what is one non-negotiable belief they hold about themselves (e.g., "I am financially conservative" or "I am a creative risk-taker")? How would you reframe your argument to confirm that belief instead of challenging it?

2. Identify a recurring number or concept in your life: a salary target, a project timeline, or a budget. Now, practice the **Anchoring Effect**. What is the highest, justified reference point you could introduce *before* stating your real target? How does simply stating the high number change your own perception of your final desired outcome?

3. Recall a complex decision you made recently. Were you rushed or distracted? Did you rely on a fast shortcut instead of slow, careful analysis (an example of **bounded rationality**)? How could a persuader have used that moment of distraction to introduce a proposal that exploited your need for speed?

4. The **Halo Effect** dictates that a single positive trait (like composure or neatness) can grant you general trustworthiness. What is the one non-verbal trait you project most consistently right now? Does it align with the persona you want (Authority, Warmth, or Competence)?

Section 2: Activating the Core Compliance Drivers

The six compliance drivers (Reciprocity, Commitment, Social Proof, Liking, Authority, Scarcity, and Consistency) are universal mechanisms for securing action. Mastery means knowing which one to deploy and when.

5. **Commitment and Consistency** requires you to secure an **active, public, and effortful** initial step. Identify a goal you have for the next month that requires the support of another person (a co-worker, a partner, or a client). What is the smallest, most effortful action you can ask them to take *today* to commit to that goal? How would you ensure this action is public, making them feel accountable to maintain consistency?

6. **Reciprocity** is activated by providing an initial, unexpected concession or gift. Think about a recent interaction where you felt obligated to someone. What did they give you that created that pressure? Now, plan an immediate, small, personal favor you can offer a potential contact in the next 48 hours to create a sense of unsolicited obligation on your terms.

7. **Social Proof** is most effective when the target is uncertain. Identify two distinct social groups you belong to: one professional, one personal. Who are the **social arbiters** in each group? If you wanted to start a new trend or idea, which arbiter

would you approach first, and how would their adoption influence the rest of the group?

8. The most potent trigger for instant action is **Loss Aversion**, where the fear of losing is stronger than the desire to gain. Describe a proposal you need to make soon. How can you shift the language to frame non-compliance as a guaranteed, quantifiable loss (e.g., losing the current discount, losing their status) rather than framing compliance as a potential gain?

Resistance is a signal that your framing or timing is wrong. Mitigation requires pre-emption and reframing the target's objection.

9. Think of a common objection you hear often (e.g., "It costs too much," "It is too risky," or "We do not have the time"). Practice the **Firebreak Strategy** (Chapter 6). Write out how you would:

    o Acknowledge the objection neutrally.

    o Validate the target's responsibility.

    o Immediately refactor the context (e.g., expense becomes investment; risk becomes mitigation).

10. **The Communality Buffer** is essential for tempering competence with warmth, particularly when a woman is asserting a high-status position . If you needed to present a non-negotiable directive, how would you start and end your statement using language of shared goals and collaboration to neutralize potential status resistance ?

11. **Linguistic Resonance** suggests using simple, concrete language reduces cognitive friction. Take a paragraph from a recent email you sent that contained abstract or overly formal language. Rewrite it using only concrete nouns, action verbs, and specific numbers, ensuring the message is delivered without demanding extra cognitive work from the reader.

BOOK TWO

MAGNETIC CHARISMA:
NON - VERBAL RESONANCE

INTRODUCTION
TO MAGNETIC CHARISMA

You see them walk in. They might not be the loudest person. They might not be the highest-ranking. Yet, when they speak, people lean in. When they ask for something, they get it. This is not luck. This is **Magnetic Charisma**.

Charisma is often seen as a gift, something you are born with. That idea is wrong. Charisma is a technical skill. It is a precise, learned display of silent signals that tell others exactly how competent, trustworthy, and authoritative you are. While the first book focused on the strategy of language, what you say, this book focuses on the strategy of projection: who you are.

Think of it this way: your words handle the logic. Your body handles the trust. If your posture or your gaze communicates anxiety, your perfectly crafted argument from Book 1 collapses. Charisma makes your physical presence align exactly with your verbal authority. It is the ability to communicate intense trust and competence without needing to speak a word.

In any social setting, judgments start long before the conversation does. This initial assessment is entirely based on non-verbal behavior. These silent signals determine whether a connection is started, maintained, or ended.

In a professional setting, non-verbal cues directly influence how people perceive your status and ability. You can assert your expertise endlessly. If your physical presence communicates hesitation, people will trust the non-verbal message over the verbal one. Charisma ensures your presence backs your words.

The Quiet Power of Non-Verbal Bias: Non-verbal behavior is particularly potent because it functions below the level of conscious thought. It can systematically favor or put down certain social groups or ideas without anyone realizing it.

Imagine a subtle, continuous change in proximity, a hesitant blink, or a slight change in the rhythm of your gaze. These micro-behaviors can signal superiority or submission. The important point is that the strong effects of non-verbal bias occur even when the bias remains **inaccessible to conscious awareness**. The target feels the impression, they feel that they should trust you or follow you, but they cannot consciously challenge or analyze that feeling.

Since this influence is silent and unconscious, it is a subtle but powerful form of social control. If you strictly regulate your posture, your breathing rhythm, and your eye contact, you can consistently implant specific, positive perceptions, like reliability and composure, directly into the target's mind.

To acquire magnetic charisma, you must master three main areas: controlled presence, emotional transfer, and physical connection.

1. Controlled Presence: Status Through Stillness

The first pillar of charisma is managing how you simply exist in a space. This is **Controlled Presence**. It requires regulating your physical stillness, your movement, and your posture to project specific, high-value traits.

The Antidote to Anxiety: We know from Book 1 that negative feelings, like anxiety, heavily influence social judgments. When a person feels anxious or unsure, they naturally look for someone who projects certainty. Controlled presence is the immediate antidote to that anxiety. It means eliminating all nervous energy.

- Avoid excessive hand movements.
- Stand or sit with symmetrical, open posture.
- Maintain a steady, measured gaze.

When you move deliberately and speak calmly, you communicate that you are in total control of yourself and the environment. This projection of composure instantly addresses the target's need for safety.

Posture as a Status Signal: Your posture is an immediate, non-verbal signal of your status. An open, symmetrical posture communicates confidence and authority. You are taking up space without apology. Conversely, slumping or a guarded posture signals lower status or defensiveness. By ensuring your physical bearing is always open and intentional, you communicate to the target that you are a competent, safe resource.

This strategy immediately activates the **Halo Effect**. The target infers positive traits like trustworthiness and capability from the single, impressive trait of your composure. This positive social judgment accelerates the foundational trust needed for any persuasion attempt. When you project high composure, you reduce the target's need for an impulsive, biased social assessment. They defer to your calm authority.

2. Emotional Transfer: The Contagion of Charisma

Charisma is not static. It is infectious. The process is known as **Emotional Contagion**, the automatic transfer of emotional states from one person to another. This emotional transfer is an essential part of charismatic and transformational leadership. Charismatic people deliberately and continuously project specific, positive emotional states, such as optimism, focused energy, or calm confidence, onto those around them.

The Charismatic Cascade: Studies in real organizations have tracked this process. Researchers found that a leader's charisma actually **cascaded down** to followers over time. The followers of a charismatic figure eventually became perceived as more charismatic themselves. This confirms that charisma is a set of observable behaviors and emotional states that can be adopted and replicated throughout a social system.

This emotional momentum is crucial for large-scale influence. You do not need to individually motivate a hundred people. You need to emotionally charge a dozen key individuals, whose energy then spreads the emotional state to the rest of the group.

The Role of Self-Monitoring: Emotional contagion works faster or slower depending on the target's personality. We use the trait of **self-monitoring** to diagnose this susceptibility.

- **High Self-Monitors:** These people are highly aware of social cues. They are more susceptible to both positive and negative emotional contagion. They are fast emotional amplifiers. They quickly absorb and reflect the projected state, whether it is urgency or enthusiasm. They are excellent for **immediate emotional mobilization** because they instantly accept the charismatic state.

- **Low Self-Monitors:** These individuals are less focused on adapting their behavior to social cues. They might resist immediate emotional shifts. However, once they finally adopt the behaviors and attitudes of the charismatic figure, those traits become stable and internalized parts of their persona. They provide the **structural support and stability** for the group long-term.

Your strategic plan must use these differences. You focus on emotionally charging the high self-monitors first, who then disseminate the perception of charisma to the broader, slower-moving group.

3. Haptic Connection: The First Language of Trust

Beyond what we see, what we *feel* can dictate trust. **Haptics**, or strategic touch, plays a fundamental role in building immediate connection. This sense of touch is the first form of communication developed in infancy.

Babies explore the world and their own identity through touch. This physical interaction is crucial for developing self-identity, security, and emotional well-being. Research confirms that a lack of physical touch, or tactile deprivation, is even associated with low confidence and learning problems.

The appropriate, strategic use of touch can therefore dramatically **accelerate the building of trust**. By identifying socially acceptable, low-risk haptics, the persuader can quickly establish a fundamental sense of security and connection. This physical resonance bypasses the slow, verbal process of building rapport.

The Calibration of Touch: The use of haptics requires careful calibration. Appropriate touch must be contextually and culturally relevant. A handshake is the universal professional haptic. Its firmness, dryness, and duration should communicate composure. Other forms of touch, such as a brief, supportive touch on the forearm, may be appropriate in closer social settings.

The goal is to use low-risk, physical contact to tap into the fundamental human need for security. This brief physical connection creates a rapid bond, making the target feel immediately safer and more secure in your presence.

4. The Unifying Role of Humor

Charisma uses humor as a sophisticated social tool. Humor serves powerful social functions, from unifying people to creating division. We focus exclusively on the unifying functions.

Identification Humor: This function is essential for building magnetic appeal. **Identification humor** builds group cohesion by appealing to a set of shared values and common perceptions. This happens when a joke or story addresses a slight violation of a social expectation, confirming that everyone present shares the same baseline understanding of the world.

When the target laughs at the same social pattern or violation, they confirm alignment on core values. This mutual reinforcement strengthens the relationship and reduces uncertainty about the other person.

Increased Attraction and Cohesion: A perceived good sense of humor is an invaluable social resource. People naturally gravitate toward those who project a positive, engaging vibe. Positive humor styles are strongly associated with desirable traits, including high self-esteem and extroversion, and greater relationship satisfaction.

Crucially, **shared laughter** increases interpersonal attraction, enhances group cohesion, and assists in conflict resolution. By employing positive, unifying humor, the persuader projects both psychological stability and social desirability. This increases attraction and facilitates stronger connections.

The System of Projection

Magnetic Charisma is the art of precise, non-verbal projection. It is the ability to send silent signals of competence, authority, and warmth that are absorbed by the target below conscious awareness.

The techniques we have discussed, from Controlled Presence to Emotional Contagion, must become automatic. They ensure that the target perceives you as trustworthy, capable, and stable before the verbal exchange even begins. This non-verbal foundation makes all the persuasive techniques from Book 1 exponentially more effective. You guide the choice with your words, but you secure the trust with your presence.

The following chapters will break down these elements into precise, actionable steps. We will detail how to use posture to **Broadcast Authority**, how to manage your emotional state to **Transfer Energy** into the group, and how to **Build Trust** using strategic haptics. Mastery of the silent signal is the key to effortless social influence.

CHAPTER 1
BROADCAST AUTHORITY:
MASTERING NON - VERBAL RESONANCE

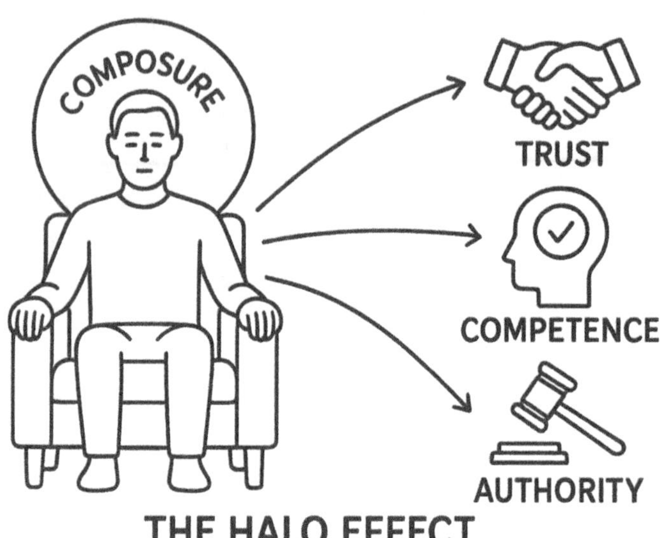

Charisma is a shield and a weapon. It protects you from doubt and guides the target toward trust. This defense and offense are built on mastering your **non-verbal resonance**. This means controlling the subtle signals that your body sends out constantly. These signals tell people how competent, calm, and authoritative you are.

The simple fact is this: you cannot decide what someone thinks of you, but you can entirely control the information they use to form that thought. Non-verbal behavior is particularly subtle, but it is a highly influential form of social messaging. It dictates the initial evaluation of your presence, and that evaluation is often absorbed below the conscious level.

To broadcast authority, you must manage three core non-verbal elements: stillness, posture, and gaze. These elements work together to project competence and composure, which immediately mitigates the target's natural anxiety and activates the powerful psychological shortcut known as the **Halo Effect**.

The Power of Stillness: Composure as Competence

In Book 1, we learned that people often rely on quick, biased judgments, especially when they feel anxious or uncertain. When a target is under pressure, they look for safety. The most immediate sign of safety and competence is stillness.

Stillness communicates that you are in control of yourself. Nervous energy, fidgeting, rapid head turning, or excessive hand gestures, sends a signal that you are not in control of the situation. This instantly undermines any verbal claim of expertise you might make. Conversely, a measured, still demeanor projects a quiet confidence.

This controlled presence serves as a powerful antidote to the target's anxiety. If you are calm, the target feels their own anxiety subside in your presence. They begin to attribute your composure to competence. This is how the **Halo Effect** starts: the single positive trait of composure causes the target to infer other positive qualities, like trustworthiness and knowledge, without needing evidence.

Actionable Stillness:

1. **Eliminate Micro-Jitters:** Become aware of small, nervous habits, tapping feet, clicking pens, or adjusting clothing repeatedly. These are energy leaks that broadcast anxiety. Practice standing or sitting with minimal movement, allowing your weight to settle completely.

2. **Controlled Transitions:** When you move, move with intention. Do not drift from one point to another. Stand up slowly. Sit down deliberately. Each movement should look like a planned action, not a nervous reaction.

3. **Vocal Control:** The voice is a primary non-verbal tool. When people are nervous, their pitch often rises and their speaking rate increases. To project composure and authority, you must maintain a low, resonant pitch and speak slightly slower than the average conversational pace. Use strategic pauses. A pause, when controlled, signals that you are thoughtful and certain, not hesitant.

Stillness ensures that the target's first, rapid judgment of you is always positive. They see competence and safety, which makes them highly receptive to your message.

Posture: The Non-Verbal Status Marker

Your posture is an immediate, non-verbal representation of your status and confidence. It dictates how much psychological space you feel entitled to take up.

Openness and Symmetry: The projection of authority requires two key features in posture: openness and symmetry.

- **Open Posture:** Avoid crossing your arms tightly across your chest or holding objects directly in front of your body like a shield. Openness communicates that you are receptive, confident, and not defensive.

- **Symmetrical Posture:** Standing or sitting with balanced shoulders and a straight back communicates physical control and mental stability. An asymmetrical posture, like leaning heavily on one side, can suggest casualness or a lack of focus.

The Space Dynamic: Posture is often measured by how effectively you utilize the space you are in. When you are standing, keep your feet planted firmly, slightly apart. When you are sitting, use the back of the chair fully. This physical settling communicates that you feel completely at ease and entitled to your space.

People subconsciously defer to those who communicate physical entitlement. By constantly practicing an open, symmetrical posture, you project a deep-seated confidence. This signals that you are not simply acting competent; you genuinely believe in your own competence.

Gaze Control: The Directed Focus

The eyes are the most powerful tool for non-verbal control. Your gaze dictates engagement, sincerity, and power dynamics.

The Measured Gaze: A nervous or subordinate gaze darts around the room, avoiding direct contact. This communicates distraction or anxiety. The gaze of authority, conversely, is controlled and measured. It is directed precisely at the target.

You do not need to stare intensely, which can feel aggressive. You need to maintain consistent, intentional eye contact throughout key parts of the interaction.

- **Establish Connection:** Use strong eye contact when you are initiating a major point or asking a critical question.

- **Signal Sincerity:** Maintain eye contact during the first sentence and the final sentence of your argument to bracket the point with sincerity.
- **Release Pressure:** In longer conversations, naturally break eye contact every few seconds by looking briefly at the side or the target's hands, then returning your gaze. This provides a brief moment of relief for the target and makes your eye contact feel intentional, not aggressive.

The Gaze of Validation: Gaze control is also essential for activating the **Liking** principle (Chapter 3). By maintaining steady eye contact while the target is speaking, you non-verbally communicate high levels of interest and respect. You are signaling that their words are the most important input in the environment. This validation increases their liking and trust in you.

The Architecture of Charismatic Projection

Broadcasting authority is the fusion of these three elements. It is the ability to project composure, competence, and confidence simultaneously.

1. **Pre-Emptive Trust:** By rigorously controlling stillness and posture, you ensure that the target's initial, rapid judgment is favorable. This pre-emptive trust makes them more receptive to your verbal message. Non-verbal behavior can be systematically biased to favor certain stimuli, and by controlling your presence, you become that favored stimulus.

2. **The Halo Effect Activation:** Your projected composure acts as the single positive trait that triggers the **Halo Effect**. The target infers that you are reliable, trustworthy, and knowledgeable because you look and sound calm. This effect significantly reduces the evidential burden you must meet later in the conversation.

3. **The Social Prime:** Your controlled presence helps set the social prime of the environment. A controlled, formal, and authoritative demeanor helps set the environment for thoughtful processing, which is often associated with the **male gender role prime**. If you require a thoughtful, long-term commitment, your non-verbal cues must support a setting where careful analysis is expected.

Mastering non-verbal resonance means treating your body as a precision instrument. Every muscle movement, every pause, and every adjustment of your gaze must be intentional. This controlled projection is the silent language of authority. It is the necessary preparation for the emotional and social influence we will discuss next.

The following chapter, **Transfer Energy: Inciting Emotional Contagion in Groups**, builds on this foundation. We move from controlling your own singular presence to actively transferring your emotional state to those around you. We will show you how to use enthusiasm, confidence, and urgency to mobilize groups and amplify your charisma through **Emotional Contagion.**

CHAPTER 2
TRANSFER ENERGY: INCITING EMOTIONAL CONTAGION IN GROUPS

FOCUSED ENTHUSIASM

The last chapter dealt with being calm. It taught you how to look steady, composed, and absolutely in control. But charisma is more than just standing still. It needs movement. It needs feeling. It needs energy.

Magnetic charisma is the ability to change the feeling of a room. It shifts the atmosphere instantly. It is not enough to simply manage your own emotional state. You must actively manage the emotions of everyone around you.

This ability to spread feeling is called **Emotional Contagion**. Think of it as an emotional current. If you project confidence, optimism, or a focused sense of urgency, that feeling automatically passes from you to the people you are talking to. This process is a fundamental, measurable mechanism of social influence. Researchers recognize it as a key ingredient in charismatic leadership. A truly magnetic person intentionally guides the collective feeling of the group. They know that a group unified by a shared emotion is much stronger than a group merely unified by an idea.

The charismatic individual is a highly efficient emotional broadcaster. They send out a clean signal. The target absorbs and then mirrors that emotional state. This ensures the collective mood aligns perfectly with the persuader's objective.

The Infectious Nature of Charisma

Charisma does not stop with the first person you meet. It creates a **cascade effect** that spreads through a social structure. This is how a small number of influential people can change the direction of a large organization or group.

Studies looking at leaders and their followers in large organizations found that the leader's charisma actually spread down through the ranks over time. This is interesting: followers of a charismatic leader eventually started to be seen as more charismatic themselves.

What does this tell us? It proves charisma is a set of observable behaviors. It is not an innate, magical quality. It is a persona, a set of emotional and physical actions that can be adopted and replicated throughout the entire group.

When you project focused energy and confidence, the influence does not stop at one person. It initiates a sequence of emotional replication. Your influence spreads without you needing to work continuously on every individual.

The Power of Behavioral Modeling: The emotional transfer ensures that the target starts acting like you. They absorb your confident posture, your calm way of speaking, and your positive emotional outlook. This behavioral modeling reduces anxiety across the group. It increases overall cohesion. People feel safer when they act the way the charismatic leader acts. They feel they are following an established, successful pattern.

Diagnosing Who Will Move Fastest

Emotional contagion works at different speeds for different people. To maximize the spread of your energy, you must quickly figure out how susceptible a person is to social cues. We rely on the personality trait known as **self-monitoring** to do this.

High Self-Monitors: The Amplifiers

High self-monitors pay intense attention to social cues. They are constantly adjusting their behavior to fit the situation. Because of this focus, they are more susceptible to both positive and negative emotional transfer.

- **Their Role:** High self-monitors are your immediate emotional amplifiers. They rapidly absorb and reflect the emotion you project, whether it is extreme urgency or deep enthusiasm. They are perfect for **immediate emotional mobilization.** If you need the group excited about a major deadline right now, focus your energy projection on the high self-monitors first. They quickly disseminate the feeling to everyone else. They are the fastest way to change a group's mood.

Low Self-Monitors: The Stable Foundation

Low self-monitors are just the opposite. They are not highly concerned with adapting their behavior to social cues. They value consistency between their internal beliefs and their external actions. They want their actions to match their identity.

- **Their Role:** Low self-monitors resist immediate emotional shifts. They are slower to be influenced by emotional contagion. But this slowness is a hidden strength. Once a low self-monitor finally adopts the behaviors and attitudes of the charismatic figure, those traits become stable. They are fully internalized. They provide the **structural support** for the group long-term. They are not the fast responders, but they are the reliable ones.

The Strategic Plan: A successful charisma strategy uses a dual approach to manage both groups.

1. **Fast Charge:** Focus immediate, clear energy projection (enthusiasm, high confidence) toward high self-monitors for quick activation and broad spread of the emotional state.

2. **Long-Term Internalization:** Use consistency arguments and secure small commitments (Book 1) with low self-monitors. Their gradual, steady adoption ensures the new behaviors and emotional states become a permanent, stable part of the group's identity.

This combined strategy ensures you get both instant energy mobilization and reliable, long-term support for your charismatic persona.

How to Engineer Emotional Projection

Emotional transfer does not happen by accident. It must be engineered through precise, non-verbal delivery. You must project your intended emotion with absolute clarity and complete consistency.

The Constant Projection of Calm: Composure is the most important foundation for emotional transfer. We know that the target's anxiety often triggers irrational social judgments. Your controlled presence is the way to counteract that anxiety. By projecting extreme calm, you activate the **Halo Effect**. The target infers that your composure comes from a source of deep competence and control, which makes them trust you instantly.

Projecting Focused Energy: Charisma needs enthusiasm, but it must be focused. Energy that is all over the place suggests anxiety. Energy that is directed and clear suggests passion and control.

- **Vocal Delivery:** Vary your tone and volume with intention. Speak slightly slower than average for authority, but increase the inflection and volume when describing the specific *benefit* of the action. This communicates that the outcome is exciting and valuable.

- **Gestural Pacing:** Use intentional, controlled hand gestures to emphasize your main points. Avoid small, nervous, repetitive movements. Use large, open hand gestures when talking about a shared objective or the future of the group. This physically reinforces the idea of collaboration.

Managing Different Affective States: Emotional contagion also depends on the target's existing emotional baseline. Some people naturally have a high **trait positive affect** (generally optimistic). Others have a high **trait negative affect** (generally critical or skeptical).

- **Positive Targets:** When engaging people who are already generally positive, amplify your enthusiasm. They will absorb and reflect it easily. This creates a positive feedback loop.

- **Negative Targets:** When talking to targets who are generally skeptical, focus more on projecting unwavering, calm authority. This addresses their skepticism with stability and competence. Do not try to overwhelm them with enthusiasm they may resist.

Humor as the Ultimate Emotional Unifier

Humor is one of the most effective tools for managing and transferring emotion in a group. It serves crucial social functions, mostly by unifying people.

Identification Humor: This specific type of humor is essential for building magnetic appeal. **Identification humor** builds group cohesion because it appeals to a set of shared values and common perspectives.

When a story or joke succeeds, it means everyone present confirms they share the same underlying social expectation or norm. This shared experience is a powerful emotional adhesive.

- **The Shared Value Check:** Shared laughter acts as a psychological test. If the target laughs at the same social violation or pattern, they confirm they align on core values. This mutual reinforcement strengthens the connection and reduces uncertainty about the other person.

The Positive Social Resource: A perceived good sense of humor is an invaluable resource in any social context. People naturally look for those who project a positive, engaging feeling. Positive humor styles are strongly associated with highly desirable personality traits, including high self-esteem and extroversion. People who use positive humor generally experience greater satisfaction in their relationships.

- **Emotional Stability:** By consistently using positive, unifying humor, you project both psychological stability and social desirability. This increases attraction and makes stronger connections easier. You must strictly avoid hostile, negative, or self-deprecating humor styles, as these suggest internal conflict or low self-esteem.

Cohesion and Conflict Resolution: The emotional value of shared laughter is supported by research showing that it increases interpersonal attraction, enhances group cohesion, and helps resolve conflicts. When people laugh together, they form stronger bonds and develop a **shared identity** that is bigger than their individual differences.

- **Creating Rituals:** Inside jokes often develop from unique group dynamics, reflecting common experiences. The charismatic leader can actively encourage these shared humorous rituals. They serve as reliable, quick ways to re-establish trust and affection, reinforcing the group's relationship and shared perspective.

The Synthesis of Energy Transfer

Transferring energy is the key to mobilizing others. It ensures the group is emotionally prepared to accept the structural arguments and decisions from Book 1.

1. **Project Composure:** Start with stability. Your calm presence is the necessary foundation that mitigates the target's anxiety and activates the Halo Effect.

2. **Target Susceptibility:** Identify high self-monitors for quick emotional spread. Use low self-monitors for long-term structural commitment.

3. **Use Humor:** Employ identification humor to confirm shared values, build group cohesion, and increase attraction.

4. **Sustain the Cascade:** Ensure your enthusiastic energy is focused and projected consistently through controlled voice and intentional gestures. This guarantees the emotional state spreads and lasts.

This mastery of emotional transfer ensures that when you move to the next stage, building deep, physical trust, the target is already emotionally receptive and unified with your purpose. This prepares the ground for the immediate, deep connection that only strategic haptics can provide. The next chapter, **Build Trust: Employing Strategic Touch and Presence**, details how to use the earliest form of human communication to accelerate rapport beyond what words can achieve.

CHAPTER 3

BUILD TRUST: EMPLOYING STRATEGIC TOUCH AND PRESENCE

Charisma must be physically grounded. It must feel real, immediate, and safe. This physical grounding is achieved through two complementary systems: strategic touch and the calculated exchange of personal information. If Book 1 taught you how to secure a choice, this book teaches you how to secure the person.

We begin with the most immediate and fundamental form of human connection: **haptics**, or touch. The strategic use of touch can accelerate trust faster than words ever could. It bypasses the slow, verbal process of building rapport. It connects directly with the target's most basic psychological need for security.

I. Haptics: The First Language of Trust

Of all the ways humans communicate, touch is the first one developed in infancy. Long before we form words, we explore our own bodies and the environment through touch. This physical interaction is crucial. It is the beginning of achieving self-identity, security, and overall well-being.

The psychological impact of touch cannot be overstated. Research even links tactile deprivation, a lack of physical touch, to developmental issues. It can lead to learning problems and a lack of trust or confidence later in life. Touch is tied directly to our foundational needs for safety and identity.

Because touch is so fundamental, the appropriate, strategic use of haptics can dramatically speed up trust building. A brief, intentional physical connection instantly establishes a fundamental sense of security between two people. This immediate physical resonance bypasses the slow, careful verbal process that logic requires.

The Necessity of Safety: Since touch is tied to deep-seated feelings of security, its use must be safe, appropriate, and low-risk. Any misuse of haptics instantly triggers an alarm in the target, and the connection is broken. The persuader must treat touch as a precision instrument, not a blunt tool.

The Controlled Handshake: The handshake is the universal professional haptic. It is the only guaranteed, appropriate opportunity for physical connection in most formal settings. You must maximize its effect.

1. **Symmetry and Firmness:** The handshake should be firm, but never crushing. It should feel symmetrical, indicating a balance of power. Avoid the submissive, "dead fish" hand. Avoid the aggressive, overly dominating grip.

2. **Dryness and Warmth:** Ensure your hand is clean and dry. A cold, clammy hand broadcasts anxiety and physical discomfort. This immediately compromises the Halo Effect you established with your composure. A warm, dry hand signals calm physical stability.

3. **Duration and Gaze:** The handshake should last approximately three seconds. During this contact, maintain direct, steady eye contact. This combination of physical contact and focused gaze communicates sincerity and intent. It locks the trust signal in place.

Low-Risk, Intentional Contact: Beyond the handshake, other forms of touch must be used carefully, adhering strictly to cultural and social norms. In appropriate social settings, a brief, supportive touch on the forearm or a gentle touch on the shoulder can be used to emphasize a shared point or to signal congratulations.

This intentional physical contact reinforces the idea of partnership. It communicates: "We are literally in this together." This creates an immediate physical bond that makes the target feel safer and more secure in your presence.

II. Controlled Presence: Non-Verbal Bias and Trust

The physical environment, including your body, is constantly influencing the target. This subtle, pervasive influence is achieved through **non-verbal bias**.

Non-verbal behavior sends signals about competence and status. This bias happens even when the target is not consciously aware of it. The target is influenced by the message, but they cannot consciously challenge or argue against it. This makes your physical presence a potent, subtle form of social control.

Maintaining Stillness and Composure: We return to the concept of Controlled Presence (Chapter 2). It is the foundation for haptics. Your body must project unwavering composure.

- **No Nervous Leakage:** Eliminate nervous gestures, fidgeting, excessive self-touch, or restless movement. These signals are leaks that broadcast anxiety.
- **The Calm Gaze:** Maintain a measured, intentional gaze. Nervous eyes dart around, broadcasting low status. A controlled gaze signals that you are focused and fully in command of the situation.

This projected composure serves a vital psychological function: it mitigates the target's internal anxiety. When the target sees your calm, controlled presence, it triggers the **Halo Effect**. They infer trust, competence, and reliability from your stability alone. This favorable initial social judgment accelerates trust and makes them more receptive to any subsequent request.

III. Strategic Disclosure: The Architecture of Charm

Once physical presence and basic haptics establish foundational trust, you must accelerate the relationship verbally. This is achieved through the strategic exchange of personal information, or **self-disclosure**. Charm is essentially the calculated use of vulnerability to create intimacy and attraction.

Frequency Over Intimacy: The goal of early self-disclosure is to rapidly establish familiarity and closeness. Research shows that **disclosure frequency** is the factor that predicts familiarity and closeness, provided the disclosures are perceived as appropriate.

The volume of shared details is more important than the depth of those details in the early stages. You must maximize the number of minor, low-stakes disclosures to build familiarity quickly. Sharing simple, non-intimate facts, your favorite type of coffee, a mundane weekend hobby, a funny anecdote about your travel routine, builds a dense foundation of connection.

The Danger of Premature Intimacy: While intimate disclosure *can* increase closeness, it carries a high risk. If disclosure is too intimate too soon, it often **reduces social attraction** because the target perceives it as inappropriate. Sharing deep, raw, or vulnerable details before a foundation of trust is established makes the target uncomfortable. They sense a lack of boundaries, and they retreat.

- **Rule of Thumb:** Intimate details (core fears, professional failures, deep relationship anxieties) must be reserved until the target explicitly signals a reciprocal readiness for that level of depth. The risk of sharing personal depth often outweighs the potential benefit in the early stages of a relationship.

IV. Narrativity: The Entertainment Value of Charm

It is not just *what* you say, but *how* you say it. The way you present personal information is key to building magnetic attraction. People appreciate being entertained.

Narrativity and Attraction: Disclosure narrativity, the telling of personal information as a structured story, increases perceived closeness and social attraction. This positive effect happens because the narrative format possesses **perceived entertainment value**. Simple, dry facts are uncompelling. Stories capture attention and create emotional connection.

The Strategy of Framing Mundane Facts: You must frame all personal information, even basic details, as engaging, short narratives rather than simple statements.

- *Instead of:* "I lived in Boston." (Dry Fact)
- *Try:* "I lived in Boston for five years. That city taught me that five minutes of rain can instantly turn into two feet of snow. I learned to keep an extra coat in the trunk, a lesson I learned the hard way after one miserable, freezing walk." (Narrative, short, entertaining, reveals minor detail).

This technique ensures the interaction remains compelling. By consistently delivering entertainment value, you maximize the psychological impact and increase social attraction toward you, the source of the story.

V. The Calibration Test: Diagnosing Appropriateness

The effects of self-disclosure are critically constrained by the target's **perceived appropriateness**. This metric is subjective. You must actively monitor the target to ensure the level of intimacy is correct.

Reciprocal Disclosure as a Gauge: The best sign of appropriateness is **reciprocal disclosure**. A target who matches your level of disclosure, in both frequency and depth, implicitly confirms that your current level of intimacy is acceptable.

The Testing Sequence:

1. **Slight Deepening:** You should test the boundary of intimacy gently. Offer a disclosure that is slightly deeper than the one you offered previously.

2. **Observe Response:** Watch the target's reaction. Do they match the depth of your new disclosure? Do they offer an equally personal, though non-intimate, detail? Do they ask a follow-up question that indicates comfort?

3. **Adjust:** If the target matches the depth, you may proceed to the next level of intimacy. If the target retreats, redirects the conversation, or offers only short, closed answers, the intimacy level was inappropriate. You must immediately reduce the depth of future disclosures back to a safe, frequent level.

This calibration process ensures you build closeness rapidly without triggering the alarm bells of inappropriate vulnerability. You maintain social attraction while escalating the relationship toward greater trust.

VI. Charisma in Non-Physical Spaces

The structure of charm changes when the physical presence is removed, such as in text messages or virtual correspondence. Here, haptics and immediate non-verbal signals are absent.

Research confirms that in the virtual medium, attraction relies almost entirely on "words, charm, and seduction" and not on physical presence. The entire burden of building rapport and signaling attraction shifts to the linguistic architecture of the message.

Linguistic Charisma in Text:

- **Narrative Focus:** Narrativity becomes even more crucial. Every message must be crafted to provide entertainment value and familiarity.

- **Emotional Density:** Since tone of voice is absent, you must ensure the language itself conveys the emotional state (e.g., using specific, active words, or light, positive humor).

- **Frequency Management:** Frequent, low-stakes digital communication maintains familiarity. It keeps you present in the target's mind without demanding deep cognitive effort.

When physical tools are gone, linguistic mastery must compensate. You must use the principles of framing and concrete language (Book 1) to build a compelling virtual persona that ensures the target's continued interest.

The Physical and Psychological Blend

Building trust through strategic presence is the blending of the physical and the psychological. It begins with the simple, fundamental act of touch: a signal that communicates security and identity deep within the target's mind. It is sustained by projecting unwavering, controlled composure and competence. It is accelerated by the calculated flow of personal information, maximizing frequency and narrativity while meticulously managing appropriateness.

Charisma is the system that ensures the target feels safe, entertained, and seen. This deep, non-verbal connection makes the persuasive ideas you introduce feel less like external demands and more like shared, safe opportunities. The following chapter, **Shape Perception: Using Posture to Signal Competence**, will return to the visual cues, detailing exactly how specific body positions and movements can permanently install perceptions of capability and status in the target's mind.

CHAPTER 4

SHAPE PERCEPTION: USING POSTURE TO SIGNAL COMPETENCE

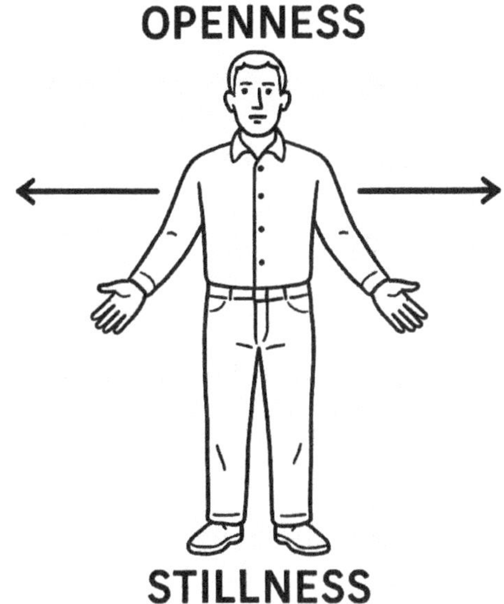

Your body is your silent resume. It speaks louder than your title and faster than your words. This silent communication is the foundation of magnetic charisma. If Book 1 taught you how to frame a choice, this chapter teaches you how to **frame yourself**. You must learn to control the visual information you send out. This information shapes the target's perception of your competence, your authority, and your general status.

The way you stand, sit, and move dictates how much psychological space you feel entitled to occupy. This perception influences power dynamics in any setting, from a negotiation to a simple social exchange. When you master your non-verbal signals, you are not simply looking confident. You are actively installing the perception of competence directly into the target's mind.

The Silent Power of Non-Verbal Bias

Charisma relies heavily on a unique feature of non-verbal communication: it is a particularly subtle form of social influence. The messages are often sent and received **below conscious awareness.**

This is crucial. Since the influence operates outside the target's conscious thought, they cannot consciously challenge or argue against the impression created. They simply accept the feeling that you are trustworthy or capable. Non-verbal behavior can be systematically biased, making people favor or put down certain social cues or individuals. By rigorously controlling your posture and gaze, you become the favored cue. You inject specific, positive perceptions into the target's mind without triggering their critical analysis.

The goal is to move the perception of competence from an abstract idea to an unquestioned reality.

Posture as Architectural Status

The first step in shaping perception is mastering your posture. Posture is a physical marker of status. High-status posture communicates that you are settled, prepared, and fully in command of your current space.

1. The Mechanics of Openness:

High competence is signaled through **openness**. You must avoid closed or guarded postures. These include tightly crossed arms, clasping hands directly in front of your body, or using objects (like a coffee cup or portfolio) as a shield. Closed posture signals defensiveness, anxiety, or low status.

Open posture means allowing your chest and torso to face the target without obstruction. Your arms should be relaxed, resting loosely at your sides when standing, or placed on the arms of the chair when sitting. This openness communicates that you are receptive, confident, and have nothing to hide. You are physically inviting connection, which lowers the target's psychological barrier.

2. Symmetry and Stability:

Authority is often signaled through **symmetry**. A balanced posture communicates physical control and mental stability. An asymmetrical posture, like leaning heavily on one foot, resting your entire weight on one elbow, or constantly twisting your body, suggests a lack of focus or casualness.

When you are seated, sit back completely, using the full depth of the chair. Keep your shoulders level. When you are standing, plant your feet firmly, distributing your weight evenly. This physical stability communicates that you are grounded and prepared for whatever happens next. You are not waiting to spring into action. You are already in command.

3. The Space Dynamic:

Posture dictates how much **space** you claim. People subconsciously defer to those who communicate physical entitlement. An effective persuader occupies their space completely, whether it is a small chair or a large platform.

This physical settling communicates that you are entirely at ease and believe you belong exactly where you are. This signals competence and influences power dynamics in professional settings. By physically claiming your space, you non-verbally assert status, and that non-verbal assertion is accepted much faster than a verbal declaration would be.

Stillness: The Composure Antidote

Composure is the single most effective trait for triggering the **Halo Effect**. The Halo Effect is a social bias where a general positive impression is inferred from a single positive trait. The trait you control is composure.

The Threat of Anxiety: As we have established, anxiety and negative feelings are deeply linked to social judgments. When a target is anxious, they make quick, biased assessments to find safety. They look for someone who projects certainty and stability. Nervous energy, fidgeting, adjusting clothing, scratching, or rapid head movements, broadcasts anxiety. This instantly undermines your verbal claims.

The Value of Stillness: Controlled **stillness** communicates that you are in total control of yourself. Your calm demeanor acts as the antidote to the target's anxiety. When the target sees your composure, they feel their own internal anxiety begin to subside. They begin to infer that your lack of nervousness is a result of deep competence and control over the situation. They think, "This person is calm because they know exactly what to do."

Actionable Stillness Techniques:

1. **Eliminate Energy Leaks:** Become ruthlessly aware of all micro-movements. Use self-monitoring to identify habits like pen-clicking, toe-tapping, or hair-touching. Eliminate these leaks.

2. **Controlled Hand Gestures:** When you use your hands, use them only to punctuate key ideas. When you are not actively gesturing, return them to a neutral, open position (e.g., resting lightly on the table or at your sides). Intentional movement is good; reactive movement is bad.

3. **Vocal Pacing:** The voice must support the stillness of the body. To project authority, you must maintain a low, resonant pitch. Speak slightly slower than the average conversational pace. Use strategic pauses before and after key phrases. A pause, when controlled, signals that you are thoughtful and certain, not hesitant.

Stillness ensures the target's first, rapid social judgment, made under conditions of potential anxiety, is a positive one. You have successfully activated the Halo Effect and accelerated the trust process.

Gaze Control: The Directed Focus of Authority

Your eyes are the most immediate indicator of your intent, sincerity, and status. Gaze control is essential for directing attention and signaling authority.

The Measured Gaze: A nervous or low-status gaze avoids direct contact or flits rapidly around the room. This communicates distraction or a lack of conviction. The gaze of authority, conversely, is controlled and measured. It is directed precisely at the target.

You do not need to maintain continuous, unbroken eye contact. That can feel aggressive and threatening. You need to maintain **intentional** eye contact during key communicative moments.

1. **Establishing Connection:** Make clear, consistent eye contact when you initiate a major point, ask a critical question, or introduce a major proposal.

2. **Signaling Sincerity:** Maintain eye contact during the final sentence of your argument. This brackets your point with a clear signal of sincerity.

3. **Releasing Pressure:** In longer exchanges, look briefly to the side, perhaps at an object or a note, and then return your gaze to the target. This brief release of pressure is intentional. It makes the target feel that your eye contact is a deliberate act of focus, not a nervous tic.

Gaze and Validation: Gaze control is also essential for activating the **Liking** principle. By maintaining steady, attentive eye contact while the *target* is speaking, you non-verbally communicate a high level of interest and respect. You are signaling that their input is the most important element in the environment. This validation increases their liking and trust in you, reinforcing the connection established by your composure.

The Subtlety of Non-Verbal Bias

We must address the fact that this influence is often outside the target's awareness. This is the definition of **non-verbal bias**.

Non-verbal bias means that exposure to your controlled presence contributes heavily to the *attitudes and beliefs shared within a culture*. If you consistently project high-status competence, you are not just influencing one person's perception of you. You are subtly reinforcing a general cultural ideal that links composure and stillness to power.

The Danger of Leaks: Because non-verbal behavior is so influential, any leak, any moment of unguarded anxiety or weakness, can damage the perception quickly. The mind absorbs the unconscious signal as truth faster than the conscious word. If your posture collapses slightly at a moment of stress, the target receives the signal: *insecurity*. This is why continuous self-monitoring is essential. You must maintain the controlled presence regardless of the internal conversational pressure.

The Role in Power Dynamics: Research confirms that non-verbal communication is vital in professional settings, specifically influencing power dynamics and perceptions of competence. By using open posture and stillness, you assert non-verbal power. This assertion, because it is silent and subtle, is often accepted without challenge.

The Integrated Visual Signal

Shaping perception is the intentional fusion of stillness, posture, and gaze. It moves influence from the realm of verbal debate to the realm of physical reality.

1. **Stillness** projects composure, neutralizing anxiety.
2. **Open Posture** claims status and signals confidence.
3. **Controlled Gaze** directs attention and signals authority and sincerity.

This integrated visual signal ensures that the target's first, non-verbal impression of you is one of high competence and stable authority. You have established a foundation of trust that makes all subsequent persuasive arguments easier to deliver and more readily accepted.

This mastery of self-projection prepares us for the social dimension of charisma. The following chapter, **Unify Groups: Leveraging Humor for Social Cohesion**, details how to use humor not just for entertainment, but as a precise psychological tool to confirm shared values, increase attraction, and create a powerful sense of group identity.

CHAPTER 5

UNIFY GROUPS: LEVERAGING HUMOR FOR SOCIAL COHESION

Charisma is the glue that holds people together. It is what moves a room full of separate individuals into a single, unified group that is easy to talk to and guide. The fastest, most effective tool for this unification is **humor**.

Humor is not just about making people laugh. It is a calculated, sophisticated social tool. It manages the dynamics of a group, confirms shared values instantly, and raises the level of attraction between people. If you use humor correctly, you are not just telling a story. You are running a psychological test. You confirm that the target and the entire group share the same basic outlook on the world. This mutual agreement builds powerful, immediate cohesion.

The Unifying Purpose of Laughter

Humor serves several critical social functions. It can be unifying or it can be divisive. A charismatic leader focuses exclusively on the unifying functions. These are mainly **identification** and **clarification**.

1. Identification Humor: Checking the Shared Beliefs

Identification humor is the process that builds group cohesion. It works because participants share a common perception or value that is revealed when the joke is told. When everyone laughs at the same joke, it often happens because the joke points out a minor, shared violation of a social expectation or norm.

- **The Vetting Process:** Shared laughter confirms alignment. If the target laughs at the same social violation, they confirm that they share your core values and baseline expectations. This mutual reinforcement strengthens the relationship instantly and reduces any uncertainty about the other person. This shared perspective creates a solid, shared worldview, which is what cohesion needs most.

- **How to Apply It:** Use humor that references a small, shared inconvenience or a common expectation that applies to everyone in the room. For example, making a light joke about a well-known technical problem that the whole team faces. By making a shared joke about the external problem, you confirm that everyone agrees on the norm (the problem is annoying) and that you are all together in the experience. This confirmation is powerful, and it raises attraction toward you.

2. Clarification Humor: Reducing Uncertainty

Humor also helps to **clarify expectations**. This function reduces uncertainty about others by appealing to common values. When a joke successfully clarifies expectations and reinforces mutual understanding, it quickly establishes what is "normal" and acceptable within the group.

In tense or awkward social settings, using unifying humor can quickly clarify what is expected and reinforce mutual understanding. When anxiety is high, humor provides a quick, acceptable moment of shared identity. This allows the group to relax and reset its emotional tone.

Humor and Personal Attraction

A perceived good sense of humor is an incredibly valuable social resource. People naturally look for those who project a positive and engaging feeling in conversation.

The Link to Emotional Health: Humor styles are deeply connected to personality and psychological health. **Positive humor styles**, humor that is gentle, inclusive, and unifying, are strongly linked to desirable traits like high self-esteem, cheerfulness, and high satisfaction in relationships.

- **Projecting Stability:** By consistently using positive, unifying humor, the charismatic person projects **psychological stability** and **social desirability**. They signal that they are emotionally secure. This makes them highly attractive and makes strong connections easier to form. You must strictly avoid humor that is hostile, negative, or self-deprecating, as these actions often suggest internal conflict or low self-esteem. Your humor must lift the group's mood, not criticize it.

The Therapeutic Value: The emotional value of shared laughter is supported by research showing that **shared laughter** increases attraction between people, enhances group cohesion, and even helps resolve conflicts. When people laugh together, they form stronger bonds and develop a **shared identity** that is greater than their individual differences.

Creating Shared Rituals

The goal is to move beyond a moment of laughter to create lasting bonds. This is best achieved by creating shared rituals and "inside jokes."

Inside Jokes as Identity Markers: Inside jokes develop naturally from unique group experiences, reflecting common ground and bringing joy to the group. A charismatic person can actively encourage the development of these shared humorous rituals. They serve as fast, reliable ways to re-establish trust and affection, especially when tension is present. The shared perspective reinforces the group relationship and confirms mutual loyalty.

- **How to Apply It:** When a funny, accidental moment happens, a small, shared error, or an unusual clash of ideas, do not let the moment pass. Reference it again later in the conversation or the next day. This repeated reference elevates the small moment into a **shared ritual**. This ritual confirms mutual loyalty and affection quickly and establishes a specific group memory.

Humor and the Non-Verbal System

Humor cannot exist in isolation. It relies entirely on the non-verbal foundation established earlier in this book.

Stillness and Delivery: Humor needs perfect **composure** for delivery (Chapter 2). If you deliver a joke with nervous energy, the anxiety compromises the effectiveness of the humor. The audience senses the instability and does not laugh with the content. Controlled stillness and a measured vocal pace ensure the humor is perceived as intentional and stable.

Emotional Contagion: Humor is a highly effective tool for initiating positive **Emotional Contagion** (Chapter 3). If you project genuine amusement, the people in the group who are easily influenced by social cues (high self-monitors) will immediately absorb and reflect that emotion, spreading the positive feeling throughout the room.

The Halo Effect: The positive feeling created by unifying humor reinforces the **Halo Effect**. The target now connects the positive emotional state (joy, connection) directly with your presence (composure, competence), which further cements the inference of trustworthiness and reliability.

Humor and Cultural Sensitivity

Humor is a universal tool, but its specific application must be highly sensitive to the group's specific context. The humor must align with the group's norms and values.

- **Targeting the Norm:** Identification humor works best when it targets a minor violation of an *external* norm or expectation, something outside the group that everyone can agree upon. Never use humor that targets a group member or that uses humor meant to divide or criticize. That instantly destroys group cohesion and trust.

- **The Unspoken Agreement:** The successful use of humor proves your social intelligence. It proves you understand the target's baseline values without them having to state them explicitly.

The Cohesive Force

Humor is the cohesive force of charisma. It moves a collection of individuals from separate self-interest into a unified, emotionally connected group. By employing identification humor, you confirm shared values, reduce uncertainty, and raise attraction. This creates a powerful shared identity that makes the group highly receptive to your influence.

The final step in mastering charisma is integrating all these concepts, posture, emotional transfer, touch, and humor, into a single, effortless persona. The next chapter will provide the final synthesis of these non-verbal strategies, detailing how they function together to create truly magnetic, lasting influence.

CONCLUSION
THE INTEGRATED CHARISMATIC PERSONA

This book was about making your presence count. We started by looking past the idea that charisma is some accidental gift. It is clear now that it is a set of specific, learned behaviors. We have moved entirely from the strategy of argument (Book 1) to the strategy of projection. You learned how to control your body, manage emotional energy, and connect with people instantly.

The person who possesses true magnetic charisma is not doing these things one at a time. They are blending them all into one seamless, powerful presence. This chapter brings together the core systems we built: **Controlled Presence, Emotional Transfer, Haptics, and Strategic Disclosure**. The entire point is to create a persona that generates trust and makes people want to listen to you, long before you even get to the logical proposal.

I. The Silent Authority: Establishing Pre-Emptive Trust

The first, non-negotiable step of charisma is making sure your body projects competence and stability. You must master **Controlled Presence**.

The Body's Hidden Message: Your body is speaking constantly. It is sending out signals that influence the target's judgment, and most of the time, the target is not even aware they are receiving the message. These non-verbal cues determine how others see your authority and competence faster than anything you could say in an introduction. If your body broadcasts nervousness, fidgeting, restless movement, or avoiding eye contact, it instantly cancels out any claim of expertise you might make.

The Fusion of Stillness and Symmetry: Authority is not loud. It is still. It is symmetrical.

1. **Stillness is Self-Control: Stillness** communicates that you are in total control of yourself. This controlled demeanor is the best possible way to counter the target's anxiety. When people are nervous, they look for safety. Your visible calm makes them feel safe. This safety triggers the **Halo Effect**: the target infers deep competence and trustworthiness from the single trait of your composure.

   - *Action Check:* Practice eliminating energy leaks. Every unnecessary micro-movement, such as pen clicking, shifting weight constantly, is a loss of psychological status. Be still.

2. **Posture Claims Space: Posture** must be open and balanced. You must avoid closed positions like tightly crossing your arms or using objects as a shield. By standing or sitting with an open, symmetrical posture, you non-verbally claim your space. This silent assertion of status is often accepted without challenge. This gives you an immediate, non-verbal advantage that supports your entire interaction.

3. **The Intentional Gaze: Gaze control** signals both focus and sincerity. A measured, intentional gaze directs the target's attention and reassures them that you are fully present. This focus is a form of non-verbal validation, which instantly increases their liking and trust in you.

Controlling your presence ensures that the target's initial, rapid judgment is positive. You secure pre-emptive trust, making the target receptive before the conversation even begins.

Charisma is not static. It spreads like a wave. The second stage involves actively moving your desired emotional state to those around you through **Emotional Contagion**.

The Charismatic Cascade: Studies show that charisma spreads from leaders to followers, who then become perceived as more charismatic by others. This proves that charisma is a set of reproducible behaviors, not an innate personal trait. You are not just managing your own mood. You are mobilizing the emotional energy of the group to align with your objectives.

Targeting the Energy Transfer: To maximize this spread, you must quickly figure out how the target processes emotion. We use the **self-monitoring** trait to categorize this:

1. **High Self-Monitors: The Amplifiers:** These people are quick to absorb and reflect the emotion you project (enthusiasm, confidence). Use them for **immediate emotional mobilization** to spread the mood rapidly throughout the group.

2. **Low Self-Monitors: The Foundation:** These people are slower to shift, but once they adopt a behavior or emotional state, it becomes fully internalized and stable. Focus on them for **long-term structural stability**.

By directing focused, positive energy toward the right people, you guarantee the collective mood aligns with your goals.

The Emotional Unifier: Humor: The most efficient tool for emotional unification is **Identification Humor**. This specific type of humor builds cohesion because it appeals to a set of shared values.

- **Actionable Result:** Shared laughter confirms that the entire group agrees on core values and expectations. This consensus reduces uncertainty, builds deep cohesion, and makes everyone like each other more. By using positive, unifying humor, you project psychological stability and social desirability, making yourself a desirable social resource.

III. The Trust Accelerator: Haptics and Disclosure

The charismatic persona must feel physically and psychologically connected. This is achieved through calculated physical signals and the calculated flow of personal information.

Haptics: The Security Signal: Touch is the most basic form of human communication, tied directly to our earliest sense of security and identity. The appropriate, strategic use of haptics, especially a firm, intentional handshake, can accelerate trust faster than any language. This physical resonance taps into the target's fundamental need for safety.

Strategic Disclosure: Intimacy by Design: Charm uses the calculated exchange of personal information, or **self-disclosure**. You must prioritize **disclosure frequency** over **disclosure intimacy** in the early stages to quickly establish familiarity.

- **The Danger:** Sharing deep, intimate details too early is often seen as inappropriate and can instantly *reduce* social attraction.
- **The Solution:** Use **Narrativity**. Frame minor personal facts as engaging, short stories that offer perceived entertainment value. This maintains interest and builds familiarity without the risk of inappropriate vulnerability.

You must continuously monitor the target's **reciprocal disclosure** to gauge appropriateness. If they match your depth, you can proceed. If they retreat, you must immediately pull back. This process ensures you build closeness rapidly while protecting social attraction.

IV. The Integrated System and Flexibility

The charismatic persona must be flexible enough to handle predictable social resistance.

The Need for Flexibility: Remember the lessons from Book 1: successful communication requires the ability to switch influence styles. You must be able to move from **push energy** (assertion, direction) to **pull energy** (collaboration, inquiry) at the right moment. The charismatic person is not locked into one single style.

The Communality Buffer: A woman asserting high competence may face predictable social resistance from male targets. This is not about the idea; it is about status.

- **Mitigation:** The solution is the **Communality Buffer**. This involves intentionally blending assertive communication with displays of warmth, empathy, and collaboration. This use of shared language neutralizes resistance by making competence feel like a shared resource, rather than a challenge to the target's status.

The Social Prime Control: Your projected composure and demeanor help set the social context. If you project a very formal, analytical approach (the male gender role prime), both men and women will process your messages more thoughtfully. If you require rapid, non-critical agreement, you must set a context that encourages less careful processing. The charisma you project controls the depth of the target's thought.

V. Conclusion: The Launch Platform

Charisma is the launch platform for influence. It ensures the target is emotionally stabilized, socially unified, and psychologically receptive. Your stillness and composure secure pre-emptive trust. Your shared humor and energy mobilize their emotion. Your careful disclosure creates deep, personal connection.

The target attributes your success to your magnetic personality, not to your careful technique. They feel safe, unified, and ready to follow.

We now transition from the visual and non-verbal to the precise control of the word. The next book, **Linguistic Influence**, will give you the tools to secure commitment using scientifically grounded principles of language. We move from the physical control of the self to the precise psychological control of the message.

REFLECTION QUESTIONS

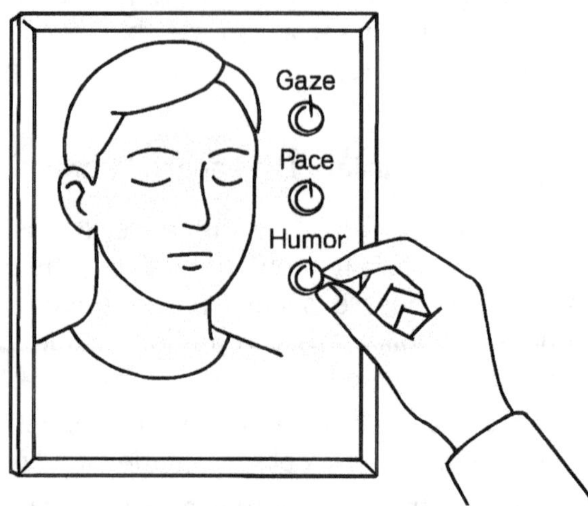

We have just finished the second book. We moved from the architecture of choice to the architecture of self. You now understand that charisma is not an accident; it is a technical output of mastering your non-verbal signals, managing your emotional energy, and initiating connections through the earliest forms of human communication.

Before we move on to the precision of language in Book 3, you must internalize these lessons. The skills of charisma, stillness, haptics, and emotional transfer, must become automatic reflexes. Use these questions to personalize the material, mapping the concepts onto your own interactions. The objective is to make the charismatic persona effortless and consistent.

Section 1: Controlled Presence and Authority

Charisma begins with control over your own body. Your presence broadcasts competence and authority. This is the foundation that triggers the **Halo Effect**, making people trust you instantly.

1. **Stillness Audit:** Recall the last three times you felt genuinely nervous in a conversation: a presentation, a job interview, or a difficult social exchange. What **energy leaks** did you exhibit? (e.g., did you shuffle your feet, play with your ring, or rush your words?) Now, describe three specific, actionable steps you can take to replace that nervous energy with intentional, controlled stillness in your next high-stakes interaction.

2. **Posture and Status: Posture** dictates how much psychological space you claim. When you are sitting in meetings, are you typically closed (arms crossed, leaning away) or open (symmetrical, hands resting on the table)? How does changing your posture to a more open, symmetrical position, physically claiming the space, change your internal feeling of authority? Practice standing in an open, powerful posture for two minutes every morning this week.

3. **Gaze Control:** Think about a recent time you had to deliver a critical point. Did you maintain continuous, intentional eye contact throughout the key phrase? If not, where did your gaze shift? For your next serious conversation, plan the exact three moments (e.g., the introduction, the critical number, the final question) where you will hold your gaze for an extra count to project absolute certainty and sincerity.

4. **The Halo Effect:** The **Halo Effect** infers competence from composure. If you walked into a room where everyone felt anxious, how would your current non-verbal presence, your vocal pace, your stillness, your open posture, act as the single calming trait that causes them to instantly trust your competence?

Charisma spreads emotional energy. It unites separate people into a cohesive, receptive group.

5. **Emotional Contagion:** When you enter a room, what is the *single* emotional state you project most consistently right now (e.g., focus, caution, or enthusiasm)? Now, identify a **high self-monitor** in your network: someone who quickly picks up and reflects the mood of the room. For your next group interaction, plan how you will direct your intended emotional state (e.g., focused optimism) specifically toward that high self-monitor to initiate the **charismatic cascade**.

6. **Humor and Shared Values: Identification Humor** is used to confirm that a group shares the same beliefs. Think about a social norm or expectation that your current work or social group finds slightly ridiculous. Plan a light, short story that gently references this norm violation. How would the **shared laughter** from that joke confirm that everyone agrees on the norm, reducing uncertainty and strengthening your **shared identity**?

7. **The Stability of Low Self-Monitors: Low self-monitors** are slow to move but provide long-term stability once committed. Identify a low self-monitor in a group you lead or belong to. What structural, verifiable evidence (data, verifiable consistency) must you provide them to ensure they internalize the new behavior, rather than simply adopting it superficially?

Section 3: Haptics, Disclosure, and Connection

Building trust requires physical and psychological closeness. This must be managed with absolute precision.

8. **Haptics as Security: Touch** is the first language of human security. Recall your last handshake. Was it symmetrical, firm, and intentional, or was it rushed? For your next handshake with a new contact, focus entirely on two things: ensuring your hand is warm and dry (to avoid broadcasting anxiety), and maintaining steady eye contact for the full three seconds of contact. How does this controlled focus change your sense of psychological presence during the introduction?

9. **Disclosure Frequency vs. Intimacy: Disclosure frequency** drives early closeness, but intimacy must be controlled. Name two minor, low-stakes facts about yourself (e.g., a mundane hobby, a favorite local coffee shop). Now, frame those two facts as short, engaging narratives that provide **entertainment value**. Commit to sharing these two narratives frequently this week to build rapid familiarity without the risk of inappropriate vulnerability.

10. **The Calibration Test:** If you were to slightly deepen your personal disclosure (e.g., sharing a minor professional challenge you overcame), how would you monitor the target's **reciprocal disclosure** to determine if the intimacy level was appropriate? What are the specific non-verbal or verbal signs that would signal you need to immediately **retreat** from that level of intimacy?

BOOK THREE

NLP MIND CONTROL:
THE SCIENCE OF FRAMING AND BELIEF

INTRODUCTION

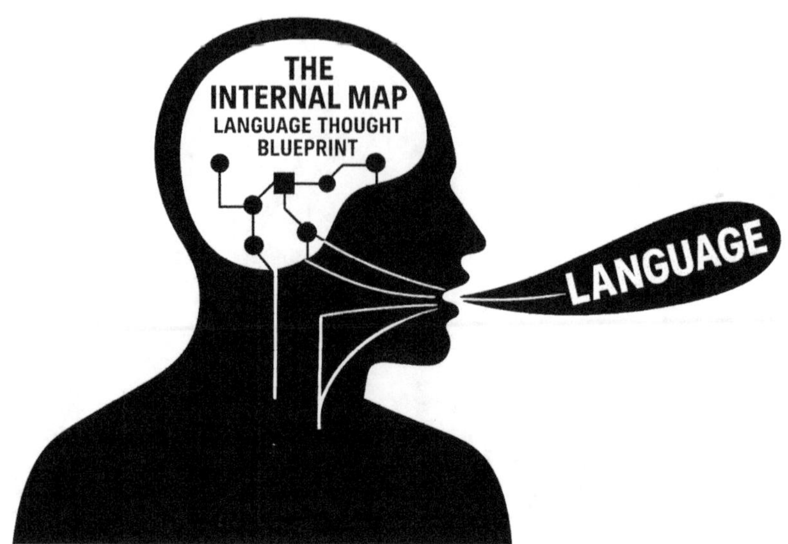

Do you ever watch someone walk into a room and instantly command attention? They get the contract. They secure the commitment. They leave others feeling energized and ready to follow. This ability is not simply a natural gift. It is a practiced skill. It rests on specific, verifiable knowledge of how the human brain works.

What if you could consistently predict the reactions of the people around you? What if you knew exactly what to say to move a choice from "maybe" to "yes"?

This book is the definitive answer to those questions. It is not an abstract theory or a philosophical treatise on success; it is a dedicated study in **predictive human behavior**, built upon the science of language, neurology, and decision-making. We are moving beyond the realm of hopeful persuasion and entering the domain of **verifiable influence**.

For too long, the true mastery of influence has been shrouded in misconception, luck, or charismatic appeal. For the serious student of human interaction, for the individual committed to achieving excellence through communication, this obscurity is unacceptable. You are not looking for chance; you are looking for a lever. This book hands you that lever. It is the culmination of decades of research, refining the art of influence into a **verifiable science**: the science of **Advanced Neuro-Linguistic Programming (NLP)**.

The acronym **NLP** stands at a fascinating crossroads, pointing to both the foundational human influence field of **Neuro-Linguistic Programming** and, in a completely separate discipline, the computational field of **Natural Language Processing**. This book is dedicated to the former, positioning it as the **master blueprint for human influence**.

The pioneers of NLP gave us a brilliant, early map for understanding how language, neurology, and behavior interconnect. This foundational work, introducing powerful concepts like **Anchoring, Reframing, and Strategy Elicitation**, provided essential insights that first mapped out how our language shapes our internal experience and, consequently, our results. This is the positive legacy we honor and build upon.

However, any field that promises mastery must be prepared to face rigorous scrutiny. The early models of Neuro-Linguistic Programming, while groundbreaking in their time, often relied heavily on analogy and non-specific observations. They presented powerful techniques but occasionally anchored those techniques to metaphorical, and sometimes scientifically outdated, concepts of brain function.

This reliance on anecdotal success, rather than empirical validation, is what fueled the skepticism from the wider scientific community, which, in some cases justly, pointed to a lack of rigorous, independently repeatable evidence for all of its claims.

This challenge is precisely where **Advanced NLP** begins. We do not ask you to simply *believe* in a system; we ask you to **master the science that now validates, refines, and supersedes** the original models. We strip away the unverified, anecdotal elements and fuse the powerful, actionable core of NLP with the most reliable findings from **cognitive science, behavioral economics, and contemporary linguistics**.

This book is the next evolution of NLP, providing the evidence-based framework that allows you to confidently apply techniques with the expectation of a **predictive outcome**.

The computational field of **Natural Language Processing** has, in its own way, validated the core premise of human influence: by using computers to analyze vast datasets of human speech and text, it has confirmed that **specific word patterns reliably correlate with specific psychological states and purchasing decisions** (Loftus & Palmer, 1974). Our goal is to take that computational precision and make it an intuitive human skill for you. You are moving from a rudimentary map to the GPS-level accuracy of modern science, ensuring that every linguistic and non-verbal maneuver you make is backed by verifiable data on how the human brain processes information and makes decisions.

The Three Pillars of Predictive Influence

The ability to "consistently predict reactions" is possible only because human decisions are fundamentally **algorithmic**. They are not random acts of free will in a vacuum; they are the result of highly systematic **cognitive shortcuts** developed by the brain to conserve energy. To master influence is to master the architecture of these shortcuts. Our methodology in Advanced NLP is built upon three irrefutable scientific pillars:

Pillar 1: Behavioral Economics and The Architecture of Framing

For decades, the assumption in much of the business and psychology world was that human beings were essentially rational actors, *Homo economicus*, who made decisions based on a clear, logical assessment of utility. **Behavioral Economics** shattered this myth.

The pioneering work of Nobel laureate Daniel Kahneman and Amos Tversky, specifically their development of **Prospect Theory**, provided the mathematical proof that decision-making is **framing-dependent** (Kahneman & Tversky, 1979). Their most critical finding is the principle of **Loss Aversion**: the finding that the pain of a loss is psychologically approximately **twice as powerful** as the pleasure of an equivalent gain.

This principle is the ultimate verifiable lever of influence, and it is the scientific refinement of the classic NLP technique of **Reframing**.

In traditional NLP, Reframing taught you to change the *meaning* of an event by shifting its context. In **Advanced NLP**, we use the mathematics of Prospect Theory to consciously frame our proposals. We stop focusing solely on what a person *gains* by saying "yes" (which only taps into 1x motivational power), and we strategically focus on what they **lose or miss out on** by saying "no" (which activates 2x motivational power).

Consider a classic sales scenario:

- *The Legacy Frame (Gain-Focused)*: "If you sign this contract, you will **gain** three new clients in the first month."
- *The Advanced NLP Frame (Loss-Aversion Focused)*: "By **not** signing this contract today, you are actively choosing to let your competitor **capture** the three new clients that are currently ready to come on board. This is what it **costs** you to wait."

This is not manipulation; it is an application of a fundamental, mathematically verified principle of human motivation. The ability to structure your language to activate this powerful, predictable bias is the essence of verifiable framing. Mastering this pillar allows you to engineer the context of the decision, making your desired outcome the path of least motivational resistance.

Pillar 2: Cognitive Science and The T.O.T.E. Algorithm

The promise of predicting reactions requires a system that is not only built on science but is also **algorithmic**, a system you can run repeatedly with the expectation of a consistent result. The foundational understanding comes from **Cognitive Science**, which views the brain as an information processing system.

Early NLP borrowed heavily from the work of George A. Miller, Eugene Galanter, and Karl Pribram, specifically their **T.O.T.E. Model (Test–Operate–Test–Exit)** (Miller, Galanter, & Pribram, 1960). We use the T.O.T.E. model as the master blueprint for all influence strategies, transforming the vague process of persuasion into a closed-loop system of feedback and refinement:

1. **TEST (The Initial Calibration):** This phase is about gathering accurate data, not making assumptions. Before you speak, you must **TEST** the subject's current frame, emotional state, and predictable cognitive biases using verifiable non-verbal and linguistic cues (which we cover in detail later).

2. **OPERATE (The Intervention):** You apply a strategic intervention, a specific linguistic frame, a Meta-Model question, or a non-verbal shift, designed to move the subject from State A to State B.

3. **TEST (The Feedback Loop):** Crucially, you immediately **TEST** for the effect. Did the subject's breathing deepen? Did you see a flash of a micro-expression of agreement? This is the moment where your **Sensory Acuity** (rooted in Ekman's research) confirms or denies the success of your intervention.

4. **EXIT (Commitment Secured or Rerun):** If the Test confirms success, you move to secure the commitment ("yes"). If not, you immediately cycle back to **OPERATE** with a refined intervention.

This T.O.T.E. structure is what makes influence a **practiced, reliable skill** rather than an improvisational art. It ensures that every action is purposeful, measurable, and adaptive, eliminating the need to guess what the other person is thinking. You gain an architecture for success.

Pillar 3: Psycholinguistics and The Programming of Language

The third pillar addresses the core concept of **Linguistic Programming**. The classic NLP models (like the Milton Model) offered powerful suggestions on how to use vague language to bypass conscious resistance. While effective, the underlying *mechanism* was often vaguely attributed to non-specific 'unconscious' factors.

Modern **Psycholinguistics** provides the precise, verifiable explanation: **Semantic Priming** (Neely, 1977). Studies consistently show that the words and concepts you introduce immediately prior to a critical decision, the "prime", unconsciously influence the speed and favorability with which a person processes a subsequent, related concept. Your language doesn't just convey information; it actively **primes** the listener's brain for the next thought, creating a favorable cognitive context.

We use this principle to transform the classic NLP technique of **Presupposition** into a highly advanced tool. Presuppositions are linguistic structures that require the listener to accept a hidden premise in order to make sense of the sentence.

For example, asking, *"Which solution do you prefer, A or B?"* presupposes that the person has already agreed to a solution. The psycholinguistic proof is that the brain, in its effort to conserve energy, expends more cognitive resources challenging the premise ("I don't agree to a solution") than simply engaging with the choice ("A or B").

By strategically loading your language with **Presuppositions** and embedding terms like "value," "agreement," and "commitment," you are, in effect, laying down neurological primes that make agreement the path of least cognitive resistance. You are not arguing for the decision; you are **programming the decision pathway** through verifiable linguistic structures.

The Architecture of Mastery: Why This Book Changes Everything

The pursuit of influence is a pursuit of power: the power to achieve your goals, to shape consensus, and to guide others toward mutually beneficial outcomes. This book is the definitive, authoritative manual for that pursuit. It is written for the individual who demands measurable results and rejects the ambiguity of traditional methods.

We have consciously created a system that is robust against academic scrutiny yet profoundly practical in the field. This book is a declaration that the most potent techniques of human influence are not mysterious, but scientific. They are waiting for the disciplined practitioner to learn, integrate, and deploy them.

Mastering the Logic of Belief

In the chapters that follow, we will begin by meticulously dismantling the concept of **Belief Systems**. We move past the idea of fighting beliefs and instead learn to see them as the mental *frames* they truly are. We will dive deep into **Cognitive Biases** (Thaler & Sunstein, 2008): the systematic, predictable errors in judgment that govern 90% of human decisions.

By understanding the brain's predictable logic (Chapter 2), you learn to structure your proposals to align perfectly with its natural tendencies, making refusal a cognitive dissonance.

The Precision of Language

You will be handed the ultimate diagnostic tool: the **Meta-Model**. Rooted in the linguistic work of Noam Chomsky, the Meta-Model teaches you the **verifiable structure of vague language** (Grinder & Bandler, 1975). When a person says, "I can't do that," they have performed three linguistic acts: they have Generalized, Deleted information, and Distorted reality.

We teach you the precise, structured questions to reverse-engineer their internal experience, forcing them to reveal the exact, missing information you need to guide their choice. This is not interrogation; it is **linguistic diagnosis**, giving you the power to find the exact pinhole in their logic where commitment can be secured (Chapter 3).

Sensory Acuity: The Predictive Edge

Perhaps the single greatest differentiator of the master influencer is the ability to read the moment-to-moment impact of their words. We train your visual system in **Sensory Acuity** (Chapter 5), turning your observations into real-time feedback data. We teach you to ignore polite words and instead focus on the **micro-expressions** (Ekman, 2003) and physiological shifts that betray a subject's *true* internal state.

This is the **'Test' phase** of the T.O.T.E. model that gives you your **predictive edge**, the ability to know exactly when your intervention has landed and when you need to adjust, all before the subject even finishes their sentence.

Finally, we address the often misunderstood concept of **Anchoring** (Chapter 6). Stripped of its mystical connotations, anchoring is simply the sophisticated application of **Classical and Operant Conditioning** (Pavlov, 1927). We will show you how to reliably associate specific emotional states (confidence, focus, agreement) with environmental triggers.

This allows you to *engineer* the emotional state of a room or a subject, ensuring that when you make your final proposal, their emotional state is perfectly calibrated for acceptance.

This is the commitment of this book. We have not merely refined old techniques; we have reconstructed the science of influence from the ground up, demanding verifiable proof at every step.

By mastering this **Advanced NLP** framework, you will acquire the specific knowledge that transforms your ability to communicate from an unreliable effort into a **practiced, predictable skill**. You will know, with certainty, exactly what to say to secure the commitment you seek. Your journey to mastery begins now.

CHAPTER 1
THE LOGIC OF BELIEF:
INTRODUCING COGNITIVE FILTERS AND FRAMING

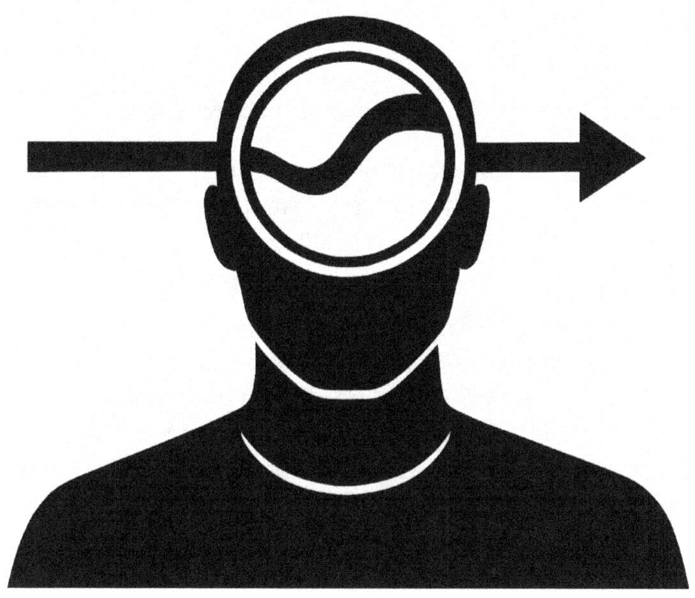

The great lie of persuasion is that you must change someone's mind.

The truth, as revealed by cognitive science and behavioral economics, is far more elegant: you don't change the mind, you change the architecture of the decision.

If you believe that influence is a battle of logic, where the person with the superior argument wins, you are already fighting a losing war. Human beings are not pure logical machines.

Our brains are efficient, flawed, and easily steered. To consistently predict reactions and move a choice from "maybe" to "yes," we must discard the fantasy of the rational actor and embrace the reality of the predictable human mind.

This chapter is the foundation of Advanced NLP because it provides the blueprint for prediction. It moves beyond the subjective concept of a "limiting belief" and into the verifiable reality of Cognitive Filters, the mental shortcuts and biases that govern every single decision your subject makes. By mastering these filters, you gain the power to structure your communication to align with their brain's path of least resistance.

2.1 The Two Systems of Decision-Making

To understand the predictable nature of human choice, we must first understand the two core mechanisms responsible for making decisions. Nobel laureate Daniel Kahneman, building on decades of psychological research, popularized this model: System 1 and System 2 thinking (Kahneman, 2011).

System 1: The Intuitive, Fast Machine

System 1 is your autopilot. It operates automatically and quickly, with little or no sense of voluntary control. It handles the vast majority of our cognitive load, from driving a car to reading a simple emotion.

- **Characteristics:** Fast, intuitive, emotional, effortless, heuristic-driven (shortcut-driven).
- **Role in Influence:** System 1 generates immediate impressions and feelings. When you encounter high resistance or immediate rejection, it is System 1 that is saying "no." Effective influence often seeks to bypass or align with this system's snap judgments.

System 2: The Deliberative, Slow Machine

System 2 is the conscious, thinking part of your brain. It is responsible for effortful mental activities that require attention, such as complex calculations, comparisons, and deliberate choices.

- **Characteristics:** Slow, effortful, logical, calculated, requires attention and energy.
- **Role in Influence:** System 2 is what approves or rationalizes the choices made by System 1. It is the gatekeeper of final commitment. When your subject says, "Let me think about it," they are handing the decision over to the slow, energy-expensive System 2.

The core objective of Advanced NLP is to present a framed proposition that is instantly accepted by the fast, emotional System 1, and then use verifiable linguistic and non-verbal cues to provide the logical scaffolding that the slow, rational System 2 needs to approve and ratify that initial "yes."

The greatest obstacle is that System 2 is fundamentally lazy. It prefers to conserve energy. This leads us directly to the concept of Cognitive Filters.

2.2 Cognitive Filters: The Predictable Shortcuts

A Cognitive Filter is a systematic pattern of deviation from norm or rationality in judgment. They are the mental shortcuts, or heuristics, that the brain relies on to save energy (Tversky & Kahneman, 1974). We rely on them because calculating every decision from scratch would paralyze us.

These filters are not weaknesses; they are entry points. When you understand the filter, you can predict the distortion it creates, and structure your proposition to fit perfectly through the warped lens.

2.2.1 Loss Aversion: The Double Weight of Loss

As introduced in Chapter 1, Loss Aversion is the most powerful cognitive filter in the realm of influence. Rooted in Prospect Theory, it states that people feel the psychological pain of a loss approximately twice as powerfully as the pleasure of an equivalent gain (Kahneman & Tversky, 1979).

- **The Filter:** The human brain is a survival organ. It prioritizes protection over acquisition. A threat to what we already possess registers as a far more urgent signal than the opportunity to acquire something new.

- **Advanced NLP Application (Framing):** To leverage this, you must shift your frame from "what they will gain" to "what they are currently losing or risk forfeiting."

Situation	Traditional (Gain) Frame	Advanced NLP (Loss) Frame
Hiring a Consultant	"You will **gain** a 20% efficiency boost."	"Your current system is causing you to **lose** 20% of your budget every month due to inefficiency."
Buying a Product	"This membership gives you **access** to exclusive content."	"If you don't secure your spot now, you will be **excluded** from this vital information when your competitors get it."

Fact Check: The Endowment Effect is a corollary of Loss Aversion, demonstrating that simply owning something (or feeling like you own it) drastically increases its perceived value (Thaler, 1980). This means that if you can frame your offer as something they **already possess** or are merely *testing* (e.g., "Take your new system home for a 30-day trial period"), their immediate sense of ownership makes the return of the item feel like an unacceptable loss.

2.2.2 The Confirmation Bias: Seeking Validation, Not Truth

The **Confirmation Bias** is the filter that ensures our beliefs remain robust. It is the tendency to search for, interpret, favor, and recall information in a way that confirms or supports one's prior beliefs or values (Nickerson, 1998).

- **The Filter:** The brain seeks consistency above all else. Once a subject has adopted a belief (e.g., "I am not a salesperson," or "That strategy is too risky"), they will unconsciously screen out all evidence that contradicts it and actively seek out evidence that supports it. They are not looking for truth; they are looking for validation.

- **Advanced NLP Application (Pacing and Leading):** You cannot directly attack a subject's core belief; it triggers immediate System 1 defensiveness. Instead, you must first **pace** their reality, validate their *experience*, and then subtly **lead** them to a new conclusion.

    - **Pace:** Start by articulating the *validity* of their current belief. If they say, "I'm worried about the risk," you pace them by saying, *"It's absolutely smart to be worried about risk. Every successful person I know is risk-averse."* (This bypasses the Confirmation Bias by confirming their self-image as a "smart, successful person.")

    - **Lead:** Once they feel heard and confirmed, you introduce the new information that re-contextualizes their belief. *"The smart, successful people I work with, however, manage risk by ensuring their investment is not a risk, but a measured step toward a guaranteed outcome."*

By pacing their belief, you gain credibility. By leading with a slight reframe, you allow them to incorporate the new idea without feeling they had to abandon their original identity.

2.2.3 The Anchoring Heuristic: The Primacy of First Data

The Anchoring Heuristic refers to the tendency to rely too heavily on the first piece of information offered (the "anchor") when making decisions (Tversky & Kahneman, 1974). Subsequent judgments are then made by adjusting away from that anchor, regardless of its relevance.

- **The Filter:** The brain dislikes cognitive heavy lifting. The anchor provides an immediate, easy reference point. All data that follows is unconsciously measured against that first point.
- **Advanced NLP Application (Value and Expectation):** You must consciously choose and deploy a strategic anchor before a proposal is made.
  - **Pricing:** If you are selling a service, the initial price you mention sets the high anchor. Even if you later negotiate down, the subject's System 2 will judge the final price not against the market value, but against the initial, high anchor.
  - **Time/Difficulty:** If you are asking a person to undertake a task, anchor the difficulty first. *"This process usually takes most people six months, but we can fast-track it in three."* You have anchored the expectation of **six months** as the normal baseline, making the three-month reality feel like a significant discount of effort.

Key Rule: Anchor High, Adjust Low. The power of the anchor remains even if the initial figure is clearly arbitrary or exaggerated. Its primary role is to set the scale.

2.2.4 The Availability Heuristic: The Vividness of Memory

The Availability Heuristic is a mental shortcut that relies on immediate examples that come to mind when evaluating a specific topic, concept, method, or decision (Tversky & Kahneman, 1973).

- **The Filter:** If something is easily recalled (highly *available* in memory), the brain assumes it is more common, more probable, or more important. Media coverage, personal trauma, and vivid storytelling all make memories more available.
- **Advanced NLP Application (Narrative Framing):** If you want a subject to choose "Yes," you must ensure that all the available mental images associated with "Yes" are vivid, recent, and positive. If you want them to avoid "No," you must make the available images associated with the *consequence of "No"* equally vivid and unpleasant (activating the Loss Aversion filter).

o **Use Vivid Stories:** Instead of saying, *"This strategy is effective,"* use a short, sensory-rich story (a form of **Narrative Priming**): *"I saw a client just last week, and the relief on her face when she closed that deal, the moment her stomach unknotted, that's what this strategy delivers."* This anchors a potent, available emotional response.

2.2.5 The Bandwagon Effect (Social Proof)

The **Bandwagon Effect** or **Social Proof** describes a phenomenon where people do something primarily because other people are doing it, regardless of their own beliefs (Cialdini, 1984).

- **The Filter:** When uncertainty is high, the brain is programmed to look to the tribe for validation. If others are doing it, it must be the correct, safe course of action. This is an evolutionarily beneficial shortcut.

- **Advanced NLP Application (Pre-Framing Consensus):** Never present a choice as an isolated decision. Always frame it within a context of established consensus.

  o **Weak Frame:** *"I think this is a good idea for you."*

  o **Strong Frame:** *"This is the exact protocol we implemented with [Successful Company A] and [Successful Competitor B]. They are already ahead of you on this, and their results are why you're considering this today."*

Fact Check: Social proof is most potent when the people in the "tribe" are perceived as similar to the subject (Festinger, 1954). If your subject is an engineer, cite other engineers. If they are a parent, cite other parents. This amplifies the cognitive shortcut.

2.3 Framing: The Master Key to Belief Architecture

Understanding these cognitive filters leads us to the master skill: Framing.

Framing is the intentional act of structuring how information is presented to influence the choices people make. It is the language used to surround a concept, setting the interpretive context that dictates how the subject processes the data.

2.3.1 Positive vs. Negative Framing

The difference between emphasizing gains (positive framing) and emphasizing losses (negative framing) is the most fundamental application of the Loss Aversion filter.

- **Example (Medical Context):**
  - *Positive Frame:* "This procedure has a 90% success rate." (Focus on the gain/success).
  - *Negative Frame:* "This procedure has a 10% failure rate." (Focus on the loss/risk).

Research shows that when decisions involve potential gains (or positive outcomes), people tend to be risk-averse (choosing the guaranteed 90% success). Conversely, when decisions involve potential losses (or negative outcomes), people tend to be risk-seeking (gambling on the 10% chance of avoiding loss) (Tversky & Kahneman, 1981).

The Advanced NLP Strategy: You must be aware of your subject's current emotional state and the nature of the decision:

1. **To Secure a Safe, Guaranteed Outcome:** Use **Positive Framing**. *"Let's secure this 90% guaranteed result now."*

2. **To Motivate Action to Avoid a Threat:** Use **Negative Framing**. *"We must act to reduce the 10% risk you are currently facing."*

2.3.2 The Zero-Risk Bias

A powerful application of framing is the Zero-Risk Bias: the tendency to prefer to reduce a small risk to zero rather than to accept a greater reduction in a larger risk (Viscusi, Magat, & Huber, 1987).

- **The Filter:** The emotional satisfaction of eliminating a problem entirely is so high that the brain will trade logical utility for it. Eliminating all risk registers as a psychological **absolute**, which System 1 loves.

- **Advanced NLP Application:** If your proposal has multiple risks, focus your language on the one risk you can reduce to zero, even if it is minor. Frame this elimination as the central, most critical benefit.
  - *Instead of:* "Our software reduces your overall operational risk by 40%."
  - *Frame as:* "We guarantee our security architecture reduces your data breach risk to zero, a complete elimination of your single greatest liability."

The total risk reduction of 40% may be logically superior, but the emotional impact of the **Zero-Risk Frame** will be more potent in securing the commitment from System 1.

2.3.3 The Default Bias (Inertia Framing)

The Default Bias is the powerful tendency for people to choose the option that has been pre-selected for them (Johnson & Goldstein, 2003). It is perhaps the strongest form of cognitive laziness.

- **The Filter:** Choosing the default requires no energy, no thought, and therefore no stress on System 2. It is the path of absolute non-resistance. The brain prefers inaction (status quo) over the effort of decision-making.

- **Advanced NLP Application (Action Framing):** When presenting an option, frame the desired choice as the already-established **default setting**, requiring the subject to expend effort to opt *out* rather than to opt *in*.

  - *Weak Close:* "Would you like to start the contract, or do you need more time?"

  - *Default Frame:* "The standard protocol here is to begin the implementation phase now so we capture the upcoming Q4 window. If you wish to delay, you'll need to fill out a separate extension form. Should we just stick with the standard protocol?"

By labeling the desired path as the "standard protocol" or "our recommendation," you establish it as the psychological default. Any deviation requires the subject to consciously exert energy to challenge the status quo, which their System 2 is programmed to avoid.

2.4 The Ecology of Belief

The final layer of the Logic of Belief involves the Ecology, how a new belief or decision fits into the subject's existing world and identity.

A true belief is not an isolated idea; it is a key piece in the subject's self-concept. If your proposal requires the subject to fundamentally believe something about themselves that is contradictory to their identity (e.g., if you frame a conservative investor as "high-risk gambler"), your influence attempt will fail, regardless of how expertly you framed the language.

Advanced NLP recognizes that influence must be congruent with the subject's self-concept. This is achieved by linking the proposed action to their highest-held values (e.g., stability, family, expertise, freedom).

- **Example:** If your subject values "Stability" above all else, do not frame your proposal around "exciting growth" or "bold changes." Frame it around "securing your current position," "reducing long-term volatility," or "building a stable legacy."

The objective is to allow the subject to maintain their core identity while seamlessly integrating the new decision. You are not asking them to become a new person; you are simply showing them that your proposal is the most logical and verifiable path for the person they already are to achieve what they already value.

This chapter has provided the essential knowledge of the Cognitive Filters that allow you to predict human behavior. In the next chapter, we move from the architecture of belief to the surgical tools of language: Mastering the Meta-Model to accurately diagnose and resolve the linguistic ambiguity that prevents commitment.

CHAPTER 2

MASTERING THE META - MODEL: PRECISION IN QUESTIONING

In Chapter 2, we established that human decision-making is not a purely logical process, but one governed by predictable Cognitive Filters and the energy-saving default of System 1 thinking. Our goal as advanced communicators is to frame our propositions so they align with these biases, effortlessly guiding the subject toward "yes."

But what happens when the subject gives you ambiguous or resistant feedback? What if their language is vague, their beliefs are hidden, or their objections are generalized?

The master influencer doesn't guess; they diagnose.

This chapter introduces the Meta-Model, the most powerful diagnostic tool in the Advanced NLP arsenal. Rooted in the verifiable principles of Transformational Grammar and Psycholinguistics, the Meta-Model teaches you to use language as a precise, surgical instrument to cut through ambiguity. It moves the conversation from the foggy realm of opinion and generalization into the clear, actionable structure of

108

specific thought. By mastering this model, you gain the power to retrieve the exact, missing information you need to collapse a limiting belief or secure a commitment.

3.1 The Linguistic Foundation: From Surface to Deep Structure

To understand the Meta-Model, we must first understand the relationship between what is said and what is meant.

In the 1950s and 60s, linguist Noam Chomsky revolutionized the understanding of language by distinguishing between **Surface Structure** and **Deep Structure** (Chomsky, 1957).

- **Surface Structure:** This is the language actually spoken or written, the words you hear. It is often vague, incomplete, and simplified.

- **Deep Structure:** This is the complete, internal neurological representation of the speaker's intended meaning, including all the sensory data, experiences, and contexts that were omitted in the Surface Structure.

The gap between the rich Deep Structure and the poor Surface Structure is inevitable. Our brains are efficient: we rely on three natural linguistic processes to simplify and shorten our communication. The problem is that when we apply these same simplification processes to our internal thought process, we inadvertently create **cognitive bottlenecks**: vague internal statements that limit our choices.

The Meta-Model is a set of specific questions designed to reverse these three simplification processes. When a subject speaks, they have inevitably performed one or more of these three transformations, creating a doorway for you to enter their internal logic.

Linguistic Process	Definition	The Problem (Cognitive Filter)	Meta-Model Goal
1. Deletion	Omitting key information from the statement.	Hides the specifics necessary for action.	**Recover Missing Information** (The WHO, WHAT, WHERE, WHEN)
2. Generalization	Drawing universal conclusions from one or two instances.	Creates limiting "rules" that block new choices.	**Challenge the Universal Scope** (Find the exception)
3. Distortion	Misrepresenting reality, often by exaggerating, linking unconnected events, or substituting cause/effect.	Creates false barriers, false causation, or false meaning.	**Identify the Source of the Error** (The HOW and WHY)

3.2 Category 1: Deletion — The Missing Data Points

Deletion is the process of leaving out critical pieces of information. The speaker is not lying; they are simply assuming the listener knows what they know. When a subject deletes information, they rob their own statement (or their belief) of the very specificity needed to take action or change.

3.2.1 Simple Deletion (Missing Nouns or Verbs)

The subject omits the specific person, object, or action.

- **The Statement:** "I am stressed."
- **The Problem:** The statement has deleted *who* or *what* is causing the stress, making the problem feel abstract and unsolvable.
- **The Meta-Model Question:** "Stressed by *whom*?" or "Stressed about *what specific situation*?"

By forcing the subject to make the vague feeling specific, you collapse the emotion tied to the abstract concept. You move the problem from a pervasive feeling ("I am stressed") to a solvable scenario ("I am stressed about the 3 pm meeting with the finance team").

3.2.2 Lack of Referential Index (Missing Actor)

The subject refers to something or someone without explicitly naming it.

- **The Statement:** "**They** are blocking the deal."
- **The Problem:** This vague pronoun prevents responsibility from being assigned or action from being taken. Who is "they"? A committee? A person? A mood?
- **The Meta-Model Question:** "**Who specifically** is blocking the deal?"

The Value for Influence: Often, subjects use vague references to avoid confronting the true source of resistance, which might be themselves. When you ask this question, they are forced to either name the external source (allowing you to address it) or recognize that the resistance is internal.

3.2.3 Unspecified Verbs (Missing Process)

The subject uses a verb that does not specify *how* the action occurred.

- **The Statement:** "The competition **failed** our client."
- **The Problem:** How did they fail? Was it slow delivery? Poor quality? Hidden fees? The lack of specificity prevents you from offering a targeted counter-solution.
- **The Meta-Model Question:** "**How specifically** did they fail your client?"

Advanced Application: When the subject is vague about a negative outcome, Meta-Model the verb to elicit the precise details that allow you to frame your own product or service as the explicit solution. If they say the competition "disappointed" them, your response must address the *specific mechanism* of that disappointment ("We guarantee all delivery is tracked in real-time to avoid the kind of **slow delivery** you experienced").

3.3 Category 2: Generalization — The Universal Lie

Generalization is the process of taking a singular experience and applying it to all similar instances. This is how we learn (e.g., "fire is hot"), but it is also the primary mechanism for creating limiting beliefs (e.g., "all opportunities are risky").

Generalizations are the biggest obstacles to securing a "yes," because they frame your proposal as a guaranteed failure before you even start.

3.3.1 Universal Quantifiers (The Absolutes)

These are words that imply a universal, absolute scope: *all, every, never, none, nobody, always.*

- **The Statement:** "**Nobody** in this industry uses that approach." or "That strategy **never** works."
- **The Problem:** The words "nobody" and "never" are almost always false, but they serve as a perfect cognitive barrier, preventing the subject from even considering a different path.
- **The Meta-Model Question (The Counter-Example):** "**Nobody?** So, if I could show you **one person** who successfully implemented it, would you consider it then?" or "**Never?** Can you think of **just one time** when that approach had a partial success, even if it wasn't perfect?"

The Value for Influence: This is the most direct way to collapse a limiting belief. By asking for a single, small counter-example, you force System 2 to search for an exception. If the subject finds one, the Universal Quantifier collapses. If they cannot, the burden of proof shifts to them, softening their rigid stance.

3.3.2 Modal Operators of Necessity (The Rules)

These words convey a sense of obligation, rule, or necessity: *should, shouldn't, must, mustn't, have to, need to, it is necessary to.*

- **The Statement:** "I **must** consult with my team before I commit."
- **The Problem:** This statement establishes a rigid internal rule. While consultation may be wise, the word "must" implies a necessity that feels non-negotiable and outside their control.
- **The Meta-Model Question (The Consequence):** "**What would happen if you didn't** consult with your team?" or "**What specifically** makes this a *must* rather than a good idea?"

By forcing the subject to articulate the consequence, you make the hidden rule visible. The answer often reveals a fear (e.g., "I'd get blamed if it went wrong"). Once the fear is known, you can frame a solution that eliminates the fear ("We can structure the agreement so the liability rests with us for the first 90 days").

3.3.3 Modal Operators of Possibility (The Limits)

These words define the subject's perceived limits of what is possible: *can't, couldn't, won't, couldn't, it is impossible to.*

- **The Statement:** "I **can't** afford your service right now."
- **The Problem:** The "can't" implies an environmental impossibility, often hiding a choice or a fear.
- **The Meta-Model Question (The Challenge to Possibility):** "**What exactly stops you?**" or "**What would happen if you did?**"

This question forces the subject to take ownership of the perceived limit. The "can't" is usually a **choice** or a **fear of consequence** framed as a rule. The subject might respond: "I'd have to rearrange my entire budget." Now, you have actionable data (their budget needs rearranging) instead of a brick wall ("I can't afford it").

3.4 Category 3: Distortion — The Map is Not the Territory

Distortion is the process of misrepresenting the relationship between events or ideas. The subject may connect two unrelated events, assign emotional meaning where none exists, or assume causation without proof. This is where the most irrational resistance is hidden.

3.4.1 Cause and Effect (False Causation)

The subject falsely links one event to another, claiming one *causes* the other.

- **The Statement:** "**Your tone of voice** makes me feel anxious."
- **The Problem:** This statement distorts reality by placing the locus of control externally. It denies the subject's own emotional response mechanism (their internal map) and places responsibility on the speaker. **Fact Check:** The verifiable truth is that "Your tone of voice" is an *input*, and "makes me feel anxious" is an *internal response* chosen by the subject's system.
- **The Meta-Model Question (The Internal Process):** "**How specifically** does my tone of voice cause you to *choose* to feel anxious?" or "**What is the process** that goes on inside you between my tone and your feeling?"

The Value for Influence: This question gently returns ownership of the emotion to the subject. Once they are forced to articulate the internal process (e.g., "Well, when you speak loudly, I remember a boss I used to have..."), the distortion collapses. You can then frame your solution around the *real* problem, the memory or belief, not the surface-level event.

3.4.2 Complex Equivalence (False Meaning)

The subject equates two unrelated events, stating that one *means* the other.

- **The Statement: "The fact that the committee didn't call me back** *means* they don't value my work."
- **The Problem:** A lack of a phone call (Event A) has been equated with a monumental failure of value (Event B). This leap of logic is a cognitive error that creates crippling internal resistance.
- **The Meta-Model Question (The False Link): "How specifically** does the fact that they didn't call back *mean* they don't value your work?" or "**What else** could their silence mean?"

This question forces System 2 to analyze the evidence supporting the equation. Since the committee's silence could mean they are busy, on holiday, or lost the number, the original conclusion ("they don't value my work") loses its force. This technique is a form of cognitive restructuring, directly collapsing the self-imposed barrier to commitment.

3.4.3 Mind Reading (False Assumptions)

The subject claims to know the internal state, thoughts, or intentions of another person without any external validation.

- **The Statement: "I know** you are only telling me this to get my money."
- **The Problem:** This is a distortion that creates an immediate wall of skepticism, based entirely on the subject's projection of intent.
- **The Meta-Model Question (The Source of Knowledge): "How do you know** my intentions?" or "**What specific evidence** gave you that information?"

The Value for Influence: This is a crucial question for establishing rapport and integrity. It forces the subject to admit their statement is based on assumption or their own past experience, not verifiable reality. The answer often reveals the subject's own fear or a painful memory from a past interaction, which you can then address directly to build trust.

3.5 The Surgical Application: Using the Meta-Model in the T.O.T.E.

The Meta-Model is not a tool for confrontation; it is the essential **TEST** phase in the **T.O.T.E. (Test–Operate–Test–Exit)** framework (as introduced in Chapter 1). It is the diagnostic test you run to retrieve the specific data necessary for your **OPERATE** phase (the reframed proposal).

Case Study: Closing a Hesitant Client

Client Statement (Surface Structure): "We've looked at your proposal, but frankly, **it's too expensive.** We **can't** afford the commitment right now. My colleagues **always** say that these kinds of partnerships **never** work out."

Meta-Model Diagnosis and Sequence:

1. **Diagnosis 1: Distortion (Complex Equivalence):** "Too expensive" is a false equation. It *means* "I don't perceive the value to be equal to the cost," not "I have no money."

   - **Question (Addressing Value):** "Compared to **what exactly** is this too expensive? Are you comparing the price to the **cost of staying where you are**?" (This applies the Loss Aversion Frame from Chapter 2).

2. **Diagnosis 2: Generalization (Modal Operator of Possibility):** "We **can't** afford the commitment."

   - **Question (Addressing Possibility):** "**What exactly stops you** from rearranging the budget to acquire this? If you had the results we promise guaranteed, **would you then find the resources?**" (This isolates the decision from the immediate budget barrier).

3. **Diagnosis 3: Generalization (Universal Quantifiers):** "My colleagues **always** say that these partnerships **never** work out."

   - **Question (Challenging the Absolute):** "**Never?** Can you recall **one partnership**, even a small one, that gave you a partial success or taught you a crucial lesson?" (This collapses the "never" and opens the door to your solution).

The Result: By running this sequence of precise questions, you have retrieved the Deep Structure:

- The client is not blocked by money, but by a **perceived lack of value** relative to the cost of inertia (Diagnosis 1).
- The **"can't afford it"** is really a **choice** to prioritize their current budget allocation (Diagnosis 2).
- The core resistance is based on an unverified, generalized past failure, not a rational assessment of your specific proposal (Diagnosis 3).

Once this Deep Structure is revealed, your **OPERATE** phase is surgical. Instead of arguing about price, you return to the **Loss Aversion Frame** and focus exclusively on the specific pain point that the Meta-Model revealed.

3.6 Ethics and Congruence in Precision

It is crucial to emphasize that mastering the Meta-Model is an ethical pursuit. It is not designed to corner or confuse the subject. The power of these questions lies in their ability to bring clarity: to the subject, and to you.

When an internal belief is vague, generalized, or distorted, it creates psychological pressure and limits choice for the subject. When you ask a precise Meta-Model question, the subject's System 2 is engaged, and the belief is forced to become specific. This act of clarification is often experienced by the subject as insightful and even therapeutic, as they are finally able to articulate the true source of their confusion.

The Golden Rule of Precision: Always use the Meta-Model to find the positive intent behind the limiting statement. The subject who says, "I can't afford it," has the positive intent of financial security. Your final frame must honor that positive intent while showing them that saying "yes" to your proposal is the best, most verifiable way to achieve that security.

Mastering the Meta-Model is the key to unlocking the power of the next chapter: Linguistic Programming. Once you know the precise internal map of your subject (Chapter 3), you can then use language to surgically implant the necessary resources, ideas, and presuppositions for commitment (Chapter 4).

CHAPTER 3
LINGUISTIC PROGRAMMING:
THE HIDDEN STRUCTURE OF INFLUENCE

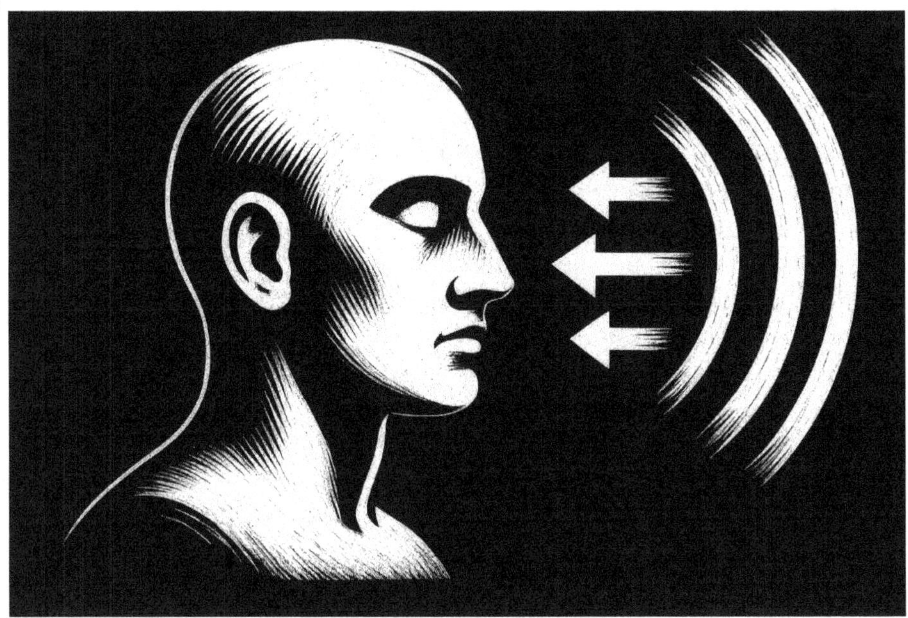

In Chapter 3, we armed ourselves with the **Meta-Model,** turning our questioning into a precise surgical instrument capable of diagnosing the hidden structure of a subject's belief (the Deep Structure). We learned that vague resistance is merely incomplete information waiting to be retrieved.

Now, we move from diagnosis to intervention.

This chapter introduces the tactical side of Advanced NLP: **Linguistic Programming.** This is the **OPERATE** phase of the T.O.T.E. model: the moment you deploy scientifically verified language structures to reshape the subject's internal experience. Our goal is to move beyond mere conversation and use language as a precise, algorithmic tool to structure choices and implant ideas.

We are not teaching linguistic parlor tricks. We are teaching the systematic application of **Psycholinguistics,** the study of the relationship between linguistic behavior and psychological processes. By

117

understanding how the brain processes sentence structure and embedded meaning, you gain the ability to pre-determine the cognitive pathway a subject must take, making your desired conclusion the path of least cognitive resistance.

4.1 The Cognitive Power of Presupposition

The most elegant and powerful tool in Linguistic Programming is the **Presupposition**.

A **presupposition** is an assumption taken for granted within an utterance. It is a concept that must be accepted as true for the sentence itself to make sense. Crucially, presuppositions work by leveraging the inherent laziness of the brain's **System 2**.

When you hear a sentence, your System 2 is engaged to process the main, conscious meaning. However, it often permits the peripheral, implied assumptions to slip through unverified. The conscious mind focuses on the surface meaning, allowing the deeper premise to be accepted as a non-negotiable fact.

Think of it this way: to challenge a premise, System 2 must expend significant energy by stopping the flow of communication and returning to an earlier point in the conversation. Because the brain constantly seeks to conserve energy, it defaults to accepting the presupposed reality simply to keep the communication moving.

The Linguistic Science

The linguistic foundation for this lies in the difference between a declarative statement and a presupposition. If I say, "My phone is black," the truth or falsehood of that statement is the focus. If I say, "When my black phone rings, I'll answer it," the focus shifts to the *action* (answering the phone), and the existence of a phone is automatically accepted as a fact necessary to process the rest of the sentence.

Mastering presuppositions allows you to elegantly achieve an agreement on a core premise *before* you ever ask for a conscious commitment.

4.1.1 Temporal Presuppositions (The Inevitable Timeline)

These are arguably the most effective form of presupposition for moving a prospect from "maybe" to "yes" because they establish the desired outcome as inevitable, requiring the subject to focus only on the timing or sequence of events.

Keywords: *when, before, after, during, since, while.*

Example Frame	Hidden Premise Accepted
"**When** you start seeing the positive quarterly reports..."	**Premise:** You *will* start seeing positive quarterly reports.
"**Before** we finalize the remaining details..."	**Premise:** The decision to move forward has already been made.
"I'm curious, **after** you integrate this new system, what will you tackle next?"	**Premise:** Integration *will* occur.

Application Strategy: If a subject is hesitating on the *decision* to buy, shift the language entirely to the *timing* of the process. Do not ask, *"Are you going to buy?"* Ask, *"When is the best time for us to finalize the delivery?"* The question presupposes the finalization, and the subject's System 2 will default to answering the simpler question about time.

4.1.2 Ordinal Presuppositions (The Irrelevant Choice)

This category uses sequence, number, or selective description to force the subject to accept the validity of the premise while choosing a less important element.

Keywords: *first, second, another, one, two, the other, a different, still.*

- **Example 1 (Choice of Time):** "Do you want to begin the initial onboarding session **first** thing Tuesday, or should we schedule it for **another** time this week?"
  - **Hidden Premise:** The onboarding session is happening. The only choice is *when*.
- **Example 2 (Choice of Focus):** "We've seen the success of this strategy with Client A. **Another** benefit you'll experience is..."
  - **Hidden Premise:** The first part (success with Client A) is an accepted fact, and you are now discussing *additional* established facts.

The Power of the Irrelevant Choice: This is often called the "embedded command of choice." By giving the subject two options, both of which lead to your desired outcome, you fully satisfy the brain's need for control (System 2 feels involved) while guiding them away from the possibility of "no." The ultimate goal is to remove "No" from the menu entirely.

4.1.3 Awareness Verbs and Adjectives

These verbs and adjectives presuppose the truth of the statement they govern, forcing the subject to agree with the premise if they wish to answer the question.

Keywords (Verbs): realize, know, discover, understand, be aware, regret.

Keywords (Adjectives/Adverbs): easily, quickly, successfully, fortunately.

Example Frame	Hidden Premise Accepted
"What made you **realize** this product was the superior option?"	**Premise:** You *did* realize this product is the superior option.
"Why do you **regret** waiting so long to start?"	**Premise:** You *are* regretting waiting so long to start.
"**Fortunately**, our team has already prepared the paperwork."	**Premise:** The preparedness of the team is fortunate (i.e., beneficial to you).

Application Strategy (The 'Realize' Trap): Asking a subject, "When did you **realize** this was the right decision?" is infinitely more powerful than asking, "Is this the right decision?" The subject is forced to search their mind for the *time* of realization, confirming the decision in the process.

4.2 Embedded Commands: The Stealth Directive

While presuppositions handle the *premise* of the conversation, **Embedded Commands** handle the *action*. An Embedded Command is a specific, actionable directive hidden within a longer, grammatically complex sentence.

This technique is rooted in the verifiable mechanism of **Semantic Priming** (Neely, 1977). As discussed in Chapter 1, psycholinguistic studies confirm that exposure to certain words or phrases (the prime) can unconsciously influence the processing of subsequent, related information. When you embed a command, you are essentially inserting a high-value, actionable prime into the subject's stream of consciousness.

The directive bypasses the critical, analytical System 2 because the command is presented as a component of a larger, seemingly innocent statement. System 1, which processes the language rapidly, registers the command as a directive, while the slower System 2 is busy parsing the full sentence structure.

4.2.1 Delivery is Everything: The Non-Verbal Highlight

The most critical component of a successful Embedded Command is the **delivery mechanism**. Because the command is grammatically integrated into a sentence, you must non-verbally highlight the command phrase to ensure System 1 registers it as distinct.

Highlighting Techniques (The Advanced Calibration):

1. **Vocal Tonal Shift:** Slightly lower the pitch of your voice, slow the tempo, and increase the volume on the command phrase. (Example: "I want you to **feel comfortable** making this choice.")

2. **Kinesic Cue:** Briefly gesture toward the subject, lean slightly in, or hold brief, intense eye contact precisely during the command phrase. This non-verbal punctuation separates the command from the surrounding text.

3. **Pausing:** Use a short, deliberate pause immediately before and after the command. (Example: "You might find it helpful to... **take action now**... on this specific point.")

4.2.2 Structuring the Command

Embedded Commands should be structured to be easy for System 1 to process and act upon. They typically involve clear, immediate action verbs.

Full Sentence Frame	Embedded Command (Targeted Action)
"As a professional, I know you will **find this information useful** later."	**FIND THIS INFORMATION USEFUL**
"You might be surprised how **easy it is to decide now**."	**EASY IT IS TO DECIDE NOW**
"It's important that you **understand the value** before we move forward."	**UNDERSTAND THE VALUE**
"I want you to **take all the time you need** to review this proposal."	**TAKE ALL THE TIME YOU NEED**

Application Strategy: Embed the command just before or immediately after a statement of validation or empathy. For example, by first saying, *"I know you've been extremely busy,"* and following with, *"and that's why it's important to **act fast** to secure this opportunity,"* you link the validation of their difficulty to the urgency of your directive.

4.2.3 Pacing and Leading with Commands

This technique blends the Pacing and Leading principle (from Chapter 2) directly into the command structure.

- **Pace (Verifiable Fact):** State a verifiable fact about the subject's current reality.
- **Lead (Embedded Command):** Link the fact to your desired directive using a soft conjunction.
- **Example: "You are looking at this screen right now** (Pace) and **you can relax and commit to this process** (Lead)."
  - The subject must accept the first, verifiable fact (they are looking at the screen). System 1 carries this acceptance over to the next part, making the embedded command feel like a natural, logical continuation of their current state.

4.3 Comparative Negation: The Unfavorable Contrast

Comparative Negation is a specialized framing technique that relies on the **Loss Aversion** principle (Chapter 2) to bias a choice. It involves framing a choice by implicitly or explicitly contrasting it negatively with an undesirable alternative.

This technique uses language to create an immediate, internal cost-benefit analysis where the cost of the *undesired option* is amplified by the sheer negative connotation of the language used to describe it.

4.3.1 The Mechanism of Unfavorable Contrast

The human brain processes negative comparisons more quickly and with more emotional weight than positive ones, precisely because of the $2\times$ power of Loss Aversion. If I frame Choice A as *"less risky"* than Choice B, the primary focus shifts to the negative idea of "risk," and Choice A gains favor simply because it reduces the negative load.

Keywords: *less than, not like, unlike, rather than, instead of.*

Comparative Frame	Hidden Negative Premise	Application
"This approach is **less complicated** than your existing method."	**Premise:** The current method is 'complicated' (a known negative).	You are selling the *avoidance of complication* (a psychological gain).
"You can choose this streamlined process **rather than** the frustrating bottlenecks you've been dealing with."	**Premise:** The subject has been experiencing 'frustrating bottlenecks' (a psychological loss).	You are selling the *elimination of frustration.*

4.3.2 Comparative Negation of Identity

This is a highly potent form of framing that ties the undesirable option to a negative self-identity or self-concept. It leverages the **Confirmation Bias** (Chapter 2) by suggesting that selecting the undesired option would be inconsistent with the subject's own high opinion of themselves.

- **Example (Targeting 'Professionalism'):** *"A **less professional approach** would be to delay this decision, but given the results you need, we should finalize the timeline now."*
  - **Effect:** The desired action (finalizing the timeline) is subtly contrasted with the negative identity ("less professional approach"). To maintain their self-concept, the subject's System 1 is pressured to comply with the positive option.
- **Example (Targeting 'Intelligence/Efficiency'):** *"We could go through the **inefficient, drawn-out process** that most people choose, but I assume you'd prefer the streamlined, efficient path that aligns with your expertise."*
  - **Effect:** The desired path is linked to their professional identity ("expertise," "efficient"), while the alternative is linked to a negative state ("inefficient," "most people").

Ethical Consideration: Comparative Negation must always be aimed at *the decision or process*, not the person. When used to contrast a product's features, it highlights the superior value. When used to compare behaviors, it must link the undesired behavior to a general, negative category ("inefficient," "delaying") that the subject naturally wishes to avoid.

4.4 Strategic Syntax: The Architecture of Agreement

While Presuppositions and Embedded Commands deal with the content of influence, **Strategic Syntax** deals with the *structure* of the sentence itself. Even simple grammatical choices significantly impact how the brain processes information, especially when building agreement.

4.4.1 Active vs. Passive Voice (Locus of Control)

The choice between active and passive voice dictates where responsibility, or the **Locus of Control**, is placed in a sentence.

- **Active Voice:** *[Actor] $\rightarrow$ [Action] $\rightarrow$ [Recipient].* (Example: "I secured the funding.")
    - **Application:** Use the active voice when discussing your positive actions, successes, or the actions you want the subject to take. It conveys certainty and clarity of action. (E.g., "You **will achieve** this result by **taking** this step.")
- **Passive Voice:** *[Recipient] $\rightarrow$ [Action] $\rightarrow$ [Actor is optional].* (Example: "The funding was secured.")
    - **Application:** Use the passive voice to distance yourself from negative events or to mitigate the impact of necessary but potentially difficult actions. (E.g., "The changes **were implemented**," instead of "We implemented the changes that caused the disruption.") It can be used as a subtle form of distortion to reduce the emotional impact of a difficult fact.

4.4.2 Conjunctions of Flow: 'And' vs. 'But'

The most subtle syntactical choices are the conjunctions we use to link clauses.

- **The Power of 'But':** The word "but" functions as a cognitive eraser. It negates everything that came before it. Psychologically, whatever follows "but" is the only thing the listener will retain.
    - *Example:* "I understand your concern about the cost, **but** the value outweighs it."
    - **Effect:** The subject only processes the second clause ("the value outweighs it"), but they feel their initial concern was dismissed.

- **The Power of 'And':** The word "and" is a conjunction of inclusion and flow. It links two ideas without negating the first, making the listener feel heard while smoothly transitioning to the next point.
    - *Example:* "I understand your concern about the cost, **and** that's precisely why we designed the system to guarantee a 300% return on investment."
    - **Effect:** The subject's System 1 feels acknowledged (Paced), and the new information (the ROI) is introduced as a logical, non-contradictory continuation of the flow of thought (Leading). **Always use 'and' to bridge an objection.**

4.4.3 Embedded Questions (The Gentle Challenge)

An embedded question is a question folded into a statement, softening the challenge and bypassing the subject's defensive System 1 response.

- **Direct Question (Challenging):** "Why did you fail to follow the protocol?"
- **Embedded Question (Softening):** "I'm curious **what prevented you from following the protocol** at that time."

The embedded format shifts the focus from blame to curiosity, facilitating a more honest and specific response, which you can then diagnose using the Meta-Model framework.

4.5 Synthesis: Linguistic Programming in Action (The OPERATE Phase)

Linguistic Programming is the toolkit for the **OPERATE** step in the T.O.T.E. Model. You use the Meta-Model to diagnose the precise nature of the subject's resistance (the **TEST**), and then you use Linguistic Programming to deliver the precise counter-intervention (the **OPERATE**).

Diagnosis (Meta-Model)	Intervention (Linguistic Program)
Problem: Unspecified Verb $\rightarrow$ *They delayed the decision.*	**Intervention:** Use Presupposition $\rightarrow$ *"**When** the decision is no longer delayed, **how quickly** will you want to start seeing the results?"* (Forces acceptance of the future result).

Diagnosis (Meta-Model)	Intervention (Linguistic Program)
Problem: Modal Operator of Possibility $\rightarrow$ *I can't find the time.*	**Intervention:** Use Embedded Command $\rightarrow$ *"I know you're a busy person, so let me show you how **easy it is to delegate this process**."* (Commands delegation).
Problem: Generalization $\rightarrow$ *That never works for us.*	**Intervention:** Use Comparative Negation $\rightarrow$ *"We could try the **old, failed method** that never works, but I recommend the proven strategy that all our successful clients use."* (Links their statement to the negative option).

By strategically deploying these language structures, you are creating a cognitive funnel. You are not *persuading* the subject; you are **architecting the mental path** they must follow to process the information, making "yes" the logical, inevitable conclusion that saves System 2 energy and honors their deepest cognitive biases.

This precision is the hallmark of Advanced NLP. We move from the surgical use of language to the surgical reading of human physiology. In the next chapter, we will master the **Science of Sensory Acuity and Calibration**, ensuring that you can instantly and accurately TEST the impact of every linguistic program you deploy.

CHAPTER 4
THE SCIENCE OF SENSORY ACUITY AND CALIBRATION

In the previous chapters, we established the blueprint for influence. We mapped the predictable Cognitive Filters that bias decisions (Chapter 2) and armed ourselves with the surgical tools of Linguistic Programming (Chapter 4) to structure the path to agreement. These are the *proactive* steps, the preparation and the intervention, of the influence process.

But what happens in the moment of contact, when your subject is speaking one thing but feeling another? What if you deploy a masterful Presupposition, and the subject's words are polite, but their body language signals resistance?

The answer is the words are the least reliable source of information.

Mastery requires a verifiable feedback system: a real-time diagnostic that tells you, without ambiguity, if your linguistic program has landed, if your frame has been accepted, or if resistance has been triggered. This system is Sensory Acuity and Calibration, and it is the absolute core of the TEST phase in the T.O.T.E. Model.

We move from the subjective notion of "reading people" to the scientific discipline of **behavioral signal analysis**. This chapter turns your eyes and ears into highly sensitive, objective instruments capable of detecting involuntary, neurological truth.

5.1 Calibration: The Predictive Feedback Loop

Calibration in Advanced NLP is the process of establishing a subject's baseline behavior (their normal, comfortable state) and then noting the precise shifts in that baseline when a specific stimulus (your proposition, frame, or question) is introduced. These shifts are your predictive data points.

If your proposition creates measurable, consistent shifts in physiology, for example, a change in breathing or a subtle facial contraction, you have secured verifiable, objective data on the subject's internal state. These non-verbal signals are reliable because they are primarily governed by the **Autonomic Nervous System (ANS)**, the control center for involuntary functions like heart rate, respiration, and blood flow. The ANS is wired for survival, and it is far too fast and primal to be overridden by the conscious intent to lie or hide emotion.

The goal here is precision, not assumption. We discard the vague metaphors of older NLP models—such as the largely non-validated eye-accessing cues (which research has failed to consistently support)—and instead focus on three scientifically verifiable pillars:

1. **Micro-Expressions (The Face):** Involuntary, fleeting facial muscle movements.

2. **Physiological Shifts (The Body):** Changes in breathing, posture, and tension.

3. **Behavioral Synchronization (The Rapport):** Alignment or misalignment of movement patterns.

The critical insight is that your influence strategy fails not when the subject says "no," but when you **fail to TEST** their internal response and proceed with the wrong intervention. Calibration is the constant, quiet confirmation of your strategy.

5.2 Pillar 1: Facial Calibration and the Science of Micro-Expressions

The most direct and rapid window into a subject's emotional state is the face. Research pioneered by Dr. Paul Ekman confirmed the existence of **universal micro-expressions**: involuntary facial displays of emotion lasting between 1/25th and 1/2 a second (Ekman, 2003). These expressions are universal across cultures, proving they are hardwired into the human nervous system.

Training your acuity to spot these fleeting signals is the single fastest way to run the **TEST** phase of the T.O.T.E. model.

5.2.1 The Big Six (Plus One) Universal Emotions

Mastery requires familiarity with the facial muscle groups associated with the seven universal emotions. While many emotions are subtle, the following are the most critical to detect during high-stakes influence:

1. **Contempt:** This is the most damaging micro-expression to spot during a pitch. It is often visible as a unilateral (one-sided) tightening of the corner of the mouth, causing a slight sneer. **Contempt signals superiority, disdain, and moral disgust.** When a subject flashes contempt, they are internally thinking, *"This is beneath me,"* or *"You are unqualified to present this to me."*

   o *Action when detected:* Stop the current line of argument immediately. Use a Meta-Model question to acknowledge their expertise and reposition yourself as a peer or consultant, not an instructor.

2. **Disgust:** The tightening and raising of the upper lip and the wrinkling of the nose (like smelling something foul). **Disgust signals an internal rejection of a concept or idea.** It means the brain is rejecting the input.

   o *Action when detected:* Your language, the frame you used, or the product detail you mentioned triggered a rejection response. Immediately link the proposal to something clean, reputable, or high-status to cleanse the emotional frame.

3. **Fear:** Raised inner eyebrows, pulled together, causing horizontal wrinkles in the center of the forehead. The lower eyelids tense, and the lips are stretched horizontally. **Fear signals a threat to safety, status, or resources.**

   o Action when detected: Your proposition is activating the **Loss Aversion** filter too strongly. Immediately shift the frame to risk mitigation and guaranteed safety. Focus on what you control and how you will protect them.

4. **Anger:** Eyebrows are lowered and pulled together; eyes glare; lips press firmly together. **Anger signals a block to a goal the subject desires.**

o *Action when detected:* The subject feels blocked or unjustly treated by your terms, the price, or the process. Use the Meta-Model to diagnose the source of the blockage ("What specifically about this clause creates the greatest difficulty for you?").

5. **Surprise:** Eyebrows flash high and curved; eyes widen, exposing the whites of the eyes above the iris; jaw drops open. **Surprise signals an unexpected event.**

   o *Action when detected:* If positive, proceed rapidly. If negative, immediately address the unexpected issue before they consciously process the implication.

5.2.2 The Calibration Baseline: Finding the Default

You cannot measure a shift until you know the norm. Before deploying your Linguistic Programming (your **OPERATE** phase), spend the first 60 seconds establishing the subject's baseline for their "neutral" or "comfortable" state:

- **Vocal Baseline:** What is their resting pitch, tempo, and volume?
- **Facial Baseline:** What is the resting tension around their eyes and mouth? Are their lips slightly parted or pressed together?
- **Body Baseline:** What is their primary breathing locus (chest or belly)? How is their weight distributed (balanced or leaning)?

Once the baseline is set, every subsequent flash of contempt, every tightening of the jaw, and every shift in breathing constitutes verifiable, objective feedback that tells you the truth about your intervention.

5.3 Pillar 2: Physiological Calibration — The Body's Involuntary Signals

Beyond the face, the rest of the body, controlled by the involuntary ANS, provides a constant stream of predictive data. These physiological shifts are harder to mask than words or deliberate posture.

5.3.1 Respiration: The Engine of Emotion

Breathing is the most reliable external marker of internal arousal (Grossman, 1983). A subject cannot consciously maintain a false, relaxed breathing pattern when their ANS is triggered by stress or anxiety.

- **Rate and Depth:** Increased rate and decreased depth signal anxiety, stress, or excitement (System 1 activation). A sudden, audible **sigh or deep exhalation** often signals resignation or relief—a definitive shift in state.

- **Locus Shift:** A relaxed person breathes from the diaphragm (belly/abdomen). When stress is introduced, the breathing shifts up to the chest and shoulders (thoracic breathing). This **locus shift** is a clear signal that the subject has moved from a relaxed, receptive state to a state of **alertness or defensiveness** ("fight or flight").

- *Action:* If you see the breathing shift from the diaphragm to the chest, you have triggered high resistance. You must immediately **pace** the subject's internal state, "I can see this is requiring a lot of thought", and then shift your frame to a lower-threat topic before attempting to proceed.

5.3.2 Skin Tone and Capillary Action

Although subtle, changes in skin tone are involuntary responses governed by the capillary blood flow—the foundation of the traditional NLP concept of **"VAK" (Visual, Auditory, Kinesthetic)**, now grounded in science.

- **Paling (Blanching):** A loss of color in the face, neck, or ears signals that blood is being pulled away from the extremities and non-essential organs to the major muscle groups. This is a classic **"flight"** response, the body preparing for confrontation or escape.

- **Flushing (Reddening):** An increase in blood flow, usually signaling anger, embarrassment, or high arousal. This is a classic **"fight"** response.

- *Action:* If a subject suddenly blanches after you deploy a Loss Aversion frame, you have successfully activated their survival instinct. This is the **TEST** confirmation that the threat is real to them. You must now quickly move to the **OPERATE** phase of offering protection or a safe way out (the "Exit" step).

5.3.3 Tension and Micro-Movement (The Leaking Channels)

Unconscious tension is a leakage channel for stress.

- **Jaw Clenching:** A firm pressing of the lips or clenching of the masseter muscles (jaw) signals suppressed anger or extreme mental effort (System 2 overload).

- **Shoulder/Neck Tension:** A slight lifting of the shoulders or rigid posture signals defensiveness.

- **Fidgeting:** Repetitive, small movements (tapping fingers, jiggling legs) signal mounting anxiety or a desire to release accumulated tension.

- *Action:* If you observe a subject's hand transition from resting flat on the table to clenching a pen or hiding beneath the table, the **TEST** indicates the subject is internally grappling with something. Use a **Meta-Model question** (Chapter 3) to articulate the tension for them: "I sense this is a complex point; what part of this feels the most difficult to resolve?"

5.4 Pillar 3: Behavioral Synchronization and Rapport

The third pillar of calibration relates to the spatial and movement patterns between you and the subject, which is essential for establishing and maintaining **Rapport**, the state of mutual responsiveness and trust.

5.4.1 Mirroring and the Chameleon Effect

The concept of **Mirroring** (unconsciously matching the posture, gestures, or tempo of another person) is scientifically supported by research on the **Chameleon Effect** (Chartrand & Bargh, 1999). Studies show that individuals who are unconsciously mimicked report liking the mimicker more and rate the interaction as smoother, even when unaware of the mimicry. This is because **synchronicity signals trust** to System 1.

- **Application (Rapport Building):** To establish rapport, consciously and subtly match three elements of the subject's behavior:
    1. **Rate of Speech:** Tempo and rhythm.
    2. **Posture:** The angle of the head or the position of the feet (avoid large, obvious movements).
    3. **Breathing Rhythm:** Matching the rate and locus of their respiration.

5.4.2 Mismatching: The Signal of Internal Conflict

If you are already in rapport (synchronized), any sudden, significant **Mismatch** in movement or posture signals that the subject has internally broken connection with you or your idea.

- **Example:** You are sitting with open posture and speaking calmly. The subject was mirroring you, but when you introduced the price, they suddenly **cross their arms or shift their torso away** from you.
- *Action:* This is a definite **TEST** failure. The crossed arms are an involuntary physiological barrier. You must interrupt your current intervention and address the barrier non-verbally first—

shift your own posture to a slightly less engaged position, pause, and then ask a **Meta-Model question** that addresses the shift in state: "Before we continue, I want to make sure I'm being clear; are we still aligned on the core objective here?"

5.4.3 Kinesic Momentum (Energy Shift)

Observe the **momentum** of their movement. A shift from fluid, engaged movements (gesturing, leaning in) to rigid stillness, or vice-versa, indicates a neurological shift:

- **Sudden Stillness:** Often signals intense System 2 processing, concentration, or internal conflict. They have stopped moving to conserve energy for thought.

- **Sudden Increase in Movement:** Usually signals excitement, relief, or a physical need to vent anxiety.

The key is always to **calibrate to the change**, not the behavior itself. If a person is naturally fidgety, increased fidgeting is less significant than a naturally calm person suddenly tapping their foot rapidly.

5.5 Integration: Calibration as the T.O.T.E. TEST

This entire chapter is dedicated to the moment-by-moment validation of your influence strategy. Calibration is the constant, quiet background process that confirms your **prediction** of their reaction was correct.

The Real-Time Sequence

Here is how Calibration (TEST) integrates with Linguistic Programming (OPERATE) in a real-world scenario:

Goal: Secure commitment on a high-value timeline.

1. **Baseline:** Subject's breathing is slow and deep (relaxed). Posture is open.

2. **OPERATE (Linguistic Program):** Deploy a Temporal Presupposition (Chapter 4): *"**When** we launch this system next month, the first thing you'll **realize** is the time you've saved."*

3. **TEST (Calibration Check):**

   - *Observation:* The subject's eyes widen slightly (surprise/interest), but their lips press together, and their breathing shifts slightly upward (tension).

   - *Interpretation:* **TEST** result is ambiguous. System 1 registered the high-value promise (surprise), but System 2 (lips pressed) has an immediate objection to the timeline.

4. **OPERATE (Adjustment via Meta-Model):** Since the tension is focused around the timeline, you run a diagnostic question (Chapter 3) aimed at the Modal Operator of Necessity: *"I can see you're processing the timeline. **What specifically makes** 'next month' a challenging necessity, rather than simply a goal?"*

5. **TEST (Calibration Check 2):**
    - *Observation:* The subject uncrosses their hands, exhales deeply (relief), and speaks with relaxed posture.
    - *Interpretation:* **TEST** successful. The specific question addressed the point of tension. The problem is no longer a hidden objection; it is a clear, manageable logistic.

6. **EXIT:** Now that the tension is gone, you address the logistic and secure the commitment.

The Predictive Advantage

When you master Sensory Acuity, you gain the ability to predict the subject's verbal response **before they speak it**. If you see a flash of contempt, you know the next words will be an objection, regardless of how polite they sound. This allows you to interrupt the pattern and reframe before the objection is consciously articulated and locked in by System 2.

This level of precision moves influence from an art to a science. It is the final, essential check against the cognitive biases and hidden resistance we introduced in Chapter 2. By mastering calibration, you ensure that every linguistic intervention you deploy is tested, refined, and ultimately successful.

The next step is to understand the final neurological levers, how to reliably link internal states to external cues. We will move to **Advanced Anchoring and State Elicitation**, which is the process of using verified principles of conditioning to program the subject's internal experience.

CHAPTER 5
ADVANCED ANCHORING AND STATE ELICITATION

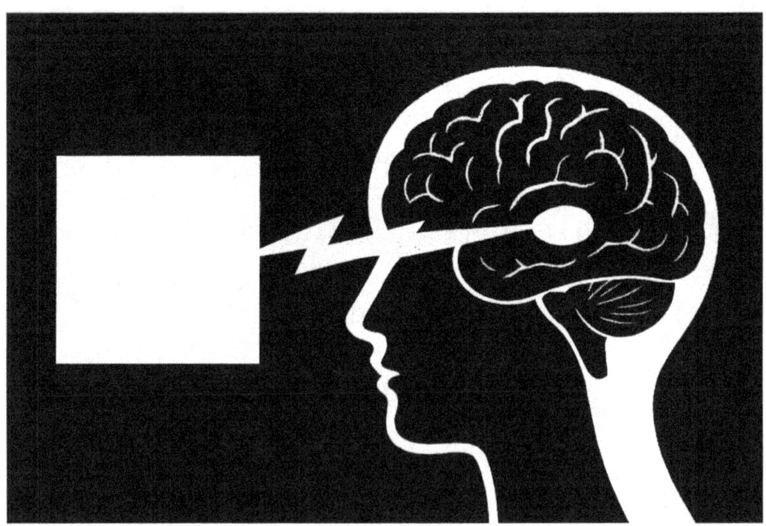

We have successfully established that influence is a predictable science. We know how to map the architecture of belief (Chapter 2), surgically diagnose resistance using the Meta-Model (Chapter 3), and deploy targeted language with Linguistic Programming (Chapter 4). Critically, we know how to TEST the impact of every intervention through Sensory Acuity and Calibration (Chapter 5).

But there is a critical vulnerability in any human interaction: state.

A subject can be perfectly aligned with your logic, but if they are currently feeling anxious, distracted, or irritated, their decision will be compromised. The rational gatekeeper, System 2, becomes impaired under high stress, often defaulting to a safety-first "no," regardless of the objective merits of your proposal.

The master influencer does not rely on chance for the subject's state; they engineer it.

This chapter introduces the science of Advanced Anchoring and State Elicitation. This is the method for reliably linking an external stimulus (a gesture, a word, a specific touch) to a highly specific, resourceful internal state (confidence, certainty, agreement). We move past the vague, metaphorical explanations of classic NLP and ground the technique in the verifiable neurological principles of Classical and Operant

Conditioning. This is the ultimate OPERATE tool for controlling the emotional environment of commitment.

6.1 Anchoring: Conditioning the Neurological Pathway

In essence, an anchor is a conditioned stimulus. It is a neurological shortcut that allows you to bypass the conscious, slow process of state management and directly access a specific emotional memory.

Traditional NLP popularized the concept of an "anchor" as a link between a unique stimulus and a potent internal experience. Our verifiable framework defines Anchoring as the deliberate application of established learning theories to create and fire these neurological associations. This process relies on two distinct, scientifically proven mechanisms:

6.1.1 Mechanism 1: Classical Conditioning (The Stimulus-Response Link)

Classical Conditioning, pioneered by Ivan Pavlov in the early 20th century, teaches us that two stimuli repeatedly paired together will eventually form an association in the nervous system (Pavlov, 1927). A previously neutral stimulus (the *bell*) becomes a **Conditioned Stimulus (CS)** that reliably elicits a powerful, involuntary **Conditioned Response (CR)** (salivation), even when the original Unconditioned Stimulus (food) is absent.

- **In Anchoring:** The **Unconditioned Stimulus (US)** is the intense, desired emotion (e.g., peak confidence) that naturally elicits an **Unconditioned Response (UR)** (e.g., physiological calmness). The **Neutral Stimulus (NS)** is your unique anchor (e.g., a specific pressure on the knuckle). By repeatedly applying the NS *precisely* at the peak of the US, the NS becomes the **Conditioned Stimulus (CS)**, capable of eliciting the calm state (**CR**) on demand.

The verifiable power here is that the response is **involuntary** and rooted in the midbrain's emotional pathways, making it a reliable way to access and shift a subject's state (LeDoux, 2003).

6.1.2 Mechanism 2: Operant Conditioning (The Behavior-Consequence Link)

Operant Conditioning, primarily associated with B.F. Skinner, teaches us that behaviors are learned and maintained by their consequences (Skinner, 1938). The frequency of a behavior is either increased through **Reinforcement** or decreased through **Punishment**.

- **In Anchoring:** This mechanism is less about emotional state and more about **actionable commitment**. If you want a subject to repeat a desired behavior (e.g., agreement, nodding, expressing certainty), you must immediately follow that behavior with a pleasant consequence (**Positive Reinforcement**), such as validating language, a non-verbal reward (a smile, a nod), or a valuable piece of information.

Operant Conditioning is how you ensure that the subject's System 2 finds the act of agreeing with you to be a **rewarding and energizing experience**, thereby reinforcing the inclination toward consensus in the future.

6.2 Advanced Anchoring: The Five Keys to Precision

The difference between accidental conditioning and advanced application lies in precision. You cannot "fire" an anchor unless it has been "set" correctly. The following five principles ensure your anchors are potent, clean, and reliable.

Key 1: Peak State Intensity (The Unconditioned Stimulus)

The power of the anchor is directly proportional to the intensity of the emotional state at the moment of conditioning. The stronger the **Unconditioned Stimulus (US)**, the fewer repetitions required to form the **Conditioned Stimulus (CS)**.

- **Elicitation Technique:** Before setting the anchor, you must verbally or contextually guide the subject into a state of **peak intensity**.
  - *Example (Eliciting Certainty):* Do not ask them to feel certain; ask them to recall a specific, detailed memory when they felt **absolute, undeniable certainty** in their life—a moment where they *knew* they were right.
  - *Meta-Model for Elicitation:* "Close your eyes for a moment, and go back to that time. Where exactly in your body did that feeling of certainty begin? What was the first sound you heard? Make that picture bright and clear. **Amplify that feeling now.**"

The **Neutral Stimulus (NS)** you choose must be unique and highly distinguishable. If you anchor peak confidence by simply tapping your desk, an action that happens countless times, the anchor will be weak and unstable.

- **Kinesthetic (Touch):** The most potent anchor. It must be a specific point (e.g., precisely two knuckles on the table, a specific pressure point on the wrist) that is not part of normal interaction.
- **Auditory (Sound/Word):** A unique, non-common phrase used only at the peak state (e.g., "Exactly right," spoken with a specific cadence).
- **Visual (Sight):** A unique gesture (e.g., interlocking fingers in a specific way) or a distinct visual prompt.

Key 3: Timing and Association (The Critical Moment)

The anchor must be applied precisely as the emotional state is **peaking**, not before it starts and not after it fades. The neurological window for effective association is narrow.

- **Sequence:** As the subject's face (calibrated via Chapter 5) shows peak intensity (deep breath, flush of color, engaged eye contact), apply the Kinesthetic anchor (e.g., the knuckle press). Hold the anchor for a few seconds to cement the association, then release it just as the state begins to subside.
- **Neurological Basis:** This simultaneous activation ensures the neural pathways for the stimulus and the response fire together, promoting rapid long-term potentiation (the strengthening of synaptic connections that form memory and learning) (Bliss & Lømo, 1973).

Key 4: Reinforcement and Testing (Solidifying the Anchor)

The anchor must be reinforced using multiple, similar emotional states and then **TESTED**.

1. **Reinforcement:** Ask the subject to recall three separate memories of certainty and apply the exact same anchor at the peak of each. This strengthens the association and makes the anchor robust against contextual changes.

2. **Testing:** Break the state (e.g., change the subject, ask a technical question). Then, **fire the anchor** (apply the CS). Your calibration (Chapter 5) must confirm the **Conditioned Response (CR)** is elicited, the subject's posture should shift, breathing should deepen, and a verifiable emotional response should appear on their face. If it fails, repeat the process.

Key 5: Stacking Anchors (The Power Chord)

To ensure maximum impact, multiple similar anchors can be applied at the peak of the same emotional state.

- **Stacking:** If you are eliciting "Confidence," you can set Kinesthetic Anchor 1 (knuckle press), Auditory Anchor 1 (the word "Precision"), and Visual Anchor 1 (a hand gesture) all at the peak of the same emotion. When you later fire all three (Kinesthetic, Auditory, and Visual) simultaneously, you create a powerful "power chord" that reliably accesses the full intensity of the resource state.

6.3 Tactical State Elicitation: Anchoring for Influence

In the context of Advanced NLP, Anchoring is used to make the subject feel the necessary emotion to commit to your proposal at the exact moment you ask for the commitment.

6.3.1 The Agreement Anchor (Operant Conditioning for Consensus)

This is the most direct application of **Operant Conditioning** in influence. The goal is to condition the subject to associate the act of **agreeing with you** with a pleasurable, rewarding consequence.

The Setup:

1. **Identify the Desired Behavior:** Nodding, saying "yes," leaning in, or expressing approval.

2. **Select the Reinforcer (Positive Consequence):** A genuine, high-value non-verbal reward, usually a specific smile, a confirming nod, or a positive, unique phrase like "Exactly right."

The Sequence (Reinforcement Schedule):

1. Ask a series of rapid, low-stakes questions designed to elicit easy, immediate agreement (**Pacing**). (*E.g., "You agree that efficiency is important, correct?" "You see the value in saving time, yes?"*)

2. Each time the subject exhibits the **Desired Behavior** (nods, says "yes"), immediately apply your **Reinforcer** (smile, confirming nod, the unique phrase "Exactly right").

3. The repeated pairing of the act of agreement with the pleasurable, positive consequence conditions the subject's system to find agreeing with you **rewarding**.

The Payoff: When you transition to the high-stakes final question, the subject's **System 1** is already conditioned to seek the reward associated with agreement, making the final "yes" the path of conditioned comfort and acceptance. This leverages the **Bandwagon Effect** on a micro-scale: the subject is following the momentum of their own reinforced behavior.

6.3.2 The Decision Anchor (Contextual Conditioning)

This technique involves setting an anchor not on the subject's body, but on the **context of the decision**.

- **The Setup:** Identify a specific object or spot in the decision environment (the contract, the pen, the corner of the table).

- **The Sequence:** Throughout the initial stages of rapport and positive value discussion, repeatedly touch, point to, or glance at the **Decision Anchor** while the subject is expressing positive emotions (e.g., excitement, comprehension, confidence).

- **The Payoff:** When you arrive at the moment of commitment, the final action required is for the subject to engage with the **Decision Anchor** (e.g., picking up the pen, signing the contract). By anchoring positive states to that object, the physical act of engaging with it elicits the positive, resourceful state you conditioned earlier, reducing hesitation and fear.

6.3.3 The Collapse Anchor (State Interruption)

This is the inverse application of Anchoring: using a **Conditioned Stimulus** to disrupt or collapse a negative state (e.g., high anxiety, fear, or rigidity).

- **The Setup:** Anchor the negative state precisely at its peak. Do not reinforce it, but simply acknowledge and anchor it.

- **The Intervention:** Once the negative state is anchored, immediately **fire a conflicting, positive anchor** (e.g., your stacked "Confidence" power chord).

- **The Result (State Collapse):** Neurologically, the simultaneous firing of two conflicting, high-intensity states (Anxiety anchor + Confidence anchor) causes both neural pathways to momentarily fire and then inhibit each other (LeDoux, 2003). The result is a brief moment of internal disorientation, forcing the subject's System 2 to find a new, neutral, or resourceful state, effectively interrupting the negative cycle.

This allows you to create a momentary **reset** in the conversation, giving you the window of opportunity to deploy a new, positive frame or a clarifying **Meta-Model** question.

6.4 Neurological Basis: The Amygdala and Emotional Memory

The verifiable science of Anchoring lies in the **Amygdala**, the almond-shaped structure in the limbic system responsible for processing and storing emotional memories.

Fear conditioning (a form of classical conditioning) has been extensively studied, showing that the amygdala is the central hub where the **Conditioned Stimulus (CS)** becomes permanently linked to the fear response (UR). This rapid, non-conscious linkage is the same mechanism at work in Advanced Anchoring (Davis, 1992).

When you successfully anchor a state of **certainty** or **excitement**, you are creating a strong neural pathway in the subject's brain that bypasses the cerebral cortex (the slow, rational part) and directly accesses the emotional memory stored in the amygdala and related structures. The goal of Advanced NLP is to intentionally create positive, resourceful conditioned responses where default environmental triggers might otherwise create negative or hesitant states.

6.5 Ethical Responsibility and the Ecology of State

Because Anchoring provides a direct, non-conscious lever into a subject's emotional experience, its application carries a profound ethical responsibility. The **Ecology of Influence**, the final test of any intervention, must be applied rigorously to state elicitation.

The Ecological Check for Anchoring:

1. **Congruence with Identity:** Is the state you are anchoring (e.g., "Decisiveness") consistent with the subject's self-concept and highest values (Chapter 2)? Anchoring a state that conflicts with their core identity will fail or create internal dissonance.

2. **Utility of the State:** Does the state you are anchoring serve a positive, long-term purpose for the subject? You should anchor **confidence** to help them commit to a beneficial decision, not **recklessness** to bypass their rational skepticism.

3. **Clean Anchors:** Avoid anchoring negative states, even accidentally. Never pair a high-intensity negative emotion (e.g., frustration) with any unique gesture, word, or location, as this will poison that resource for future use.

The master influencer uses Anchoring to ensure the subject is in their **optimal resourceful state** to make a great decision, not a manipulated one. We are clearing away anxiety and distraction so that their rational System 2 can ratify the excellent, valuable frame you have provided.

By mastering Advanced Anchoring, you now control the emotional variables of the encounter. You have the tools to diagnose resistance (Chapter 3), frame the proposition (Chapter 4), monitor the results (Chapter 5), and ensure the subject is in the right emotional state to commit (Chapter 6).

The final step is to synthesize all these tools into a single, cohesive, and predictable strategy, the architecture of long-term commitment. This will be the focus of our final, concluding chapter.

CONCLUSION

We began this journey by defining influence not as a gift of charisma, but as a **practiced, verifiable science**. Throughout the previous chapters, we have systematically dismantled the mechanisms of human decision and armed ourselves with the tools necessary to structure the path to agreement:

- We mapped the predictable decision errors, the **Cognitive Filters** and **Loss Aversion**, that define the human algorithm (Chapter 2).
- We mastered the surgical diagnosis of resistance through the **Meta-Model** (Chapter 3).
- We learned to architect propositions using the embedded commands and assumptions of **Linguistic Programming** (Chapter 4).
- We transformed our senses into real-time feedback systems using **Sensory Acuity and Calibration** (Chapter 5).
- And finally, we gained control over the emotional variables by employing **Advanced Anchoring and State Elicitation** (Chapter 6).

Now, the final, most crucial step: **Synthesis**.

A box of surgical tools does not make a surgeon; the blueprint, the protocol, and the disciplined application of the strategy do. This chapter delivers the **Master Blueprint**: the **Predictive Influence Loop**. This loop is the strategic integration of every tool in this book, governed by the relentless feedback mechanism of the **T.O.T.E. Model**, all situated within a context of deep, neurological **Rapport**. Mastery is not about deploying a single technique; it is about running this comprehensive, adaptive loop until commitment is secured.

7.1 The Master Blueprint: The T.O.T.E. Model Refined

The foundation of our strategy is the **T.O.T.E. Model** (Test–Operate–Test–Exit), originally developed by Miller, Galanter, and Pribram (1960) to describe the neurological structure of behavior. It is the definitive algorithm for self-correction and goal achievement, and we apply it directly to the process of influence.

The T.O.T.E. Model reframes the entire interaction as a continuous cycle of **checking for congruence (TEST)** and **intervening (OPERATE)** until the desired outcome is achieved. It eliminates improvisation and replaces it with **adaptive, data-driven action.**

Step 1: TEST (The Initial Calibration and Outcome Frame)

The cycle begins not with talking, but with **calibrating** and **framing**. Before any linguistic intervention, you must gather essential data.

1. **Define the Outcome (The Exit Condition):** What is the specific, sensory-verifiable commitment you need? (e.g., "The client signs the contract," not "The client feels happy.") This defines the **T.O.T.E. Exit condition**.

2. **Establish Rapport and Baseline:** Engage the subject, using subtle **Mirroring and Matching** (Chapter 5) to establish neurological synchronization. **Calibrate** their neutral/comfortable state (their breathing, posture, resting facial tension). This is the initial **TEST** of their baseline behavior.

3. **Identify the Filter/Belief:** Use soft, open-ended language to elicit the subject's initial perspective. Listen for **Generalizations, Deletions, and Distortions** (Chapter 3) and identify the controlling **Cognitive Filter** (Loss Aversion, Confirmation Bias, etc.) that will govern their decision (Chapter 2).

   - *Key Insight:* The initial **TEST** provides the data. If the data is ambiguous (e.g., the subject says "yes" but their body language signals tension), you proceed to OPERATE to clarify the internal state.

Step 2: OPERATE (The Strategic Intervention)

Based on the data gathered in the initial TEST, you select and deploy the most precise intervention.

1. **State Elicitation (The Emotional Context):** First, anchor the emotional environment. If the subject is anxious, deploy a **Collapse Anchor** or a **Confidence Anchor** (Chapter 6). If they are hesitant, utilize **Operant Conditioning** to build momentum with the **Agreement Anchor**.

2. **Linguistic Programming (The Core Message):** Deploy a precisely framed proposition that aligns with the subject's cognitive filter. If you detected a **Loss Aversion** filter, frame the proposition using **Comparative Negation** (Chapter 4), emphasizing the cost of

inaction. If the resistance was vague, use the **Meta-Model** to elicit the Deep Structure (Chapter 3).

- *Key Insight:* The **OPERATE** phase is not persuasion; it is the calculated input designed to shift the subject from their current state (State A: Hesitation) to the desired state (State B: Commitment).

Step 3: TEST (The Feedback Loop)

Immediately after deploying your intervention, you must **TEST** for the effect. This is the moment of truth where your **Sensory Acuity** proves the success or failure of the intervention.

1. **Check for Congruence:** Use your calibration skills (Chapter 5) to observe the subject's physiological response. Did the pitch of their voice drop? Did their breathing shift from thoracic (stressed) to diaphragmatic (relaxed)? Did you see a flash of **Contempt** or **Disgust**?

2. **Confirm the Shift:** If you deployed a Loss Aversion frame, you should see a subtle increase in arousal (System 1 activation). If you deployed an Agreement Anchor, you should see increased synchronization/mirroring.

3. **Diagnosis:**

   o **Success (Congruence):** The subject's verbal response and non-verbal signals align with the desired outcome. Proceed to EXIT.

   o **Failure (Incongruence):** The subject's words are positive, but their body signals resistance (e.g., they say "I agree," but their jaw clenches). Rerun the loop.

Step 4: EXIT or Rerun

The final step determines the overall flow of the interaction.

- **EXIT (Commitment Secured):** If the **TEST** confirms success (congruence is achieved), transition immediately to securing the verbal or written commitment. Use a final **Temporal Presupposition** to seal the deal (e.g., "Now that we've confirmed this, **when** is the best day to finalize the paperwork?").

- **RERUN (Adaptive Strategy):** If the **TEST** indicates incongruence or failure, the process immediately loops back to the **OPERATE** phase. The data from the failed **TEST** is now your new input. You do not repeat the previous intervention; you deploy a refined strategy (e.g., switch from a Linguistic Program to a Meta-Model question to diagnose the source of the hidden tension).

This T.O.T.E. structure eliminates guesswork. It turns every objection into data, every failure into a learning opportunity, and every intervention into a calculated move toward the desired end state.

7.2 The Context: Rapport as Neurological Synchronization

The T.O.T.E. loop operates most efficiently when the context is one of **deep, neurological rapport**. Rapport is often dismissed as mere friendly nodding, but in Advanced NLP, we define it as **interpersonal neural synchronization**, a state where the subject's brain is naturally receptive to your input.

Rapport is not an emotion; it is a **neurological precondition for influence**.

7.2.1 The Mirror Neuron System

The verifiable foundation for rapport lies in the **Mirror Neuron System (MNS)**, first mapped in macaque monkeys and later confirmed in humans (Rizzolatti & Craighero, 2004).

- **The Mechanism:** Mirror neurons are specialized cells that fire both when an individual performs an action and when the individual *observes* another performing the same action. The MNS is the brain's fundamental mechanism for empathy, understanding intent, and learning. When you observe a subject reaching for a cup, the same neurons fire in your brain as if you were reaching for the cup yourself.

- **Rapport as MNS Activation:** When you engage in subtle **Mirroring and Matching** (Chapter 5), you are intentionally sending verifiable non-verbal signals to the subject's MNS. You are, in effect, telling their brain: **"I am like you, I understand your action, and I share your internal state."** This subconscious verification of similarity is the fundamental basis of trust. When MNS activation is high, cognitive defenses are lowered, making the subject naturally more receptive to your linguistic input.

7.2.2 Emotional Contagion: The Shared State

Rapport is deepened by **Emotional Contagion**, the process by which a person's emotions and related behaviors prompt similar emotions and behaviors in others (Hatfield, Cacioppo, & Rapson, 1994). This phenomenon operates primarily through **mimicry** (facial, vocal, postural) and the subsequent **afferent feedback**, the brain's interpretation of its own bodily state.

- **The Mechanism:** If you non-verbally project a state (e.g., Calm Confidence), the subject's MNS begins to subconsciously mimic your posture and facial expressions. The subject's brain then receives feedback from their own body ("My body is adopting a calm posture; therefore, I must be feeling calm"). This allows you to **influence the subject's resource state** without ever mentioning the emotion.

- **Application (Pre-Framing):** Before you enter the **OPERATE** phase of the T.O.T.E. loop, you must first ensure your own state is optimal. Your internal state of **Certainty** (anchored via Chapter 6) is contagious. By maintaining a congruent, resourceful state, you leverage Emotional Contagion to pull the subject out of anxiety and into a state of focus and confidence, making the final commitment possible.

7.3 The Predictive Influence Loop: A Step-by-Step Strategy

The following is the integrated, seven-step protocol for running the Predictive Influence Loop, synthesizing all the tools and concepts of Advanced NLP.

Step 1: Pre-Frame and Define the Exit (Chapter 2 & 1)

- **Action:** Define the **T.O.T.E. Exit** condition (the verifiable commitment).

- **Frame:** Determine the most potent **Cognitive Filter** (e.g., Loss Aversion) that will be the central theme of your presentation. Structure your opening to hit this filter. (e.g., "The greatest cost here is the cost of staying where you are.")

- **Internal State:** Anchor your own state of **Calm Authority** (Chapter 6).

- **Action:** Spend 60-90 seconds building rapport. Subtly match the subject's rate of speech, vocal volume, and posture.
- **Calibration:** **TEST** the subject's **Physiological Baseline** (breathing, facial tension). This is your initial data for the T.O.T.E. loop.

- **Action:** Pace their reality and elicit their core belief/resistance. Use soft, non-threatening statements that confirm their experience.
- **Diagnosis:** Listen acutely for **Universal Quantifiers** ("always," "never") and **Modal Operators of Possibility** ("can't," "won't"). This initial **TEST** reveals the **Deep Structure** of their resistance.

- **Action:** If the subject is vague (a high volume of Deletions or Unspecified Verbs), use the **Meta-Model** to ask a single, targeted question that retrieves the missing information. If they show clear, low-level agreement, deploy an **Agreement Anchor** (Operant Conditioning).
- **Linguistic Focus:** Structure your **OPERATE** phase with **Temporal or Ordinal Presuppositions** to embed the inevitability of the agreement.

- **Action:** Immediately after the intervention, **TEST** their response. Check for congruence: Does the physiological signal (Chapter 5) match their verbal feedback?
- **Feedback:** If you see a **Mismatch** (e.g., verbal agreement but a flash of **Contempt** or **Disgust**), the resistance is hidden.
- **T.O.T.E. Rerun:** The detected physiological signal becomes the new input. Return to **OPERATE** with a clarifying intervention (e.g., "I can see that point is causing some internal conflict; **what specific implication** of this change requires more thought?").

- **Action:** Once the subject is congruent (non-verbal signals match verbal agreement) and the last objection has collapsed, you move to the commitment phase.
- **Final Anchor:** Fire a previously set, high-intensity **Certainty Anchor** or **Confidence Anchor** (Chapter 6).
- **Final Frame:** Immediately follow the anchor with a powerful **Default Bias Frame** (Chapter 2): *"Based on all the evidence we've covered, the next step is the standard protocol for implementation, which starts today. Is there any logistical reason we shouldn't follow the standard protocol?"*

Step 7: EXIT (The Final Seal)

- **Action:** Secure the physical commitment.
- **Final Reinforcement:** As the subject acts (signs, shakes hands, or confirms), immediately and genuinely apply a high-value **Positive Reinforcer** (a powerful, unique word and nod) to cement the reward/consequence link for future positive interactions.

7.4 The Final Leverage: Cognitive Dissonance and Commitment

The ultimate goal of the Predictive Influence Loop is to trigger the final, powerful psychological lever: **Cognitive Dissonance**.

Cognitive Dissonance is the mental stress or discomfort experienced by an individual who holds two or more contradictory beliefs, ideas, or values, or performs an action that contradicts their beliefs (Festinger, 1957). The human brain is evolutionarily compelled to resolve this dissonance, usually by changing the less strongly held belief to align with the action already taken.

The Dissonance Gap

The Predictive Influence Loop is designed to maximize the **Dissonance Gap** between the old belief and the new action.

1. **Old Belief (Resistance):** *"This proposal is too expensive and risky."* (A Generalized, Loss Aversion filter).
2. **New Action (Commitment):** The subject is linguistically and emotionally guided to say **"Yes"** and shake your hand (The Exit).

Once the subject has taken the action (the commitment), their brain must resolve the dissonance: *"I just committed to the proposal, but I still believe it is too expensive."* It is easier for the brain to retrospectively change the belief to align with the action than to undo the commitment.

The brain automatically restructures the belief: *"I committed because it's not actually expensive; it is a smart, strategic investment."*

The Law of Consistency: Influence does not stop at the signature. The act of making an initial, small commitment significantly increases the probability of making subsequent, larger commitments (Cialdini, 1984). By guiding the subject to several small, congruent agreements throughout the T.O.T.E. loop (e.g., "Yes, efficiency is key," "Yes, that's what stopped me before"), you build a powerful, verifiable track record of agreement that they are neurologically compelled to maintain.

7.5 Mastery: The Continuous Pursuit of Precision

The strategies outlined in this book transform influence from a hopeful encounter into a predictable process. The Predictive Influence Loop is your final, complete operating system. It requires the continuous, disciplined practice of:

1. **Objectivity:** Using **Calibration** to gather data, not relying on intuition.

2. **Surgical Precision:** Deploying the **Meta-Model** and **Linguistic Programming** to address the exact, verifiable cause of resistance.

3. **Adaptive Control:** Utilizing the **T.O.T.E. Model** to ensure every action is tested and corrected immediately.

The journey to advanced influence is a commitment to precision. By integrating these scientific principles, you gain the ability to predict, control, and architect consensus in any human interaction, ensuring that the path you prescribe becomes the path of least resistance for the subject's own logical system. Your mastery begins now.

SYNTHESIS AND STRATEGIC REFLECTION

You've made it. We've gone deep into the complete blueprint of predictable influence, moving all the way from the psychological foundations to the integrated, self-correcting strategy of the **Predictive Influence Loop**.

But let's be real: reading a textbook on carpentry doesn't make you a master builder. Mastery in Advanced NLP isn't about memorizing the jargon; it's about **self-calibration** and **meta-cognition**, it's about intentionally stopping and thinking about how *you* think, how *you* react, and how *you* apply these tools.

This final chapter isn't about new material. It's your surgical checklist. It's a structured set of reflection questions designed to turn the principles from neat theories into robust, reliable habits. Use a journal or a voice recorder for this. Don't let yourself get away with **Generalizations** ("It went well"). Be your own toughest **Meta-Model** coach. Dig for the specifics.

The goal here is simple: stop guessing what people want and start accurately mapping their internal reality.

1. **Framing and Loss Aversion:**
    - Think about the last three times you tried to influence a key decision. **How specifically** did you frame the conversation to make the **cost of doing nothing** (Loss Aversion) feel heavier than the price of your solution?
    - What verifiable, non-verbal signal, a flicker, a breath change, a shift in posture, did your **Calibration** pick up that confirmed your Loss Aversion frame actually landed? Did you trigger resistance instead?

2. **Meta-Model Self-Correction:**
    - Pull up a recent significant objection you received. Now, coach yourself through the **Meta-Model** diagnosis:
        - Which **Generalization** (like "We can **never** afford that") was used? What is the single, specific **counter-example** you should have asked the subject for right away?
        - What key piece of information was missing (a **Deletion**)? Who was the missing actor, or what was the unspecified process?
        - What **Distortion** (like "Their silence **means** they don't trust us") was at play? What was the true, internal fear or false logic that the subject needed to see?

3. **Identity and Alignment:**
    - Before your next high-stakes conversation, list out the subject's top three values (e.g., Security, Freedom, Innovation).
    - How will your final pitch explicitly link to reinforce **all three** of those values? Are you making sure that saying "yes" to you aligns perfectly with their self-concept (their **Confirmation Bias**)?

This section is about verifying the surgical precision and *cleanliness* of your inputs. You're checking for accidental contamination.

1. **Linguistic Precision:**

    o   Go back through a recent email or presentation script. Find every instance where you used the word **'but'** to negate a concern. Now, replace it with the word **'and.'** What does that simple change do to the mental process for the reader?

    o   Pick a crucial instruction you need to implant (e.g., "Decide now"). Formulate two or three distinct **Embedded Commands** that carry that message, then practice the **Tonal Shift** and the **Pause** that makes them covertly effective.

    o   When you use a **Temporal Presupposition** (like, "**When you start seeing the revenue increase...**"), are you absolutely sure you're bypassing an inconsequential detail, or are you actually avoiding a major objection that needs a full **Meta-Model** diagnosis?

2. **Anchoring and State Control:**

    o   Describe the last time you consciously **set an anchor** on a subject. What exact, unique **Kinesthetic Stimulus** did you use (e.g., specific knuckle press)? Was the subject truly at their **peak state** when you set it?

    o   Define your **Agreement Anchor** (the unique sound, word, or gesture you use to reward consensus). Are you being diligent enough to **only** use that reinforcer when they are genuinely agreeing, or are you accidentally polluting it with random conversation?

    o   Think about your personal state. What **Anchor** do you use to access **Calm Authority** before a big meeting? Do you **TEST** that anchor on yourself regularly to make sure it still fires instantly?

This is about turning your senses into data-gathering tools and ensuring you are always running the **Predictive Influence Loop** adaptively.

1. **The Respiration Test:**
   - In your next conversation, consciously try to ignore the words for one minute. Focus only on the subject's **Respiration.** Note the precise moment and topic when the breath **locus shifts** (from belly to chest) or when they take a sudden, deep breath. What specific **internal conflict** do you think that physiological shift represents?
   - What is your internal definition of the micro-expression of **Contempt**? Practice spotting the unilateral sneer in the mirror. If you spot it in a client, what is the fastest, non-defensive action you can take to address the **superiority signal** and reset the rapport?

2. **T.O.T.E. Adaptive Strategy:**
   - Reflect on a recent failure to close a deal or secure agreement. Plot your steps onto the **T.O.T.E. Model** flow: **Where did your first TEST fail?** Did you miss a key calibration cue?
   - Describe a situation where you successfully executed a **T.O.T.E. Rerun.** What *new, specific information* did the failure of the first **TEST** provide, and how did you use that information to make your second **OPERATE** phase surgical?
   - What is the final line you use to secure the **EXIT**? Does it ask for a simple signature, or does it leverage a final **Temporal Presupposition** and an **Agreement Anchor** to cement their commitment?

The ultimate test of true influence is its sustainability and its ethical footprint.

1. **The Ethical Calculus:**
   - Identify a situation where you used a powerful covert technique (like a **Loss Aversion Frame** or an **Embedded Command**). If the subject were to watch a replay of that conversation and understand every technique you used, would they still feel the decision was theirs and the value was real?
   - How are you actively using **Reciprocity**? List three **high-value, unrequested insights** you can deliver to a key relationship this week, insights that help them understand *their own* **Deep Structure** better.
   - Run the **Autonomy Test** on your current biggest goal: Do the interventions you plan still leave the subject with the genuine feeling of **ownership** over the final decision?

2. **Consistency and Legacy:**
   - List three small, low-risk commitments you can secure from a subject *before* asking for the final agreement. How will you make sure you immediately **reward** (Positively Reinforce) their follow-through on those small steps to build a **habit of consistency**?
   - If your entire legacy were defined by your ability to upgrade the **Internal Maps** of others, what is the single most important limiting belief (**Generalization** or **Modal Operator of Possibility**) you are committed to helping a key person overcome?

By committing to this rigorous cycle of self-reflection, you are moving beyond technique and embracing the **Adaptive Intelligence** that defines true mastery in the science of predictable influence.

BOOK FOUR

IRRESISTIBLE CHARM:
RELATIONSHIP DYNAMICS

INTRODUCTION
TO IRRESISTIBLE CHARM

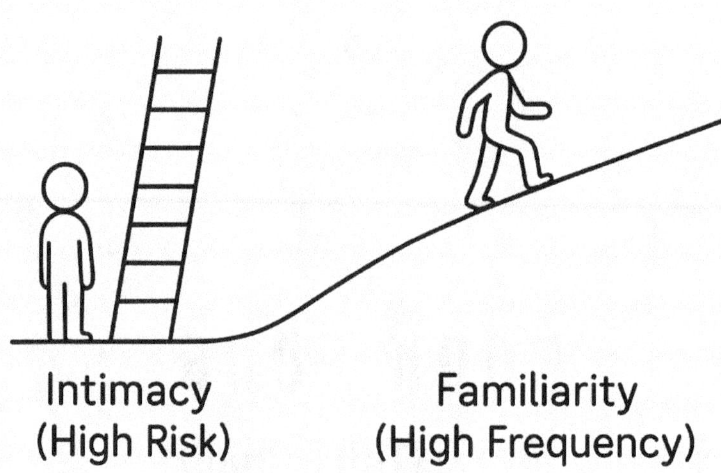

We have moved through the logical and the non-verbal. Book 1 covered the strategy of choice. Book 2 taught you the charisma of physical projection. Book 3 ensured your words landed with precision. Now, we face the hardest challenge: making people **want** to be influenced by you. This book is about building **Irresistible Charm** through the mastery of relationship dynamics.

Charm is not just a thin layer of manners. It is a fundamental psychological resource. It is the skilled use of openness, social connection, and emotional management to secure intense attraction and loyalty over the long term. Charm is the difference between a good transaction and a lasting connection. It is the mechanism that ensures people feel deeply invested in your presence and your success.

This book guides the relationship from simple professional trust to deep, personal alignment. It is built on the measurable science of **self-disclosure** and **social cohesion**. We will show you how to rapidly accelerate intimacy without setting off the target's psychological defenses. We focus on the architecture of human connection, ensuring the bond you create is resilient and self-sustaining.

The Blueprint of Intimacy: Self-Disclosure

Every deep connection, whether with a partner, a key client, or a core team member, rests on a calculated exchange of personal information. This process is called **self-disclosure**. Charm is essentially the intentional management of this exchange. It controls the pace and the appropriate depth of intimacy.

The objective is to quickly create a sense of familiarity and closeness. Research strongly confirms a key finding: **disclosure frequency**, how often you share small personal details, is the number one factor that predicts familiarity and closeness, provided the disclosures are perceived as appropriate. This means that the sheer volume of low-stakes interaction is more important than rushing to share deep secrets.

The Threshold of Appropriateness: The strategy must be precise. You must be aware of the boundary. Studies show that while intimate disclosure can increase closeness, it also carries a significant risk: it far more often **reduces social attraction** if the target perceives the disclosure as inappropriate. If you share too much too soon, you violate a boundary. You signal poor judgment, and the target immediately retreats.

Charm is the skill of navigating this delicate line. It requires maximizing the frequency of low-stakes disclosures to build rapid familiarity. At the same time, you must meticulously monitor the target's reciprocal behavior. This tells you the exact moment it is safe to increase the depth of the conversation.

The Three Engines of Magnetic Attraction

Irresistible charm relies on three core principles that elevate a relationship beyond just a functional exchange.

1. Narrativity: The Entertainment Investment: A relationship must be engaging. It must hold the target's interest over time. Simply stating dry facts is boring. Charm requires presenting personal information as a compelling story. **Disclosure narrativity**, the practice of telling short, structured stories about yourself, significantly increases perceived closeness and social attraction.

This positive effect happens because the narrative format possesses a clear **perceived entertainment value**. The goal is to frame every interaction as a worthwhile investment of the target's time and attention. This concept is extremely important in virtual or text-based settings. In those spaces, where physical presence and body language are missing, attraction depends almost entirely on "words, charm, and seduction." Linguistic crafting becomes the only tool you have.

2. Social Rituals: The Shared Identity Check: Charm secures long-term loyalty by building a **shared identity**. People feel an intense sense of belonging when they share common experiences and values. This is achieved through **shared social rituals** and **identification humor**.

Identification humor builds group cohesion because it appeals to a set of shared expectations and norms that everyone in the group recognizes. When a group laughs at the same social violation, they confirm they share the same underlying worldview. This shared psychological vetting mechanism strengthens the relationship and reduces uncertainty about the other person.

The ultimate goal of this shared laughter is to create deep cohesion. Research confirms that shared laughter increases interpersonal attraction, enhances group cohesion, and helps resolve conflicts. By encouraging shared humor and inside jokes, you help the group develop a resilient **shared identity** that is much stronger than their individual differences.

3. Projection of Psychological Stability: Charm is amplified by projecting deep psychological stability. A perceived **good sense of humor** is an invaluable social resource. People naturally gravitate toward those who project a positive, engaging feeling.

Positive humor styles are strongly associated with desirable traits: high self-esteem, extroversion, and greater satisfaction in relationships. By consistently using positive, unifying humor, the charismatic person projects stability and social desirability. This makes them a highly sought-after connection. They are seen as a psychological resource.

The Synthesis of Charisma and Strategy

This book takes the strategic systems of the previous books and applies them directly to the human heart and mind:

- **Linguistic Precision (Book 3):** The personal narratives and disclosures must use concrete language to maximize impact and avoid cognitive friction.
- **Non-Verbal Resonance (Book 2):** All disclosures must be supported by composed delivery and intentional stillness, ensuring the **Halo Effect** reinforces trustworthiness.

- **Covert Persuasion (Book 1):** The emotional commitment gained through self-disclosure and loyalty must be leveraged to secure larger, structural loyalty and adherence.

This book details the exact steps for managing this delicate process. We will show you how to structure disclosures to accelerate intimacy, how to use humor for social vetting, and how to continuously calibrate the relationship's boundaries to maintain peak social attraction.

The next chapter, **Accelerate Intimacy: Structuring Calculated Self-Disclosure**, details the precise formula for using disclosure frequency and content. It shows you how to build rapid, deep familiarity while minimizing the risk of sharing too much, too soon, which could break the connection.

CHAPTER 1

ACCELERATE INTIMACY:

STRUCTURING CALCULATED SELF - DISCLOSURE

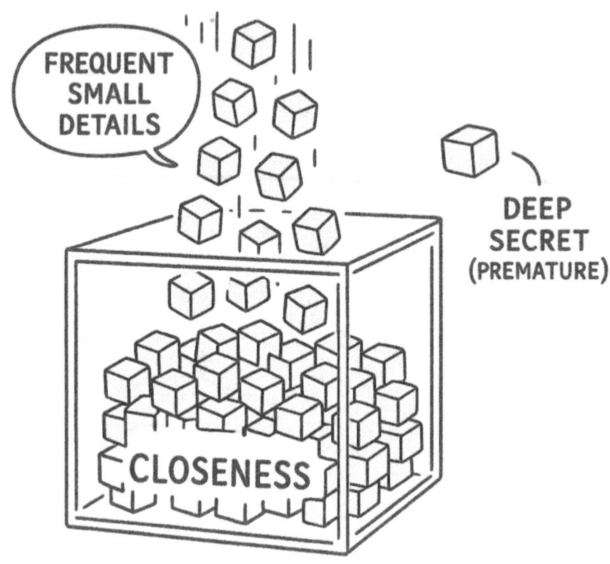

We enter the most delicate part of influence. It is not enough to guide a person logically. You must connect with them personally. This requires accelerating intimacy without rushing to vulnerability. The tool for this rapid connection is **calculated self-disclosure**.

Charm is essentially the intentional management of shared personal information. Every deep relationship, whether it is personal or professional, is built on this exchange. The objective is to establish familiarity and closeness so fast that the target feels they have known you far longer than they actually have. This process creates a resilient, strong psychological bond.

I. The Formula for Familiarity: Frequency Over Intimacy

The primary mistake people make when seeking connection is sharing too much, too soon. They confuse vulnerability with intimacy. They try to speed up the process by dumping secrets or painful details right away. This approach is often disastrous.

The Key Finding: Research consistently shows that the most powerful factor predicting familiarity and closeness is **disclosure frequency**. This is the volume of information shared, not the depth of the information. The sheer number of small, safe interactions matters more than the urgency of the deep secrets.

If you share often, about low-stakes things, your weekend routines, a minor preference, or a funny anecdote from your week, you quickly build a dense foundation of connection. The target feels they know you well because they have accumulated many small data points. This high-frequency exchange is the fastest route to perceived closeness.

The Danger of Premature Depth: While intimate disclosure can certainly increase closeness in established relationships, it far more often **reduces social attraction** if the target perceives the sharing as inappropriate for the current stage of the relationship.

If you reveal deep, personal failures or intense emotional anxieties too early, you signal a lack of boundaries or emotional instability. This sets off an internal alarm for the target, and they immediately retreat. They feel uncomfortable. They view the sharing as a social violation. The risk of sharing deep personal matters often outweighs the potential benefit in the initial stages.

Actionable Frequency Strategy:

1. **Maximize Low-Stakes Volume:** Share specific, small details about your life three times more often than you would naturally. Talk about your favorite type of coffee, the difficulty of your commute, or a small win you had this morning.

2. **Maintain Neutrality:** Ensure the content is positive, non-controversial, and not emotionally taxing. The objective is to build a large catalog of neutral shared facts.

3. **Prioritize Reciprocity:** Always leave room for the target to match your disclosure. Your small disclosure is an invitation for them to offer a small disclosure back. This mutual exchange is the engine of closeness.

II. The Necessity of Narrativity: Charm as Entertainment

It is not enough to just share facts. The words must be engaging. A relationship must be compelling enough to hold the target's sustained interest. Simply stating dry facts is boring, and boring conversations kill charisma.

The Power of Storytelling: Disclosure narrativity, the practice of framing personal information as a structured, short story, increases perceived closeness and social attraction. This positive effect happens entirely because the narrative format possesses **perceived entertainment value**. The target enjoys listening to you. They are investing their attention because they are getting a worthwhile return.

The Strategy of Framing the Mundane: The goal is to elevate mundane details into engaging, short narratives. You must frame every piece of information as an investment of the target's attention.

- *Instead of (Dry Fact):* "I was late because I had to fill out a form." (Zero entertainment value)

- *Use (Narrative Frame):* "I was almost twenty minutes late because the new security form insisted I list my dog's middle name. It was a bizarre, unnecessary five minutes of my life, but I learned that the system will shut down if I type 'None'." (Short, specific, creates a shared moment of mild frustration, possesses clear entertainment value).

By consistently delivering these small, entertaining narrative capsules, you maximize the psychological impact and dramatically increase social attraction toward you, the source of the story. The interaction is transformed from a simple exchange of facts into a valuable, engaging social resource.

III. The Calibration Test: Diagnosing Appropriateness

The effects of self-disclosure are entirely controlled by the target's **perceived appropriateness**. This boundary is dynamic. It is subjective, and it must be actively monitored. You cannot guess the boundary; you must test for it.

Reciprocal Disclosure as a Gauge: The single most reliable measure of appropriateness is **reciprocal disclosure**. A target who matches your level of disclosure, in both frequency and depth, implicitly confirms that your current level of intimacy is acceptable. Their return of information signals that the boundary is safe.

The Testing Sequence for Depth:

1. **Initial Low Stakes:** Start with high-frequency, low-intimacy disclosures (Chapter 2, Section I).

2. **The Gentle Deepening:** Once familiarity is established, you should gently test the boundary. Offer a disclosure that is *slightly* deeper than the one before it (e.g., instead of talking about hobbies, talk about a minor professional philosophy).

3. **Observe Response:** Watch the target's reaction carefully. Did they match the new depth? Did they ask a follow-up question that indicates comfort?

   o **If they retreat:** If the target offers a very short, closed answer, changes the subject abruptly, or redirects the focus back entirely to you, the intimacy level was inappropriate. **You must immediately retreat.** You pull back the depth of future disclosures to a safer, frequent level.

   o **If they match:** If the target matches or even exceeds the new depth, they have implicitly signaled the boundary is safe, and you may proceed to the next level.

This continuous calibration ensures you build closeness rapidly without violating trust. Pushing too hard or too fast reveals a lack of social intelligence, which instantly breaks the charm and reduces social attraction.

IV. Disclosure and the Compliance Drivers

Calculated self-disclosure is not just for emotional connection. It is a strategic tool that feeds directly into the compliance drivers detailed in Book 1, securing commitment and activating liking.

1. Activating Liking (Similarity): The core of the Liking principle is similarity. We like people who are similar to us. By using **disclosure frequency** to share many small, positive details, you are maximizing the surface area for finding common ground.

   • **Actionable Alignment:** You should quickly note any small detail the target shares, a favorite movie, a preferred travel destination, a shared frustration with a local service, and immediately disclose a similar, supporting detail. This instant, subtle mirroring of preferences creates a powerful, unconscious sense of connection. The target thinks, "This person is like me," which is the fastest route to trust and acceptance.

2. Securing Commitment and Consistency: Self-disclosure creates the psychological condition for **Commitment and Consistency**. For commitment to be lasting, the target must accept **inner responsibility** for the action, feeling they chose to perform it without strong external pressure.

- **Application:** By initiating a series of small, reciprocal disclosures, you are securing small commitments from the target ("I trust this person with a small detail about my life"). This establishes a pattern of positive, low-pressure commitment. The larger requests that follow feel like a logical, consistent extension of this established pattern of trust. The target believes the final, large choice originated from their own will, not from your external control.

V. The Virtual Challenge: Charm Without Presence

The architecture of charm changes when physical presence is removed. In virtual or text-based communication, non-verbal signals like haptics and eye contact are absent. The entire burden of building rapport and attraction shifts to the linguistic architecture of the message.

Linguistic Charisma is Paramount: In the virtual medium, attraction relies almost entirely on "words, charm, and seduction."

1. **Narrativity is Essential:** Since you cannot rely on composed posture (Book 2) to hold attention, your **Narrativity** must be extremely strong. Every communication must be crafted to provide entertainment value and familiarity.

2. **Concrete Vocabulary:** You must use the principles of concrete language (Book 3) to ensure the message delivers maximum emotional density. Abstract or vague language will be instantly ignored in a competitive digital environment.

3. **Frequency and Presence:** High-frequency, low-stakes digital communication maintains familiarity. It keeps you present in the target's mind without demanding deep cognitive effort, sustaining the bond.

When physical tools are gone, linguistic mastery must compensate. You must use the principles of framing and concrete language to build a compelling virtual persona that ensures the target's continued interest.

VI. Architectural Vulnerability

Accelerating intimacy through calculated self-disclosure is the first step in building irresistible charm. It is the sophisticated use of architectural vulnerability: you control the input and the pace. You maximize familiarity through **frequency**, strengthen the bond through **narrativity**, and ensure safety by constantly checking for **appropriateness**.

This process creates a bond that is psychologically deep. The target feels safe, understood, and entertained. This deep connection makes all subsequent attempts at influence feel less like external demands and more like shared, safe opportunities.

The next chapter, **Cement Loyalty: Creating Identity Through Shared Social Rituals**, details how to solidify this connection. We move from the individual exchange of information to the creation of permanent, structural loyalty by manufacturing group identity and shared experiences.

CHAPTER 2

CEMENT LOYALTY: CREATING IDENTITY THROUGH SHARED SOCIAL RITUALS

A connection between two people is weak. It can break easily under pressure. Intimacy, even deep intimacy, is fragile if it remains private. To make a bond last, to build true **loyalty**, you must move it into a strong social setting.

Loyalty is not a feeling you simply wish for. It is a structure you must build. It rests on shared experiences, confirmed values, and common rituals. When someone becomes truly loyal, they stop asking if they should support you. They just act consistent with the common identity they already share with your group.

This chapter details how to use **shared social rituals** and **group identity** to build a bond that is resilient. We move from the personal exchange of details to the creation of a powerful, unified perspective. This is how you make loyalty strong for the long term.

The Core Need for the "Us"

People have a deep, constant need to feel like they belong. They look for a collective, a group that shares a basic way of seeing the world. This **shared identity** is the essential foundation of loyalty. Once individuals feel like they belong to a group, their actions are driven by the group's goals. They stop thinking only about personal self-interest.

To secure this collective mindset, you must prove that the group is structurally unified. You must show that the target and the charismatic person are completely linked. This unification happens through shared memory and shared laughter. You must create a clear boundary that says, "We are together, and they are separate."

Loyalty becomes structural when you tie the individual's self-image to the group's identity. If a person sees themselves as "a dedicated member of this core team," challenging the team becomes challenging their own self-worth. That is a painful choice most people will avoid.

The charismatic person must constantly create this feeling of "us" versus everything else. They do this by turning small, shared moments into powerful, permanent rituals.

I. The Ritual of Belonging: Making Moments Stick

Small, accidental events often come to define a group's spirit. The shared laughter over a small accident or a strange phrase becomes a marker. The charismatic leader notices these markers. Then they turn them into **social rituals**.

Inside Jokes as Identity Markers: Inside jokes are not accidental fun. They grow naturally from unique group dynamics. They reflect common experiences. They bring a specific joy to the members that outsiders do not share. These small moments are essential social markers. They function as fast, reliable ways to re-establish trust and affection. This is especially true when tension appears in the group.

Creating the Permanent Ritual: You must not let a good shared moment simply fade away. You must use it again. You must elevate it.

- **The Ritual of Remembrance:** The charismatic individual constantly references the inside joke or a funny shared moment. They might mention it at the start of a serious meeting. They might mention it in a difficult conversation. This repeated use turns the moment into a **shared ritual**. This ritual quickly confirms mutual loyalty and affection. It signals to the target, "We share a memory that is unique. We are part of a specific, protected group."

- **Psychological Payoff:** When the group laughs at the inside joke, they get a dose of emotional warmth and affirmation. This good feeling is tied directly to the group's identity. The target learns that participation in the group ritual gives them a consistent, positive emotional reward. This consistent payoff links the group identity to feeling psychologically well. They become dependent on the group for this feeling.

The loyalty created through social rituals is structural. It is deliberately built to activate the powerful driver of **Commitment and Consistency**.

The consistency rule says people feel a constant need to align future actions with past commitments. This adherence is strongest when the commitment is **active, public, and effortful**. If the action is easy, private, or passive, the commitment breaks quickly.

Structuring the Effortful Ritual: You must design small, repeated rituals that satisfy these three demands.

1. **Active:** The ritual must require a physical action, not just agreement. This could be a unique, shared handshake used only by the core team. It could be a required verbal declaration of a positive intention before starting work.

2. **Public:** The ritual must be visible to others. A shared, positive saying repeated before a challenge is public. It creates external pressure to uphold the group's image.

3. **Effortful:** The ritual must require minor effort. This could be the small effort of memorizing a specific group history. It could be the small vulnerability of sharing one honest challenge from the previous week.

By performing these rituals, the target constantly reaffirms their commitment to the group's identity. They feel **inner responsibility** for the group's behaviors and values. They believe the commitment is their own choice. This makes the loyalty secure and self-sustaining. It is much stronger than loyalty based on external demands alone.

The Cost of Inconsistency: When rituals are established, the psychological cost of *breaking* them becomes very high. Breaking a public, active commitment causes internal conflict. The target feels pressure because their action (breaking the ritual) contradicts their self-image (a loyal member). To relieve this internal pain, they are overwhelmingly motivated to maintain the ritual.

III. The Unifying Force of Humor: Vetting Values

The most efficient tool for creating this unified perspective is **humor**. Humor is a highly sophisticated social resource. We must focus on the most unifying function: **identification humor**.

The Shared Value Check: Identification humor builds group cohesion. It appeals to a set of shared expectations and norms that everyone recognizes. When a group laughs at the same joke, it often means the joke points out an unusual violation of a norm or expectation.

- **Actionable Vetting:** The shared laughter confirms alignment. If the target laughs at the same social violation, they confirm they share your core values and baseline expectations. This mutual reinforcement strengthens the relationship and instantly reduces uncertainty about the other person. This shared perspective creates a unified worldview that is essential for trust.

- **Targeting the Norm:** The best identification humor targets a minor violation of an *external* norm or expectation. This means something outside the group that everyone can agree upon. You must avoid humor that targets a group member. You must avoid humor meant to divide or criticize. By agreeing on what is externally ridiculous or annoying, you solidify the bond inside the group.

Therapeutic Value and Conflict Resolution: Shared laughter has documented emotional value. Research confirms that shared laughter increases attraction between people. It enhances group cohesion. It helps resolve conflicts. When people laugh together, they form stronger bonds. They develop a **shared identity** that is more resilient than their individual differences. This shared emotional release acts as a safety valve, making the group feel psychologically safer.

IV. The Founding Myth: Shared Narrative

Loyalty needs a history. It is cemented by shared memory. The charismatic leader ensures the group possesses a powerful, common story of its past. This story must focus on overcoming shared, external difficulty.

Narrativity and Emotional Density: The **narrativity** of self-disclosure (Chapter 2) is used for group cohesion. By framing the group's history as an engaging, short story, you maximize the **perceived entertainment value** of the collective experience.

- **Framing the Struggle:** The leader must constantly frame past difficulties as "the time *we* all overcame that impossible deadline" or "the moment *we* realized the old system was holding *us* back." This framing turns shared difficulty into a **founding myth**. The narrative must be concrete. It must use specific dates, names, or quantifiable metrics. It must unify the group under a banner of shared achievement.

This process ensures that when the group faces a new challenge, they refer back to the shared memory (the narrative) as proof of their inherent strength and loyalty. The loyalty is cemented by the memory of shared success against an external problem.

The Anchor of Stability: The charismatic persona is seen as a source of psychological safety. This constant attraction solidifies loyalty because people naturally gravitate toward sources of stability and positive emotion.

The Positive Humor Style: Positive humor styles are directly associated with desirable personality traits like high self-esteem and extroversion. By constantly using positive, unifying humor, the charismatic person projects **psychological stability** and **social desirability**. This stability is the emotional anchor for the group. They are seen as a **safe and valuable social resource**. The natural desire to stay near this source of stability is a powerful driver of loyalty.

Loyalty as Structure

Cementing loyalty is the construction of an identity. It moves beyond individual rapport to the creation of a powerful psychological structure.

1. **Shared Rituals** provide the active, public, and effortful commitment markers that secure long-term consistency.

2. **Identification Humor** provides the social vetting that confirms shared values, reducing uncertainty and increasing cohesion.

3. **Shared Narrative** elevates group history into a founding myth, reinforcing collective strength.

This system ensures that the individual target's loyalty is not just an emotion they feel. It is a structural part of the group's running identity. They are loyal because the group's success and their participation in its rituals are now deeply tied to their self-image.

The next chapter, **Gauge Limits: Calibrating Disclosure for Optimal Attraction**, addresses the continuous maintenance of this bond. We detail the crucial skill of monitoring the relationship boundary. We ensure that intimacy is escalated just enough to maintain high attraction without violating the boundary of appropriateness. Violating that boundary could instantly destroy the loyalty built.

CHAPTER 3

GAUGE LIMITS: CALIBRATING DISCLOSURE FOR OPTIMAL ATTRACTION

We have covered the initial burst of intimacy. We know that high **disclosure frequency** builds familiarity fast. But familiarity is not the same as lasting attraction. True, irresistible charm requires constant work. You must monitor the most delicate boundary in any relationship: the line of **appropriateness**.

The biggest mistake a person can make is pushing too hard, too fast. They confuse openness with intimacy. They share deep secrets hoping to earn trust quickly. But studies show that this is dangerous. Intimate disclosure, if given at the wrong time, often **reduces social attraction** instead of building it. It sets off an internal alarm. It signals a lack of control.

This chapter teaches you how to maintain maximum attraction by mastering the art of the **Calibration Test**. You must learn to read the target's subtle signals. You must know exactly when to advance the intimacy and, more importantly, when to immediately pull back. This constant monitoring ensures the bond remains strong and safe.

Intimacy is an acceptable state only when the target feels the context is right. Appropriateness is the psychological framework that allows intimacy to proceed. Without it, the deepest secrets feel uncomfortable, like a social violation.

The High Risk of Premature Depth: If you share a deeply personal failure or intense emotional difficulty too early, the target is put in a difficult position. They feel pressure to reciprocate. They feel responsible for this sudden, unearned vulnerability. This creates anxiety. They respond by retreating. They view the sharing as a sign of poor boundaries or emotional instability on your part.

This is a risk management issue. The potential reward of gaining quick closeness is real, but the risk of destroying attraction by violating the boundary is far greater. Therefore, you must prioritize low-stakes sharing, high volume, and constant monitoring. You must secure familiarity first. Intimacy must be earned later, through controlled testing.

The Role of Context: The level of appropriate disclosure depends entirely on the setting. In a virtual setting, where attraction relies entirely on **words and charm** , disclosures must be crafted with maximum precision and minimum emotional demand. In a professional setting, the appropriate boundary for disclosure is much tighter than in a personal setting. The charismatic person always adheres to the highest level of formality required by the environment, adjusting only slowly.

II. The Calibration Test: Monitoring Reciprocal Behavior

You cannot guess where the boundary lies. You must test for it gently, then confirm the safety of the boundary through the target's reaction. The best gauge for appropriateness is **reciprocal disclosure**.

A target who matches your level of disclosure, in both frequency and depth, implicitly confirms that your current level of intimacy is acceptable. Their return of personal information signals that the boundary is safe for both of you.

Step 1: The Gentle Deepening

Once you have established familiarity through high frequency (Chapter 2), you test the boundary gently. You offer a disclosure that is *slightly* deeper than the one you offered previously. This must be an intentional, small step up the ladder of vulnerability.

- *Example:* You previously talked about minor preferences (favorite foods). The gentle deepening moves to minor challenges (a frustration with a professional process, or a small life lesson you learned last month). It is honest, but it is controlled. It does not carry immense emotional weight.

Step 2: Observe Verbal and Non-Verbal Response

You must watch the target's reaction carefully for specific cues. They signal their comfort level instantly.

- **Verbal Retreat:** Does the target offer a very short, closed answer? Do they change the subject abruptly, perhaps redirecting the focus entirely back to you? Do they offer an answer that is much less personal than your disclosure?

- **Non-Verbal Retreat:** Do they break eye contact and look away for a prolonged period? Do they physically shift their posture away from you (a movement away from openness)? Do they suddenly become less animated or energetic?

These are all signs that your disclosure was too much. The target is signaling, "Stop. You have exceeded the boundary."

Step 3: The Decision Point

You have two choices at this crucial moment:

- **If they Match or Exceed:** If the target offers an equal or slightly deeper disclosure, or if they ask a warm, engaging follow-up question, they have implicitly confirmed the boundary is safe. You may proceed to the next level of intimacy at the next opportune moment.

- **If they Retreat:** If you observe any verbal or non-verbal retreat, the intimacy level was inappropriate. **You must immediately retreat.** You pull back the depth of future disclosures to a safer, more frequent level. You must respect the boundary you discovered. Retreating signals that you are socially intelligent and that you respect their comfort. This respect helps preserve the existing level of trust, even if the boundary test failed.

This continuous calibration ensures you build closeness rapidly without violating trust. Pushing too hard or too fast reveals a serious lack of social intelligence, which instantly breaks the charm and reduces social attraction.

Why is inappropriate intimacy so damaging? Because it breaks the illusion of competence you built in Book 2. It triggers a strong negative psychological response in the target.

1. The Halo Effect Failure: Your charisma is built on the **Halo Effect**, the idea that people assume you are competent and stable because you are composed and controlled. When you suddenly share inappropriate, raw, or unstable information, you break your own persona. The target thinks, "If they are this unstable, they cannot possibly be competent." The entire perception of authority collapses instantly.

2. Increased Anxiety: Inappropriate self-disclosure creates anxiety in the target. This anxiety is uncomfortable. To relieve this stress, the target's mind automatically seeks distance from the source of the anxiety: you. They retreat from the interaction, or they become emotionally closed off. This defense mechanism is not rational; it is automatic.

3. Social Bias and Retreat: Non-verbal behavior is highly influential. If your behavior is suddenly inconsistent or inappropriate, it creates a **social bias** against you. The target may feel pressure to mirror the uncomfortable vulnerability you just showed, or they may feel pressure to conform to this new, negative, shared attitude about you. They retreat to avoid this psychological pressure.

The ultimate goal is to keep the target feeling secure in your presence. Boundary violation shatters this security immediately.

IV. Sustaining Optimal Attraction with Narrativity

Once the optimal level of disclosure is found, the place where the target is comfortable but still curious, you must sustain it. This is done by maximizing the **perceived entertainment value** of your disclosures.

The Power of Storytelling: Disclosure narrativity, framing personal information as a short, engaging story, increases perceived closeness and social attraction. The narrative format is inherently valuable to the target. They are investing their attention and getting a worthwhile return.

Framing the Routine: You must continuously frame small, routine details as engaging narratives. You are avoiding dry facts and focusing on short, structured stories.

- *Example:* Frame a business challenge not as a vague problem, but as "The 72-hour period last month when we almost lost the deal due to the shipping error, and how the team managed to fix it by 3 PM Friday."

This approach requires using the principles of **Concrete Vocabulary** (Book 3). Specific names, dates, and measurable facts make the narrative feel real and emotionally dense. This continuous delivery of engaging content sustains the target's interest, ensuring they remain attracted to you as a source of positive, valuable interaction.

V. The Continuous Calibration

Gauging limits is the core of sustainable charm. It is a continuous, moment-to-moment process of testing, observing, and adjusting. You are creating intimacy by design, controlling the pace to maintain high attraction without violating the boundary of appropriateness.

1. **Prioritize Frequency:** Start with high-frequency, low-stakes disclosures to build rapid familiarity.
2. **Test Gently:** Use small, incremental deepening of the conversation to find the boundary of the target's comfort.
3. **Read Reciprocity:** Use the target's verbal and non-verbal response as the final gauge for appropriateness. Retreat immediately if you detect signs of anxiety or withdrawal.

This disciplined approach ensures that the deep loyalty you cemented in Chapter 3 remains protected. You maintain the psychological security the target needs. This leaves the target feeling safe, entertained, and consistently drawn to your presence.

The next chapter, **Sustain Interest: Crafting Narrative for Entertainment Value**, will focus exclusively on the mechanics of storytelling. We will detail how to use the structure of a narrative to amplify psychological effects, ensuring every interaction, from a brief email to a long conversation, holds the target's sustained interest.

CHAPTER 4

SUSTAIN INTEREST: CRAFTING NARRATIVE FOR ENTERTAINMENT VALUE

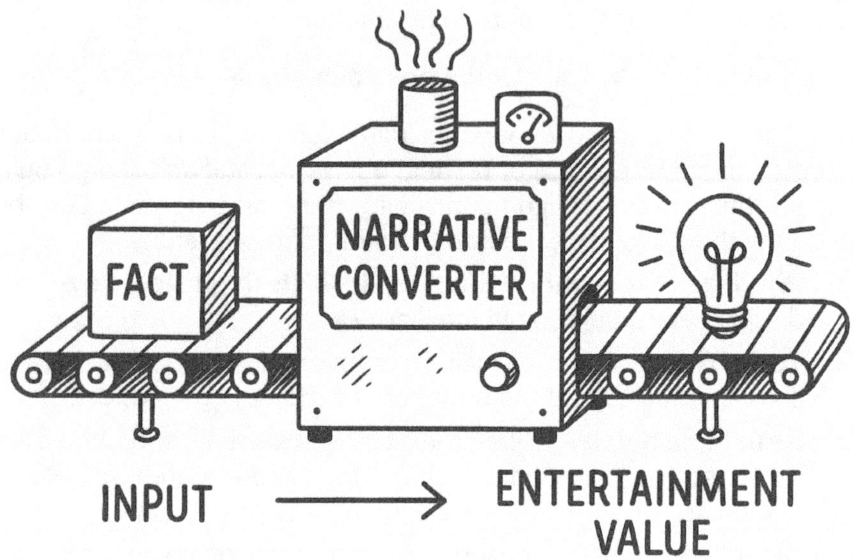

We secured the target's interest. We know they feel familiar because you shared details often. They feel safe because you carefully checked the boundaries of intimacy. Now the hard work begins: keeping them engaged over time. A strong bond will still break if the relationship becomes boring.

To achieve **irresistible charm**, you must ensure the connection provides a consistent, valuable psychological reward. This consistent reward is **perceived entertainment value**.

This chapter details the precise steps for storytelling. We stop just sharing facts. We start crafting a structured narrative. You must learn to transform the small details of your life into short, engaging stories. This steady storytelling is the engine that keeps the target's interest high. It ensures they remain attracted to you as a valuable source of positive interaction.

I. The Power of Story: Entertainment as Closeness

Why does telling a story work better than listing facts? The human brain is built for narrative. Facts demand logical effort and slow thought. Stories instantly engage emotion, memory, and imagination.

The Key Finding: Research confirms that **disclosure narrativity** significantly increases both perceived closeness and social attraction. This positive effect happens because the narrative format possesses clear **perceived entertainment value**.

The target invests their attention and time in listening to you. They receive a worthwhile return on that investment. The interaction moves from a basic exchange into a valuable, engaging social resource. They like the feeling they get when they listen to you talk.

This is especially vital in text-based or virtual communication. Physical presence and body language are missing in those settings. Attraction and interest rely almost entirely on **"words, charm, and seduction"**. Your linguistic skill must work extra hard to compensate for the lack of visual cues. If your digital communication is boring, the connection stops immediately.

II. The Architecture of the Engaging Narrative

A story is not just a sequence of events. It is a tool with a specific psychological structure. To maximize entertainment value, you must frame every small event. Use a clear, recognizable narrative structure.

The Short-Form Narrative Structure: You must compress events into short, efficient stories. They must maximize emotional payoff. Every successful short narrative should contain three basic acts:

1. **The Setup (The State of Normalcy):** Establish the scene quickly. Use concrete details to anchor the story in reality. This gives the target a clear baseline. *Example: "Last Tuesday, the 2:00 PM meeting was just a 15-minute file review with the client."*

2. **The Conflict (The Break in Pattern):** Introduce the unexpected problem or deviation from the norm. This step creates tension and curiosity. *Example: "But at 2:05 PM, the entire system crashed. It froze every single file on the shared network. We had zero access."*

3. **The Resolution (The Lesson or Outcome):** Provide a quick, satisfying end. Offer a lesson, a feeling of relief, or a moment of humor. *Example: "I spent 40 frantic minutes trying to troubleshoot. The real lesson I took away was simple: physical backups must now happen every Monday morning, without fail."*

This structure guarantees that the target's attention is captured by the conflict. Then they receive the satisfying emotional release of the resolution. This consistent delivery of structured, entertaining content keeps their interest high. It prevents the bond from becoming predictable and dull.

III. Maximizing Impact with Concrete Vocabulary

The narratives you tell must use the principles of **Concrete Vocabulary** (Book 3). Abstract, vague language instantly destroys entertainment value. Specificity makes the difference between a story that sticks and one that is forgotten.

Specific Details Engage the Senses: Concrete language uses specific names, dates, numbers, and direct verbs. It engages the target's imagination instantly. They can visualize the scene. They can feel the tension.

- *Weak Example:* "I had a bad experience with the software last year that cost us time." (Abstract, unspecific).

- *Strong Example:* "Last **September 12th**, the **budget submission** failed at 4:58 PM. It cost us **three full workdays** to recover. I learned to never trust a cloud server after 4:00 PM." (Specific, measurable, creates a clear image and gives a specific date).

This specific, measurable detail maximizes **emotional density**. The target understands exactly what three days of lost time means. This makes the narrative feel real. It strengthens the psychological bond. It increases the perceived entertainment value.

IV. Narrativity and Psychological Vetting

Storytelling is not just about fun. It is a sophisticated way to conduct subtle **psychological vetting** (Chapter 3).

The Vetting Process in Narrative: When you tell a story, you reveal your values by how you narrate the conflict and the resolution.

- If your stories consistently emphasize integrity and hard work, the target learns that you value those traits.

- If your stories consistently emphasize avoiding responsibility, the target learns to distance themselves.

The target constantly watches your narratives. They want to determine if your inner values match their own. If the values align, the psychological vetting succeeds. Then the bond deepens. This subtly reinforces the **Confirmation Bias**. The target looks for information that proves they were right to trust you.

The Shared Struggle Narrative: Narratives that focus on a shared struggle against an external problem are very potent. These stories activate the **Reciprocity** principle. By framing your vulnerability, the struggle, within a successful narrative, the resolution, you offer an emotional concession. The target feels they must reciprocate by offering their trust or continued attention.

This narrative of shared difficulty also builds group cohesion (Chapter 3). Frame the group's past difficulties as a **"founding myth."** For example: "That time we fixed the code in 48 hours to save the company." This maximizes the collective entertainment value of the group's history. It reinforces loyalty.

V. Sustaining Interest by Combating Time Delay

A crucial function of effective storytelling is combating the target's natural tendency toward **Temporal Discounting**. This is the cognitive process where people value rewards less the further out they are in the future.

Your proposal often requires action *now* for a reward that is *delayed*. Narrativity helps close this psychological gap.

The Strategy of Imminent Visualization: You must use sensory language. Make the future outcome feel present and imminent.

- *Instead of:* "If you commit to this plan, you will receive the benefit next year." (Delayed, low value).
- *Use:* "When you execute this plan, you will **see** the budget surplus number on the screen *by June 1st*. You will **feel relief** immediately when the deadline passes." (Sensory, imminent).

By making the future reward tangible, something they can see or feel, you minimize the perceived time delay. This makes the present commitment easier to accept. The narrative keeps the **reward** visually and emotionally present.

VI. The Engine of Enduring Charm

Sustaining interest through narrative is the engine of enduring charm. It moves the relationship from a functional necessity to a source of consistent psychological reward.

1. **Structure the Story:** Use the three-act model (Setup, Conflict, Resolution). This maximizes tension and release.

2. **Use Concrete Vocabulary:** Inject specific numbers, dates, and names. This maximizes emotional density. It combats cognitive friction.

3. **Frame the Values:** Ensure your stories subtly check your core values. Align them perfectly with the target's need for consistency.

4. **Close the Time Gap:** Use sensory language. Make future rewards feel imminent and emotionally present.

This disciplined approach ensures that the target remains psychologically invested in you. You are a source of positive, engaging interaction. You are not only trustworthy, but you are also rewarding to listen to. This continuous psychological return is the definition of irresistible charm.

The next chapter, **Project Desirability: Vetting Values Through Shared Laughter**, focuses on the most advanced social tool. We detail how to use humor not just for entertainment. We show how it acts as a precise instrument to confirm shared moral and social alignment. This further solidifies the bond.

CHAPTER 5
PROJECT DESIRABILITY: VETTING VALUES THROUGH SHARED LAUGHTER

We have secured the target's physical presence and controlled the flow of personal details. But a relationship built on shared facts and careful boundaries will not last if the core values clash. The ultimate test of long-term compatibility is often invisible. It is revealed through laughter.

This chapter details the most advanced social tool in the charismatic arsenal: **humor**. Humor is not just for entertainment. It is a precise instrument. You use it to confirm shared moral and social alignment. This vetting process solidifies the bond. It ensures the target sees you as a desirable, stable, and valuable psychological resource.

The quality of your humor dictates your desirability. Laughter proves that you and the target share the same baseline understanding of the world. This mutual confirmation reduces deep uncertainty. It builds intense social cohesion.

I. The Social Functions of Laughter

Humor is a sophisticated function of human society. It serves several powerful social roles. These roles fall on a spectrum. Some functions unify the group. Other functions divide and isolate. A charismatic leader uses only the unifying elements.

The two unifying functions are **identification** and **clarification**.

1. Identification Humor: The Shared Value Check

Identification humor builds group cohesion. It works because participants share a common value or perception that the humor brings out. When a group laughs at the same joke, it is often because the joke points out a small violation of a social rule or expected pattern.

- **The Vetting Mechanism:** The shared laughter confirms alignment. If the target laughs at the same social violation, they confirm they share your core values. This immediate, mutual reinforcement strengthens the relationship. It instantly reduces the natural uncertainty people feel when forming a new connection. This shared perspective evokes a solid, unified worldview that is essential for deep trust.

- **How to Apply It:** You must use humor that references an *external* problem or expectation. For example, reference a silly administrative rule everyone hates. Or mention a common frustration with a technology platform. By making a light, shared joke about the external issue, you confirm that everyone agrees on the norm. You solidify the internal group bond. This is subtle, but highly effective.

2. Clarification Humor: Reducing Uncertainty

Humor also serves to clarify expectations. This function reduces uncertainty about others. It appeals to common values. When a joke clarifies expectations and reinforces mutual understanding, it quickly establishes what is acceptable within the group.

If a social setting is tense or ambiguous, deploying unifying humor can quickly clarify what is expected. It reinforces mutual understanding. When anxiety is high, humor provides a quick moment of levity and shared identity. This allows the group to relax and reset its emotional tone.

The Spectrum to Avoid: While humor can unify, it can also divide. You must strictly avoid humor that differentiates or enforces norms through criticism. Humor that attacks an external group, or that singles out a member of your own group, instantly destroys cohesion. It breaks the feeling of safety you worked hard to build.

A perceived good sense of humor is an invaluable social resource. People naturally seek out those who project a positive and engaging feeling. The humor you use is directly tied to your psychological stability.

The Link to Positive Traits: Positive humor styles are strongly linked to highly desirable personality traits. These traits include high self-esteem, extroversion, and cheerfulness. People who use positive humor styles also report greater satisfaction in their relationships.

- **Projecting Stability:** By consistently using positive, unifying humor, the charismatic person projects deep **psychological stability** and **social desirability**. They signal that they are emotionally secure. This makes them highly attractive. It facilitates stronger connections.

- **The Anchor:** This stability is the emotional anchor for the group. When external pressure mounts, the group looks to the leader who uses positive humor. This signals competence and emotional security. They are seen as a **safe and valuable social resource**. The natural desire to stay near this source of emotional stability is a powerful driver of loyalty.

You must view humor as a tool for projecting your best self. Avoid negative, hostile, or self-deprecating humor styles. These signals often suggest internal conflict or low self-esteem. True loyalty requires the leader to project an unwavering, positive emotional outlook.

III. Cementing Loyalty: Shared Rituals and Group Identity

Humor moves beyond temporary laughter to create lasting loyalty. This is achieved by creating shared rituals and "inside jokes."

Inside Jokes as Identity Markers: Inside jokes naturally emerge from unique group dynamics. They reflect common experiences and bring a specific joy to the members. A charismatic leader can actively encourage these shared humorous rituals. They serve as reliable, quick ways to re-establish trust and affection, especially when tension is present.

The Effortful Ritual: This social alignment is structurally sound because it activates the powerful driver of **Commitment and Consistency**. Loyalty based on social rituals is strong because the target accepts inner responsibility for the commitment.

The ritual must be **active, public, and effortful**. The shared laughter and the continued use of inside jokes are active, public commitments to the group's identity. This small, continuous effort strengthens the bond. The target feels they chose this belonging themselves, making the loyalty self-sustaining.

Conflict Resolution: The therapeutic value of shared laughter is supported by research showing that it helps resolve conflicts. When people laugh together, they form stronger connections. They develop a **shared identity** that is more resilient than their individual differences. This shared emotional release acts as a safety valve. It allows the group to quickly repair itself after minor disputes.

IV. The Charismatic Delivery: Stillness and Humor

Humor requires perfect delivery. It relies entirely on the non-verbal foundation established in Book 2. If the delivery is flawed, the humor fails to unify.

Composure and Delivery: Humor needs perfect **composure** for delivery. If you deliver a joke with nervous energy, the anxiety compromises the humor. The audience laughs at the anxiety, not with the content. Controlled stillness and a measured vocal pace (Chapter 2) ensure the humor is perceived as intentional and stable.

Emotional Contagion: Humor is a highly effective tool for initiating positive **Emotional Contagion**. If you project genuine amusement, the people in the group who are easily influenced by social cues will immediately absorb and reflect that emotion. This spreads the positive feeling throughout the room.

The Halo Effect: The positive feeling generated by unifying humor reinforces the **Halo Effect**. The target now connects the positive emotional state (joy, connection) directly with your composed presence. This further cements the inference of trustworthiness and reliability.

V. Vetting Values Through Narrative and Laughter

Storytelling (Chapter 5) and humor must work together. The stories you tell reveal your values. The humor confirms that those values match the group's.

The Narrative Vetting: When you frame a story, you reveal what you value by how you handle the conflict. If you narrate a story that focuses on integrity during a financial struggle, you vet your honesty. If the target laughs at the moral outcome, they confirm that they also prioritize honesty.

The Founding Myth: Use this shared laughter to reinforce the "**founding myth**" of the group (Chapter 3). Frame the group's past struggles as a shared triumph against an external problem. This creates a strong collective narrative that reinforces loyalty.

The Anchor of Stability: This system ensures the target remains psychologically invested in you. You are a consistent source of stability, attraction, and positive emotional reward. This continuous psychological return is the definition of irresistible charm.

VI. The Desirable Persona

Projecting desirability is the art of using social tools to secure long-term loyalty. You move a collection of individuals from separate self-interest into a unified, emotionally connected group.

1. **Identification Humor** confirms shared values and reduces uncertainty.

2. **Shared Rituals** provide the active, public commitment markers that secure long-term consistency.

3. **Positive Humor Styles** project psychological stability, making you an attractive emotional resource.

This system ensures that the target's bond with you is not just based on a temporary feeling. It is a strong, structural part of their ongoing identity. They are loyal because your presence makes them feel safe, unified, and psychologically stable.

The final chapter will summarize all the techniques from Irresistible Charm. We will integrate the skills of disclosure, calibration, humor, and loyalty to finalize the architecture of the magnetic social persona.

CONCLUSION
THE ARCHITECTURE OF ENDURING CHARM

We have finished the study of Irresistible Charm. This book taught you how to build deep, lasting connections that secure loyalty. We moved the focus from temporary rapport to the creation of a resilient, shared identity. Charm is not just a polite social skill. It is a system for managing vulnerability, setting boundaries, and using social rituals to cement long-term commitment.

This final chapter synthesizes the core lessons of **Disclosure, Calibration, Loyalty, and Narrativity**. We show how these elements fuse together. This unified system ensures the target remains psychologically invested in you. The goal is simple: to create a desirable social persona that provides consistent psychological returns.

I. The Foundation: Intimacy by Design

The entire system of charm rests on the controlled management of personal information. This process accelerates closeness without the risk of emotional instability.

Synthesis of Disclosure and Frequency (Chapter 2):

1. **Prioritize Frequency:** The most powerful factor predicting closeness is **disclosure frequency**. You must maximize the number of low-stakes, safe interactions. This builds a dense foundation of familiarity quickly.

2. **Narrativity as Value:** Simply sharing facts is boring. You must use **disclosure narrativity** to frame small details as short, engaging stories. This storytelling provides **perceived entertainment value**. This ensures the target invests their attention and time in the interaction.

The Crucial Calibration (Chapter 4):

Intimacy is only safe when the target feels the boundary is right. You must constantly monitor the relationship.

1. **Test Gently:** You find the boundary by testing it. Offer a disclosure that is *slightly* deeper than the one before it.

2. **Read Reciprocity:** You use the target's reaction as the final gauge. A target who matches your level of disclosure implicitly confirms the boundary is safe.

3. **Retreat Immediately:** If you observe any verbal or non-verbal retreat (signs of anxiety or discomfort), you must immediately pull back the depth of future disclosures. Violating the boundary of appropriateness destroys social attraction and breaks the trust you built.

This disciplined approach ensures you build closeness rapidly while maintaining the psychological security the target needs.

II. The Structural Cement: Loyalty and Shared Identity

Intimacy is secured permanently by cementing the personal bond into a shared group identity. This loyalty is structural, not emotional.

Synthesis of Rituals and Commitment (Chapter 3):

1. **Build Shared Rituals:** Loyalty is built on shared experiences. The charismatic person must turn accidental, shared moments (e.g., inside jokes) into repeatable **social rituals**.

2. **Activate Effortful Commitment:** These rituals must be **active, public, and effortful**. This commitment is self-sustaining. By performing these rituals, the target continuously reaffirms their commitment to the group's identity. This makes the loyalty strong and permanent.

3. **Vetting Values with Humor:** Humor is used as a psychological vetting mechanism. **Identification humor** builds group cohesion. It works because the shared laughter confirms that everyone agrees on the same core values and norms. This immediate confirmation instantly reduces uncertainty and strengthens the bond.

This system ensures that the individual's loyalty is now tied to a strong, shared identity. The psychological cost of breaking that loyalty becomes very high.

III. The Anchor of Desirability

The magnetic persona must be seen as a source of psychological stability and positive emotion. This constant attraction solidifies loyalty.

Synthesis of Desirability (Chapter 6):

1. **Project Stability:** You must consistently use **positive humor styles**. These styles are strongly associated with desirable personality traits like high self-esteem and extroversion. This projects **psychological stability**. People naturally seek out this source of emotional security.

2. **Narrate the Myth:** You sustain interest by continuously framing the group's past struggles as a **"founding myth."** This narrative elevates shared difficulty into collective triumph. This reinforces group strength and loyalty.

This ensures the target remains psychologically invested in you. You are a consistent source of stability, attraction, and positive emotional reward.

IV. The System Integration

Irresistible Charm is the synthesis of all four books. It acts as the final relational layer for the entire influence system.

- **Charm Protects Authority:** The composure you project (Book 2) is protected by the careful boundaries you maintain (Chapter 4). If you break the boundary, you destroy the persona.

- **Charm Delivers Language:** The precise, concrete language (Book 3) is delivered through engaging narratives (Chapter 5), maximizing its appeal and emotional density.

- **Charm Secures Commitment:** The emotional connection secured through self-disclosure is leveraged to secure the structural **Commitment and Consistency** (Book 1) of the group.

The result is a relationship that is resilient and strong. The target feels safe, unified, and continuously drawn to your presence. The influence is no longer a tactic. It is a natural consequence of the deep, positive bond you have established.

We have now mastered the art of building lasting connection. The final book, **Instant Influence**, shifts the focus entirely to generating immediate, urgent action. We will explore the mechanics of time, scarcity, and loss aversion. These are the powerful psychological forces that compel rapid compliance. We move from building long-term loyalty to securing the decisive, necessary action *now*.

REFLECTION QUESTIONS

We have completed the study of Irresistible Charm. This book taught you how to build deep, strong connections that secure loyalty. You learned to manage vulnerability, set boundaries, and use social rituals to cement long-term commitment.

The skills of charm, disclosure, calibration, humor, and loyalty, must move from theory to consistent practice. Use these questions to personalize the material. Map the concepts onto your own interactions. Prepare for the final phase of influence: urgent action.

Section 1: Disclosure and Intimacy Calibration

Charm relies on accelerating closeness without violating the target's sense of appropriateness. This requires controlled self-disclosure.

1. **Frequency over Depth:** Think about a new professional contact you made last month. How often did you communicate? Was the communication focused on deep issues or **low-stakes details** (e.g., commute, hobbies, minor preferences)? How can you increase the **disclosure frequency** of small, safe details by 50% in your next week to quickly build familiarity?

2. **The Danger of Premature Intimacy:** Recall a time when someone shared too much information with you too soon. How did that make you feel? Did it **reduce social attraction**? What specific detail did they share that crossed the line of appropriateness for that early stage of the relationship?

3. **The Calibration Test:** You must use the target's reaction to find the boundary. If you were to offer a small, slightly deeper disclosure in your next meeting, what specific **verbal or non-verbal signal** would tell you that the target was retreating? What is your immediate, planned **retreat response** to protect the existing level of trust?

4. **Narrativity and Value:** Think of a routine, necessary task you completed yesterday (e.g., filing a tax document, fixing a slow computer). Rewrite the description of that task using the three-act narrative structure (Setup, Conflict, Resolution). How does framing the mundane detail as a short story increase its **perceived entertainment value**?

Section 2: Loyalty, Rituals, and Desirability

Loyalty is secured by cementing the personal bond into a resilient, shared group identity.

5. **Identification Humor: Humor** is a psychological vetting mechanism. Identify one external social norm or expectation that your work group commonly dislikes (e.g., a shared administrative burden or a specific technology glitch). Plan one piece of **identification humor** that targets this external issue. How would shared laughter over this external problem confirm alignment on your core values?

6. **The Effortful Ritual: Commitment** is strongest when it is active, public, and effortful. Think of a goal your immediate team needs to achieve next month. Design one small, **effortful ritual** that the core team can perform weekly (e.g., a specific 5-minute shared task, a specific public verbal confirmation). How does this small effort solidify their long-term commitment to the group's success?

7. **Anchor of Stability: Positive humor styles** project psychological stability, making you an attractive social resource. If pressure mounts next week, how will you consciously use positive, unifying humor to act as an **emotional anchor** for your team?

8. **The Founding Myth:** Think about a time your group overcame a significant difficulty or setback (e.g., losing a client, missing a deadline). How can you frame that negative event as a **"founding myth"**, a shared narrative of collective triumph against an external problem? Use concrete details (dates, names, metrics) to make the story emotionally dense.

BOOK FIVE

INSTANT INFLUENCE: URGENCY AND ACTION

INTRODUCTION
TO INSTANT INFLUENCE

We have finished the complex work. We have built the long game of influence. We learned how to frame a decision for consistency (Book 1). We mastered the charismatic presence needed for trust (Book 2). We secured the deal with precise language and zero resistance (Book 3 and Book 4).

But sometimes, consistency and loyalty are not enough. Sometimes, you need action **right now**.

This final book deals with the most decisive phase of influence: **Instant Influence**. This is the art of collapsing the decision window. It is about using the psychological forces that compel immediate, urgent compliance. This system relies entirely on manipulating the target's perception of time and value.

This is the shift from long-term relationship building to short-term motivational science. You stop asking, "Why will they agree next week?" You start asking, "What psychological trigger forces them to agree in the next 60 seconds?"

The Science of Impatience: Temporal Discounting

The foundation of instant influence is the human brain's flawed relationship with time. This concept is called **Temporal Discounting**. It is the cognitive process where people prefer more immediate rewards over future benefits, even if the future benefits are worth more.

This human nature tends to be impatient. Behavioral economics shows that people often make irrational choices when time is involved. Imagine you have a choice: take $100 today, or take $110 in a month. Many people will grab the immediate $100. The extra $10 seems less valuable simply because it is delayed. The value we place on future rewards drops sharply the further away they are.

This phenomenon is also known as time discounting or hyperbolic discounting. It explains why people struggle with long-term financial planning. It explains why people engage in unhealthy behaviors that offer immediate rewards, like smoking.

The persuader's job is to exploit this tendency. You must make the target act in the present by structuring the choice so that the **present action** is associated with an **immediate reward** or the avoidance of an **immediate loss**. This technique overrides the target's ability to rationally evaluate the long-term payoff.

The Dominance of Fear: Loss Aversion

While you can motivate people with positive rewards, fear is a much stronger driver. Specifically, the fear of losing something is measurably more powerful than the desire to gain an equivalent item. This is the core principle of **Loss Aversion**.

Nobel laureates Daniel Kahneman and Amos Tversky showed this: the psychological pain of losing something is generally more powerful than the pleasure of gaining an equivalent item.

The strategy for instant influence is simple: **Frame non-compliance as a guaranteed, immediate loss.**

- Do not focus on the potential money they will make next year (Gain Frame).
- Focus on the immediate money they will lose if they wait until tomorrow (Loss Frame).

This technique triggers the **Fear Of Missing Out (FOMO)**. To avoid the regret associated with missing out, people are compelled to make quick, impulsive decisions. They often overlook a thorough evaluation of the proposal's true long-term value.

Loss Aversion is amplified by **Scarcity**. We value things more when they are rare or limited.

Our brains are built to assign greater value to things that are scarce, even if their actual worth does not change. A famous experiment in 1975 showed this clearly: participants rated identical cookies from an almost empty jar as more desirable than the same cookies from a full jar. The desire was determined entirely by the perceived limited availability.

Psychological Reactance: Scarcity triggers an immediate defensive reaction. When our freedom to choose or acquire something is threatened by limited availability (e.g., "Only three left" or "Offer ends at midnight"), we experience **Psychological Reactance**. This is an innate desire to reassert that threatened freedom. We often do this by wanting the restricted item even more intensely.

The powerful combination for instant influence is: **Temporal Discounting + Loss Aversion + Scarcity.**

You create a situation where the future reward is devalued (Temporal Discounting). You ensure inaction means an immediate, guaranteed loss (Loss Aversion). You restrict the time window to challenge the target's freedom (Scarcity/Reactance). This manufactured urgency collapses the decision window entirely.

The Integration of Charisma and Urgency

The emotional stability and trust you built in Books 1 through 4 are not discarded here. They are used as anchors for the urgency.

- **Authority and Urgency:** If a target trusts your **Authority** (Book 1/2), they trust your deadlines. Your urgent demand, "You must sign this by 3 PM", is accepted as legitimate fact, not as a cheap sales tactic.

- **Commitment and Action:** The small commitments you secured (Book 1) pave the way for this urgent, large commitment. The target's mind sees the urgent action as consistent with their established pattern of following your guidance.

This book provides the final, mechanical steps for compelling this immediate action. We turn these powerful psychological concepts into actionable steps for controlling time and value.

The next chapters will break down these elements:

- **Compel Action Now:** We detail how to use **Temporal Discounting** to secure present commitment for a delayed payoff.
- **Force Urgency:** We show how to activate **Loss Aversion and Scarcity** by framing inaction as a guaranteed loss.
- **Demand Presence:** We explore techniques for minimizing the **perceived delay** of the future reward, making it feel imminent.
- **Control Deadline:** We show how to manufacture the psychological need to buy, ensuring the target feels the pressure to comply immediately.

Mastery of instant influence ensures that when the moment for decisive action arrives, hesitation is eliminated, and the choice is made immediately in your favor.

CHAPTER 1

COMPEL ACTION NOW:
EXPLOITING TEMPORAL DISCOUNTING

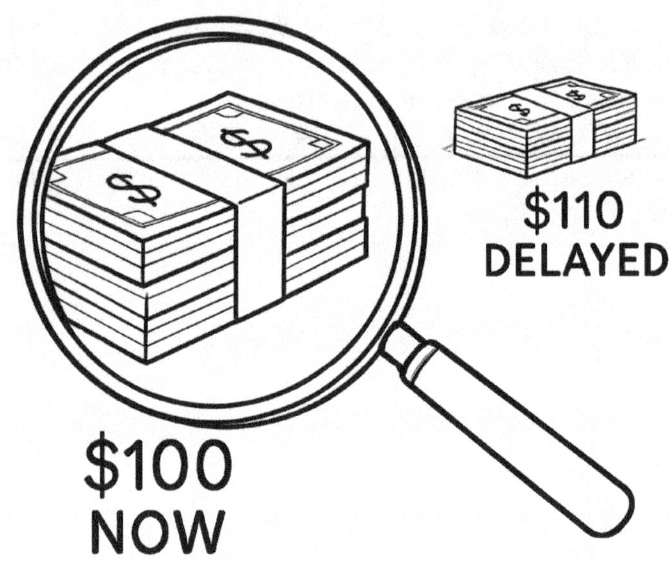

We are now focused on closing the deal immediately. The time for subtle cultivation is over. You must bypass the target's slow, rational system. This is done by exploiting the fundamental flaw in human judgment: the way we value rewards over time.

This flaw is called **Temporal Discounting**. It is the psychological reason people prefer a smaller reward right now over a larger reward later. The value of a future prize fluctuates based on how long you have to wait to get it. The longer the delay, the less the reward is worth to the target's brain.

Your job is to structure the choice so the target's innate impatience becomes the reason they act immediately. You must ensure the present action is associated with an immediate payoff, even if the main benefit is months away.

I. The Science of Present Bias

Behavioral economics confirms that human financial decisions are not always rational. This concept explains why people struggle with long-term financial planning, like saving for retirement. It explains why people engage in behaviors that offer immediate rewards, even if they have long-term negative consequences, like choosing cake over health.

The Impatience Factor: Most people will choose to take $100 today rather than $110 in a month. The extra $\$10$ seems less valuable simply because it is delayed. The value of future rewards drops sharply the further away they are. This phenomenon is also known as hyperbolic discounting.

The Strategy: Pay a Present Premium: To compel instant compliance, you must pay a small, immediate premium to secure the large, future commitment. You must associate the required action *now* with an instant, tangible gain. This gain must occur immediately upon agreement.

- *Example:* If the target must commit to a six-month project, do not focus only on the project's future completion. Focus on the immediate reward they get by signing the document *today*. This could be immediate access to an exclusive community, a small material bonus, or instant elevation of status.

This immediate payment counteracts the hyperbolic devaluation of the long-term benefit. Even if the future reward is substantial, the certainty and presence of the immediate reward motivate the necessary current decision. The immediate gain satisfies the target's impulse for instant gratification.

II. Structuring Immediate Incentives

Because human nature tends toward impatience, immediate compliance is achieved by structuring the request so that execution generates an instant psychological or material gain. This gain must satisfy the target's impulse for instant gratification.

The Strategy of Immediate Status: Status is a powerful, immediate psychological reward.

- *Example:* Frame the present action as an immediate elevation of status. "By signing this document today, you instantly move into the **Tier One Founder's Circle**, which unlocks immediate access to the lead development team." The target receives the status immediately, even if the development team does not meet for two months. The psychological reward is present.

The Strategy of Immediate Relief: Stress is a strong motivator. The target often delays action because the final decision is stressful.

- *Example*: Frame the present action as immediate relief from pressure. "The moment you sign this, the three weeks of indecision are over. We can immediately stop planning and **start building**. The burden of the final decision is lifted from your shoulders right now." The immediate reward is the removal of cognitive stress.

This structuring ensures that the target's mind views the agreement not as the start of long work, but as the end of difficult deliberation.

III. The Illusion of Presence: Minimizing the Gap

The subjective value of a reward increases sharply if it is perceived as temporally or physically close. If the future outcome feels distant and abstract, the brain heavily discounts its value.

The persuader must use visual and linguistic techniques to minimize the perceived time gap between the present action and the long-term benefit. This creates the **Illusion of Presence**.

Sensory Language: You must describe the future outcome with extreme sensory detail. This makes the future reward concrete and imminent, fighting the natural tendency toward temporal discounting.

- *Instead of*: "You will achieve budget control next quarter." (Abstract, delayed)
- *Use*: "By committing now, you will **see** the final $\$7,000$ surplus number on your screen by June 1st. You will **feel** the relief immediately when the deadline passes." (Sensory, imminent)

By making the future reward tangible, something they can see, feel, or hear, you psychologically minimize the perceived time delay. The outcome feels present, making the action required today feel less like work and more like the final step before realization.

Visual Anchors: Use physical anchors to shrink the time gap. Show the target a model, a blueprint, or a projected image of the finished result. The physical representation brings the abstract future benefit into the present moment.

IV. The Emotional Cost of Delay

Temporal discounting often leads to emotional consequences. People who prioritize short-term gratification often feel regret or guilt later. This regret can be leveraged preemptively.

The persuader must frame the *lack* of immediate action as a guaranteed source of immediate future regret. This technique activates **Loss Aversion** (Book 5, Chapter 3).

The Strategy of Preemptive Regret: The focus must be on the emotional cost of delay, not the statistical cost. Non-action is presented as a quantifiable, immediate emotional expense.

- *Example:* "If you delay this decision until tomorrow, you are accepting the **guaranteed loss** of the current pricing. You will look back at this conversation next month and know that you personally cost the project $5,000 by waiting 24 hours. That regret is immediate."

This strategy compels the target to act now to avoid the psychological pain of feeling responsible for missing out or failing to secure the present opportunity. The action is driven by the desire to avoid future guilt.

V. The Integration with Commitment and Consistency

The urgent action demanded by exploiting temporal discounting must still align with the target's need for consistency (Book 1). The target must believe the impulsive decision was still rational.

The Immediate Justification: The persuader must provide a quick, immediate justification that aligns the impulsive, present action with the target's existing values.

- *Target's Value: Efficiency.*
- *Justification:* "You are acting now because waiting would be inefficient. As an efficient manager, you know that the fastest route to the final goal is to secure the necessary resource immediately."

By providing this immediate linguistic frame, the target can quickly justify their impulsive decision, securing the action without triggering a full rational review.

Exploiting temporal discounting is the art of collapsing the decision window. You structure the choice so that the reward is perceived as present and the cost of delay is perceived as immediate and painful.

1. **Pay a Present Premium:** Secure the present commitment by offering an immediate material or psychological gain.

2. **Minimize the Gap:** Use sensory language and visual anchors to make the future benefit feel imminent.

3. **Frame Future Regret:** Present non-action as a guaranteed, immediate loss of value, triggering the desire to avoid guilt.

This ensures the target's inherent impatience works for you, compelling immediate compliance and eliminating hesitation. The next chapter will amplify this pressure by detailing the combined force of **Loss Aversion and Scarcity**.

CHAPTER 2

FORCE URGENCY:

ACTIVATING LOSS AVERSION AND SCARCITY

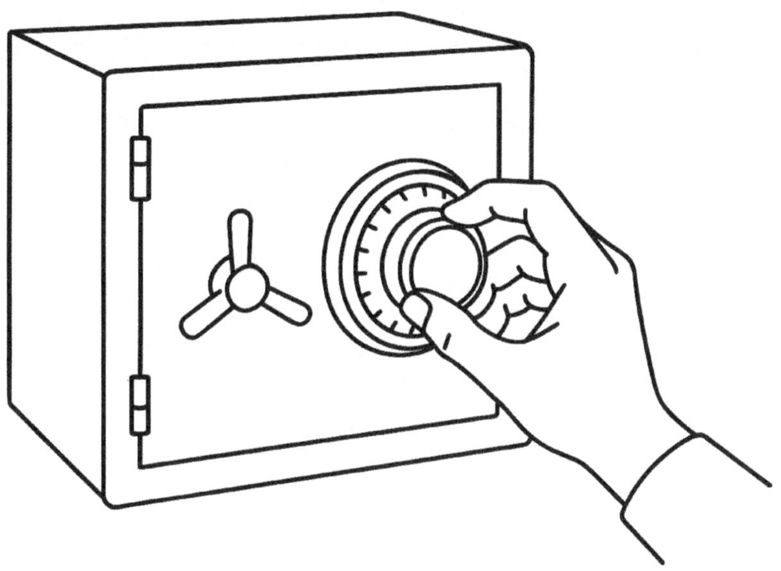

We spent the last chapter learning to use time against the target. We exploited the fact that people prefer small, immediate rewards over larger, delayed rewards. That strategy collapses the decision window by making the target impatient for the present payoff.

But impatience is a soft trigger. True, immediate action requires force. It needs psychological pressure that the target cannot ignore. This pressure is built on fear. Specifically, the fear of loss.

This chapter deals with the mechanical activation of the strongest emotional drivers for instant compliance: **Loss Aversion** and **Scarcity**. You stop motivating the target with the promise of future gain. You start compelling them with the certainty of immediate pain. This combination is the psychological force required to secure decisive action right now.

The most powerful psychological insight in motivation is this: the pain of losing something is measurably stronger than the pleasure of gaining an equivalent item. This is the core principle of *Loss Aversion.*

This concept was highlighted by Nobel laureates Daniel Kahneman and Amos Tversky. They showed that when humans make decisions, the psychological pain of losing something weighs much heavier than the pleasure of gaining an equivalent item. If you gain $100, the joy is significant. If you lose $100, the pain is usually much sharper than the previous joy was sweet.

This fundamental truth dictates your entire urgency strategy. You stop selling the positive outcome. You start selling the avoidance of the negative outcome.

Framing Non-Compliance as a Guaranteed Loss:

The persuader's job is to make non-action the most painful option available. You must frame the decision not as choosing a good option, but as choosing to **avoid a guaranteed loss**. This loss must be specific. It must be immediate. It must be quantifiable.

- **Weak Framing (Gain Focus):** "If you approve this today, you will gain an extra 5% savings over the standard price next quarter."

- **Strong Framing (Loss Focus):** "If you delay this approval until tomorrow, you **guarantee the loss** of the 5% savings currently locked in. Waiting 24 hours means you personally cost the project $2,500."

The second frame uses the target's own fear of regret against them. It immediately ties the psychological pain of loss to the present moment. Non-action becomes a quantifiable, immediate expense. The target's brain is wired to mitigate this pain instantly.

The Emotional Cost of Regret: Loss Aversion works because it triggers the **Fear Of Missing Out (FOMO)**. People make impulsive decisions to avoid the regret associated with missing out on a clear advantage. The target stops thinking about the product's long-term utility. They start thinking only about the urgent need to protect themselves from the painful consequence of inaction.

This urgency often forces targets to bypass a thorough evaluation of the proposal's true value. The emotional need to protect the status quo overrides rational analysis.

Loss Aversion is potent on its own. It becomes overwhelming when paired with **Scarcity**. We value things more when they are rare or limited in availability.

Our brains automatically assign a greater psychological value to things that are scarce. This happens even if the item's actual worth does not change. A fascinating experiment demonstrated this perfectly in 1975. Participants rated identical cookies from an almost empty jar as more desirable than the same cookies from a full jar. The desire was driven entirely by the perceived limited availability.

Engineering Scarcity Conditions:

The persuader must actively **engineer scarcity**. You must visibly reduce the perceived availability of the desired outcome. This ensures the target feels a constant pressure to act before the opportunity vanishes.

1. **Limited Quantity (Resource Scarcity):** The item or access must be presented as limited in number. Use specific, low numbers. *Example: "We only have three slots left in the founder's circle," or "Only the first five contracts signed will receive the dedicated consulting time."* This forces a calculation not just of cost, but of competitive opportunity.

2. **Limited Time (Temporal Scarcity):** The decision window must be closed with a firm, irreversible deadline. This deadline must be justified by external forces, not internal whim. *Example: "The system update happens at midnight tonight, and the price automatically adjusts 8% after that time."* This external justification legitimizes the urgency.

The Strategy of the Empty Jar: The appearance of scarcity matters more than the reality of the inventory. Ensure that the target perceives the resource as diminishing. Even if you have fifty contracts to sign, the perception that *others* are snapping up the resource increases its desirability. You are using Social Proof (Book 1) to amplify the fear of loss. If others are taking the limited resource, it must be valuable.

III. The Freedom Threat: Psychological Reactance

Scarcity does more than just trigger loss aversion. It triggers an innate defensive reaction known as **Psychological Reactance**.

We possess a deep, psychological need to feel free to choose. When our freedom to acquire or choose something is threatened by limited availability, we experience a strong desire to reassert that freedom. We often do this by wanting the restricted item even more intensely. This defensive desire overrides careful thought.

Restricting Choice to Increase Desire: The strategy is to subtly, temporarily restrict the target's perceived freedom.

- *Example*: When you announce the limited-time deadline ("Offer ends at midnight"), you are threatening the target's future freedom to acquire the item at that price. Their immediate psychological impulse is to overcome that threat by securing the item now.

The Combination Lock: The most overwhelming force for instant influence is combining the three core pressures:

1. **Time Pressure (Temporal Discounting):** The target devalues the future reward.
2. **Loss Aversion:** The target fears losing the immediate benefit or guarantee.
3. **Reactance/Scarcity:** The target feels their freedom is threatened, increasing their desire for the restricted item.

This manufactured urgency collapses the decision window entirely. It minimizes the time available for the target's rational processing system (Central Route) to interfere. The decision becomes purely emotional and impulsive.

IV. Legitimizing the Urgency with Authority

The entire system of instant influence relies on the trust established in the previous books. If the target suspects your deadline is arbitrary or a cheap sales tactic, the pressure fails. They must believe the deadline is a legitimate, external fact.

Authority Legitimizes Scarcity: Your **Authority** (Book 1/2) legitimizes the scarcity and the deadline.

- *If you have established an authoritative persona (composed, still, expert posture), your urgent demand, "The financial lock-in requires the signature by 3 PM Tuesday", is accepted as a verifiable business fact, not a personal whim. The target trusts your competence and therefore trusts your constraints.*

Commitment Secures the Impulse: The previous small **Commitments** you secured (Book 1) pave the way for this urgent, large commitment. The target's mind sees the immediate, urgent action as consistent with their established pattern of following your guidance and recommendation. The impulsive decision is instantly justified by their prior pattern of trust.

The Linguistic Frame of Necessity: You must use precise, concrete language (Book 3) to frame the urgency as necessity.

- *Avoid:* "We'd like you to sign now."
- *Use:* "The system update **requires** the signed document by 3 PM. Failure to comply locks us out of the current pricing."

The strong, precise, and concrete language reinforces the legitimacy of the constraint, further reducing the target's chance to question the urgency.

V. The Decisive Action

Forcing urgency is the art of controlling the final moment of decision. You use the scientifically verified principles of Loss Aversion, Scarcity, and Psychological Reactance to generate immense, immediate pressure.

1. **Frame Loss:** Make non-action a guaranteed, painful financial or emotional loss.
2. **Engineer Scarcity:** Introduce a legitimate, external constraint of time or quantity.
3. **Use Authority:** Ensure your established competence and authority legitimize the urgent constraint.

This system ensures that when the moment for decisive action arrives, the target is compelled to act immediately in your favor. Hesitation is eliminated because the perceived psychological cost of delay is too high. The final chapters detail how to maintain this pressure, ensuring the target follows through on the impulse.

CHAPTER 3

DEMAND PRESENCE: MINIMIZING PERCEIVED DELAY FOR FUTURE GAIN

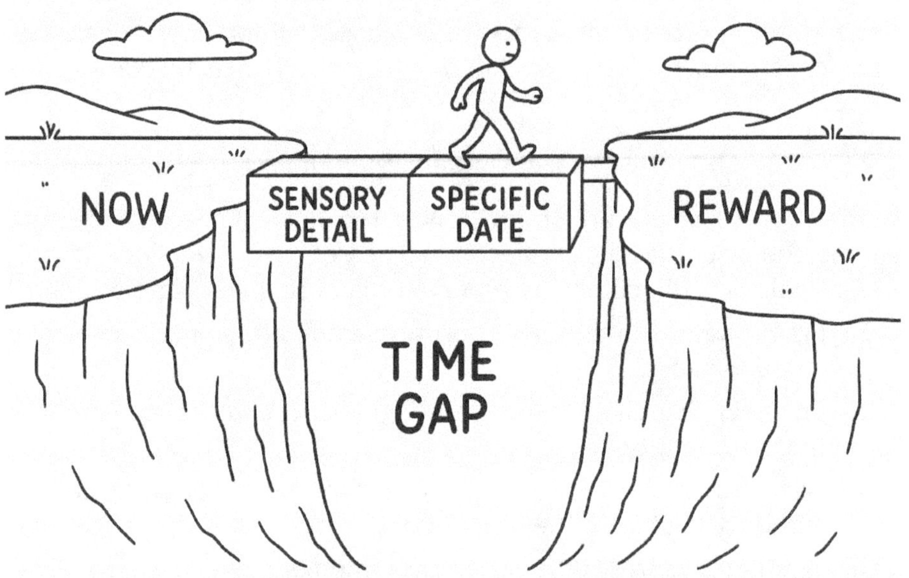

The last two chapters showed you how to collapse the decision window. You used **Temporal Discounting** to make the target impatient. You used **Loss Aversion** and **Scarcity** to make them fearful of waiting. This process forces an immediate impulse.

But impulse is fleeting. You need to solidify that impulse into commitment. The key here is making the future feel immediate. The target discounts future rewards sharply because those rewards feel abstract and distant. If the reward seems far away, the brain ignores it.

This chapter details how to create the **Illusion of Presence**. You must use linguistic and visual techniques to shrink the perceived time gap. You make the future benefit feel tangible, sensory, and imminent. This keeps the reward emotionally valuable right now. You ensure the target feels the final payoff is just around the corner.

I. The Science of the Shrinking Gap

The subjective value of a reward increases sharply when it is perceived as temporally or physically close. This is the opposite of temporal discounting. When the brain can easily visualize a reward, it assigns it higher value.

The Strategy: Sensory Immersion: You must use language that engages the target's five senses. This makes the abstract, delayed outcome feel present and imminent. This active visualization combats the natural tendency of the brain to devalue things that are not here yet.

Actionable Sensory Language:

1. **Visual and Auditory Detail:** Do not just talk about a "successful outcome." Describe what the successful outcome looks like and sounds like. *Example: "By committing now, you will **see** the budget surplus number, $8,000, on your screen every Monday morning. You will **hear** the client confirming the final agreement next week."*

2. **Tactile and Kinesthetic Detail:** Describe the feeling associated with the reward. *Example: "The final contract is not just paper. Signing it today means you **feel** the relief and the burden lifting immediately from your shoulders."*

By making the future reward tangible, something they can see, feel, or hear, you psychologically minimize the perceived time delay. The outcome feels present. This makes the present action feel less like an effort and more like the final step before realization.

II. Anchoring the Future in the Present

The brain relies heavily on immediate, concrete anchors. To demand presence, you must anchor the abstract future benefit to a specific, present moment or object.

Visual Anchors: Use physical anchors to shrink the time gap.

- *Example:* Do not just talk about the completion date next year. Show the target the **specific physical prototype,** the **final blueprint,** or the **signed legal document** that represents the finished project. Hold the physical contract and say, "This document right here is the moment the three weeks of indecision are over. Signing it right now is the same as starting the system build." The physical object makes the future benefit feel immediate.

Linguistic Anchors (Specifics): Vague timeframes, like "soon" or "next quarter," heavily discount the reward. Use specific, concrete dates and times (Chapter 5) to anchor the future.

- *Example:* "The system will be fully operational by **March 1st, 2026**." This concrete date is a much stronger anchor than "next year." The specific detail makes the future reward feel structured and certain. Certainty reduces the brain's impulse to devalue the future reward.

III. The Reciprocity of Immediate Gain

Instant influence often requires asking the target to do something hard or immediate. The target's brain wants a reward for that effort. This activates the **Reciprocity** principle.

By making the target visualize the immediate benefit, you create an emotional payoff *now*. This immediate emotional reward acts as a form of **reciprocal exchange** for the present commitment they are making.

The Strategy: Presenting the Immediate Benefit: Structure the language to emphasize what the target *gains immediately* by signing, even if the gain is psychological.

- *Example:* "By agreeing to this now, you instantly secure the **Tier One Founder's Circle** status. That status and access begin **today**." The immediate gain of status is the reciprocal "payment" for the immediate action. The target feels they have received something of value *right now* in exchange for their commitment. This eliminates the feeling that they are acting only for a distant, unverified benefit.

IV. Justifying the Impulse: The Consistency Frame

When the target acts impulsively, driven by the pressure of Loss Aversion and Scarcity, they will immediately seek justification for that choice. They need to believe their impulsive decision was still rational and consistent with their self-image.

This is where the linguistic frame of **Commitment and Consistency (Book 1)** must be deployed instantly.

The Strategy: Providing the Immediate Justification: The persuader must provide a quick, immediate linguistic frame that aligns the impulsive, present action with the target's pre-established values.

- *If the target values efficiency:* Justify the impulse: "You acted immediately because waiting would be highly inefficient. As an efficient leader, you know the fastest route to securing the resource is to commit now."

- *If the target values stability:* Justify the impulse: "You signed immediately to secure the current price lock-in. That action was necessary to **guarantee stability** and mitigate future risk, which aligns with your core goal of protection."

By providing this immediate frame, the target can quickly justify their impulsive decision. This secures the action without triggering a full, rational review later that could lead to buyer's remorse.

V. Combating Regret: The Focus on Status Quo Bias

The urgency strategy must also account for the target's natural resistance to change. Humans generally prefer things to remain the same; this is called **Status Quo Bias**. Any decision to change is hard, even when the new option is objectively better.

The Strategy: Reframing Non-Action as Change: The most powerful way to bypass the Status Quo Bias is to **reframe non-action as the true risk.**

- *Instead of:* "Sign this to move to a new, better system." (Focus on change)
- *Use:* "If you fail to sign this today, you are actively choosing to **risk instability** from the old system, which costs you $1,000 per month in maintenance fees. This action is simply securing the current, safe operational state." (Focus on preventing a negative change).

By framing non-action as the true departure from stability, you turn the target's innate preference for the Status Quo into a force that drives them toward your solution. They act immediately to protect the present, safe reality, which you have linked to your proposal.

VI. Demanding Presence

Demanding presence is the final mechanical step in forcing urgent compliance. You neutralize the natural human tendency to delay and devalue the future.

1. **Sensory Immersion:** Use language that makes the future reward tangible, imminent, and sensory.
2. **Anchor the Future:** Use specific dates and physical objects to anchor the abstract benefit to the present.

3. **Frame Justification:** Immediately provide a linguistic frame that aligns the target's impulsive action with their core values, preventing regret.

This disciplined approach ensures that when the target makes the final, urgent decision, they do so with the psychological conviction that they acted responsibly and in their own immediate best interest. The next chapter will finalize this pressure by detailing how to eliminate hesitation through precise incentive structuring.

CHAPTER 4
ELIMINATE HESITATION: STRUCTURING INCENTIVES FOR IMMEDIATE REWARD

The last few chapters focused on generating impulse. We used time pressure to make the target impatient. We used fear to make them act now. But fear fades quickly. Impulse needs to be immediately reinforced with a positive payoff. If you demand action, you must also provide an instant reward.

This chapter details how to structure incentives so they eliminate hesitation. The incentive must serve two key purposes: first, it must satisfy the target's impulse for **immediate gratification**. Second, it must provide the **rational justification** needed to defend the sudden, impulsive choice.

We are moving past abstract future benefits. We are engineering a present, concrete reward that locks in the commitment today.

We know that **Temporal Discounting** makes the target devalue future rewards dramatically. Even a large benefit planned for next year feels worthless right now. To eliminate hesitation, you must provide a payoff that happens *today*. This payoff acts as the necessary reciprocal payment for the present commitment.

The Strategy: Present Premium: To compel instant compliance, you must pay a small, immediate premium to secure the large, future commitment. You must associate the required action *now* with an instant, tangible gain. This gain occurs the moment the target agrees.

This immediate payment counteracts the heavy psychological discounting of the long-term benefit. The immediate gain satisfies the target's impulse for instant gratification and makes the decision feel immediately worthwhile.

Actionable Incentives for Today:

1. **Immediate Status Elevation:** Status is a powerful, immediate psychological reward. You must frame the present action as an instant promotion or entry into an exclusive group.

   o *Example:* "By signing this document today, you instantly move into the **Tier One Founder's Circle**. This begins your new status immediately." The target receives the status now, even if the main project deliverable is delayed.

2. **Immediate Relief from Pressure:** Stress is a strong factor in hesitation. The target often delays action because the final decision itself is stressful.

   o *Example:* Frame the present action as immediate removal of cognitive stress. "The moment you sign this, the three weeks of painful deliberation are over. We can immediately **stop planning and start building**. The burden of the final decision is lifted from your shoulders right now." The immediate reward is the removal of mental effort.

3. **Small Material Bonus:** Offer a small, unexpected material bonus that is delivered instantly. This could be a specific, immediate service or a small, non-refundable discount. This must be a concrete, measurable gift.

This structuring ensures that the target's mind views the agreement not as the start of long, hard work, but as the immediate end of difficult decision-making.

When a target acts impulsively, driven by the pressure of Loss Aversion, they will immediately feel internal pressure to justify that choice. They need to believe their sudden decision was rational and **consistent** with their self-image. If they cannot justify the impulse, they will experience buyer's remorse and may retreat later.

The immediate reward is the key to providing this justification.

The Strategy: Providing the Immediate Justification: The persuader must provide a quick, linguistic frame that aligns the impulsive action with the target's pre-established values (Book 1). The immediate incentive becomes the proof of rationality.

- *If the target values **Security***: Frame the incentive: "You acted immediately to secure the current price lock-in. That action was necessary to **guarantee stability** and mitigate future risk, which aligns with your core goal of protection."
- *If the target values **Efficiency***: Frame the incentive: "You acted now because waiting would be inefficient. You secured the **Tier One Status** immediately, proving your commitment to the fastest route to the final goal."

The immediate payoff (status, relief, or a bonus) acts as a physical anchor for the rational justification. The target can point to the immediate reward and say, "I acted responsibly because I got this." This locks in the commitment, preventing regret.

III. The Reciprocity of Instant Gain

Instant influence often requires asking the target to agree to something challenging or immediate. This activates the **Reciprocity** principle. The target needs to feel they are not being taken advantage of.

By providing an immediate incentive, you are offering a form of **reciprocal exchange** for the present commitment. This immediate payment is a psychological acknowledgment of the difficulty of the decision you are asking them to make.

The Strategy: Immediate Concession: Frame the incentive not as a bonus, but as an immediate, necessary concession you are making to them.

- *Example:* "We need your signature now for the system lock-in. Because we are asking for this immediate action, we are offering this **5% discount** that expires in the next hour. This is our concession for the urgency we require."

This framing turns the incentive into a tangible part of the negotiation process. The target feels they have forced you to make a reciprocal concession, which reinforces their sense of control over the interaction.

IV. Eliminating the Status Quo Bias

The urgency strategy must also combat the target's inherent preference for things to remain the same, known as **Status Quo Bias**. Any decision to change is hard, even when the new option is objectively better.

The Strategy: Reframing Non-Action as Costly Change: The most powerful way to bypass the Status Quo Bias is to **reframe non-action as the true risk to stability.**

- *Avoid:* "Sign this to move to a new, better system." (Focus on uncomfortable change)
- *Use:* "If you fail to sign this today, you are actively choosing to **lose the current pricing** and **risk instability** from the old, outdated maintenance system. The best action for maintaining the status quo is securing this resource immediately." (Focus on preventing a negative change).

By framing non-action as the true departure from stability, you turn the target's innate preference for the Status Quo into a force that drives them toward your solution. They act immediately to protect the present, safe reality, which you have linked to your proposal.

V. The Final Lock

Structuring incentives for immediate reward is the final lock on the impulsive decision. You neutralize the natural human tendency to delay and devalue the future.

1. **Pay a Present Premium:** Offer an immediate material or psychological gain that satisfies the need for instant gratification.
2. **Provide Instant Justification:** Use a linguistic frame that aligns the immediate reward with the target's core values, preventing regret.
3. **Combat Status Quo:** Frame non-action as the true risk to stability, forcing the target to choose your proposal to maintain safety.

This disciplined approach ensures that when the target makes the final, urgent decision, they do so with the psychological conviction that they acted responsibly and in their own immediate best interest. The next chapter will finalize this pressure by detailing how to maintain this manufactured urgency until the action is fully completed.

CHAPTER 5

CONTROL DEADLINE: MANUFACTURING THE PSYCHOLOGICAL NEED TO BUY

We have built the psychological pressure. The target is impatient for the reward. They are afraid of the loss. They feel their freedom is threatened by scarcity. These forces create the impulse.

But impulse is only the first step. You must now control the moment of final compliance. This requires manufacturing a psychological need so strong that the target feels they absolutely must buy **now** to regain control of their own environment. You do not just set a deadline. You make the target internalize the deadline as their own urgent problem.

This chapter details how to use legitimacy, consistency, and psychological reactance to finalize the urgent decision. You ensure the target completes the action before their rational mind can trigger regret or analysis.

I. Legitimizing the Deadline: Authority as Fact

The entire system of instant influence collapses if the target believes your deadline is arbitrary. If they suspect you are simply using a cheap sales tactic, they will wait, and the pressure will fail. The deadline must be accepted as a **legitimate, external fact**.

The Role of Authority: The trust you built in your **Authority** (Book 2) must legitimize the constraint. Your composure, your still presence, and your competence must support the deadline.

- **Verifiable Constraint:** The deadline must be justified by an outside force that you cannot control. This might be a financial system lock-in, a change in regulatory code, or a hard logistical cut-off.
    - *Example:* Do not say: "The price goes up when I decide."
    - *Say:* "The system wide update happens at midnight tonight. The current pricing structure is locked into the old system. The price automatically adjusts 8% after that time." This external justification makes the urgency real.

The Linguistic Frame of Necessity: You must use precise, concrete language (Book 3) to frame the deadline as an unavoidable necessity. Use direct verbs.

- *Avoid:* "We'd like you to decide soon."
- *Use:* "The system lock-in **requires** the final signed document by 3 PM Tuesday. Failure to comply locks us out of the current pricing." The strong, precise language reinforces the legitimacy of the constraint. This reduces the target's chance to question the urgency.

The target trusts your competence, so they trust your constraints. They believe the deadline exists because you, the authority figure, confirmed it.

II. Leveraging Reactance: The Freedom Threat

Scarcity not only triggers fear of loss. It triggers **Psychological Reactance**. This is the innate human desire to reassert threatened freedom. When the target perceives a threat to their freedom to choose, they want the restricted item even more intensely.

The Strategy: Restricting Future Freedom: You must briefly and subtly threaten the target's perceived future freedom. This dramatically increases their present desire for the restricted option.

- *Example*: The deadline ("Offer ends in 60 minutes") restricts the target's freedom to get the benefit later. Their immediate psychological impulse is to overcome that threat. They reassert their freedom by immediately securing the item now.

The Focus on Exclusivity: Scarcity is more effective when the threat is tied to **exclusivity**. The fact that an item is scarce suggests that others recognize its value and are snapping it up. This ties scarcity directly into **Social Proof** (Book 1).

- *Example*: "Only the first five contracts will receive the dedicated consulting time." This implies that knowledgeable people are already taking the resource. The target must act immediately to avoid being excluded from the valuable, restricted group. This compels the target to act impulsively to keep their status and autonomy.

III. The Consistency Lock: Justifying the Impulse

When the target acts on urgency, their mind immediately tries to justify the quick decision. They need to believe the impulsive choice was rational and **consistent** with their self-image. If they cannot justify the impulse, they will feel buyer's remorse and may cancel or retreat later.

The Strategy: Providing the Immediate Consistency Frame: You must immediately provide a linguistic frame that aligns the urgent action with the target's pre-established values (Book 1).

- **Immediate Payoff Justification (Chapter 5):** The immediate reward you gave (status, relief, or bonus) acts as a physical anchor for the rational justification. The target can point to the immediate reward and say, "I acted responsibly because I got this bonus right now."

- **Value Alignment:** You must connect the quick action to their core values:

    - *If the target values Innovation:* Frame the action: "You signed immediately because **innovators** secure necessary resources immediately. Delay is a tactic for the cautious, not the forward-thinker."

    - *If the target values Caution:* Frame the action: "You secured the lock-in now to prevent the 8% price increase. That action was the **most cautious and fiscally responsible** choice available."

This immediate, tailored justification locks in the commitment. It prevents the regret that stems from making an impulsive choice.

IV. The Final Barrier: Eliminating Buyer's Remorse

Buyer's remorse often occurs when the target realizes they acted impulsively. This is a cognitive clash between the quick decision (Peripheral Route) and their need for rational consistency (Central Route).

The Strategy: Closing the Cognitive Loop: You must proactively close the cognitive loop immediately after the signature.

1. **Reiterate the Loss Avoided:** Immediately remind the target of the specific loss they successfully avoided by acting now. *Example: "Congratulations. You successfully avoided the $2,500 cost increase that would have hit tomorrow."* This reinforces the positive feeling of **loss avoidance**.

2. **Affirm the Commitment Effort:** Remind them that the action was **effortful** (Commitment principle). *Example: "That was a difficult decision to make under pressure, and I commend you for securing this."* This reinforces their inner responsibility for the choice. They now feel committed to the action because they associate it with their own strong will.

3. **Future Visualization:** Use sensory language one final time to make the immediate future seem present. *Example: "We can now immediately send the first production timeline. You will see that document in your inbox in the next hour."* This shifts the target's focus from the difficult decision they just made to the immediate reward they are about to receive.

This final sequence ensures the target's rational system accepts the impulsive decision.

V. Finalizing the Urgency

Controlling the deadline is the art of finalizing the urgent decision. You transition from generating impulse to securing commitment.

1. **Legitimize the Pressure:** Use authority and external facts to make the deadline real and unavoidable.

2. **Activate Reactance:** Restrict future freedom with scarcity to increase the target's desire for the restricted item.

3. **Lock Consistency:** Immediately justify the impulsive action with a linguistic frame that aligns the choice with the target's core values.

This system ensures that the target's psychological need to buy is manufactured, controlled, and resolved instantly in your favor. This completes the entire influence system, moving from strategy and charm to decisive, immediate action.

CONCLUSION
THE FINAL SYSTEM OF DECISIVE ACTION

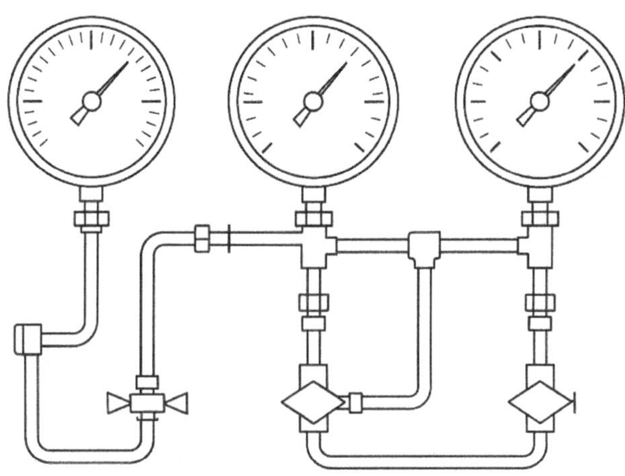

We have finished the final book, completing the entire structure of influence. This book, **Instant Influence**, was dedicated entirely to collapsing the decision window. It moved us beyond the patience of long-term strategy and into the mechanics of immediate compliance.

The core lesson is that immediate action is not rational. It is a forced psychological impulse. You stop relying on the target's slow, analytical mind. You start manipulating their perception of time and value. You ensure the action happens before regret or second thoughts can interfere.

This conclusion synthesizes the three core drivers of instant action: **Temporal Discounting, Loss Aversion, and Scarcity**. We show how to fuse these forces. This creates the overwhelming psychological need that compels the target to agree right now.

I. The Foundation: Controlling Time and Value

Instant influence begins by exploiting the fundamental flaw in how humans perceive time. This flaw is **Temporal Discounting**.

The Discounting Principle: People prefer a smaller reward right now over a larger reward later. The psychological value of a future prize drops sharply the further away it is. This impatience is human nature.

Synthesis of Temporal Discounting (Chapter 2):

1. **Pay a Present Premium:** To compel instant compliance, you must pay a small, immediate premium for the present commitment. This could be immediate status elevation, immediate relief from decision stress, or a small, measurable bonus. This immediate gain satisfies the target's impulse for instant gratification.

2. **Minimize the Gap:** You must use **sensory language** and **visual anchors** to shrink the perceived time gap. Describe the future outcome with extreme detail. Make the target *see* the budget surplus or *feel* the relief immediately. This makes the future reward feel present, keeping its value high.

This strategy uses the target's impatience against them. It ensures they view the agreement not as the start of long work, but as the immediate end of difficult deliberation.

II. The Overwhelming Force: Fear and Rarity

Impatience is a soft trigger. To secure decisive action, you must use the strongest emotional forces: fear and restriction.

Synthesis of Loss Aversion (Chapter 3):

1. **Frame Loss Over Gain:** The fear of losing something is much stronger than the desire to gain an equivalent item. You must frame non-compliance as a guaranteed, immediate, quantifiable loss. *Example: "Waiting 24 hours means you personally cost the project $2,500."* This triggers the **Fear Of Missing Out (FOMO)**. The emotional need to avoid loss overrides rational analysis.

Synthesis of Scarcity and Reactance (Chapter 3):

1. **Engineer Scarcity:** You must visibly reduce the perceived availability of the desired outcome using a legitimate, external constraint (limited time or limited quantity).

2. **Activate Psychological Reactance:** The deadline restricts the target's freedom to choose later. This threat activates their innate desire to reassert control. They do this by immediately securing the restricted item. This manufactured urgency eliminates hesitation.

This combination of forces collapses the decision window entirely.

Impulse must be secured quickly before regret can set in. This requires legitimizing the deadline and instantly aligning the impulse with the target's core values.

Synthesis of Legitimacy (Chapter 6):

1. **Authority Legitimizes Urgency:** Your **Authority** (Book 2) must legitimize the deadline. The target must believe the deadline is a verifiable external fact (e.g., a system update, a hard financial lock-in) and not a cheap tactic.

2. **Use Concrete Necessity:** You must use precise, **concrete language** (Book 3) to frame the deadline as an unavoidable necessity. *Example: "The system lock-in requires the final signed document by 3 PM Tuesday."*

Synthesis of Consistency (Chapter 6):

1. **Lock the Impulse with Justification:** When the target acts impulsively, you must immediately provide a linguistic frame that aligns their action with their core values. This is the **Consistency Frame** (Book 1). *Example: "You signed immediately because, as a cautious leader, you knew that securing the current price lock-in was the most fiscally responsible action."* This immediate justification locks in the commitment. It eliminates buyer's remorse.

2. **Combat Status Quo:** You must reframe non-action as the true risk. By linking non-action to the loss of stability, you compel the target to choose your proposal to maintain the present, safe reality.

IV. Conclusion: The Full Circle of Influence

This final book, **Instant Influence**, completes the entire system. It is the decisive application of the principles we built in the previous four books.

- **Strategy (Book 1):** The commitment drivers are used to secure the impulsive action.

- **Presence (Book 2):** Authority legitimizes the scarcity and urgency.

- **Language (Book 3):** Concrete vocabulary and framing maximize the fear of loss.

- **Charm (Book 4):** The established trust ensures the urgent demand is seen as helpful advice, not manipulation.

The result is a system where the target is guided through a comprehensive, controlled process. The final action is immediate, decisive, and fully justified by their own psychological need for safety and consistency.

We have now provided a complete, scientifically grounded guide to covert persuasion, charisma, linguistic control, irresistible charm, and instant influence. The next step is the final resource list and checklist.

REFLECTION QUESTIONS

We have completed the system of **Instant Influence**. This final book taught you to collapse the decision window. You learned to use the powerful forces of time, scarcity, and loss aversion to secure immediate action. You moved from patient strategy to forced impulse.

The skills covered here, anchoring the future, manufacturing urgency, and locking the commitment, must become instant reflexes. Use these questions to personalize the material. Map the concepts onto your own interactions. Prepare to execute with decisive speed.

Section 1: Temporal Discounting and Present Value

The foundation of instant influence is the human flaw of **Temporal Discounting**. You must make the present action feel like the immediate reward.

1. **Immediate Payoff:** Think about a proposal you need to send this week that offers a large reward six months from now. What is the immediate, small, **psychological** reward you can offer right now, today, for the signature? This could be instant status elevation or immediate relief from the decision stress.

2. **Sensory Immersion:** The target discounts abstract future benefits. Describe the final outcome of your current project using only **sensory language**. What will the target *see*, *feel*, or *hear* the moment the project is completed? Use specific details to make the future feel imminent and valuable right now.

3. **Status Quo Justification:** Humans naturally resist change. This is the **Status Quo Bias**. If your target is hesitating, how can you reframe non-action as the greater **risk to stability**? Write one sentence that links signing the document today to maintaining their current safe reality.

4. **Justifying the Impulse:** When someone acts on impulse, they need immediate justification. If a client signed quickly because of a deadline, what single, self-serving reason can you immediately provide them to align their impulsive action with their core value of **fiscal responsibility**?

Section 2: Loss Aversion and Scarcity

The strongest triggers for instant action are the fear of loss and the threat of scarcity. This pressure eliminates hesitation.

5. **Framing Loss:** Identify a goal where you need an immediate "yes." How are you currently framing the request (e.g., gain)? Now, rewrite the request entirely to focus on **guaranteed loss**. What is the specific, quantifiable financial loss or missed opportunity they suffer if they wait until tomorrow?

6. **Engineering Scarcity:** You must create an external, legitimate constraint. If you cannot use a price deadline, what is one non-monetary resource you can limit immediately (e.g., dedicated consulting time, priority access, limited slots in the pilot program)? How can you use that **scarcity** to trigger the target's desire to act now to avoid exclusion?

7. **Psychological Reactance: Scarcity** threatens freedom, which triggers **reactance**. If you announce a deadline, the target wants the item more intensely. How can you subtly reference the fact that "other interested parties" are taking the limited resource, using **Social Proof** to amplify the fear of exclusion?

8. **Closing the Cognitive Loop:** Buyer's remorse is a risk after an impulsive decision. Immediately after securing a major agreement, what two actions can you take? You must do one to reinforce the **Loss Avoided** and one to affirm the target's **effort and consistency**.

The final execution requires using established trust to legitimize the urgency and finalize the commitment.

9. **Legitimizing the Deadline:** Your **Authority** must support the deadline. If you set a deadline of 3 PM on Friday, what is the single **external, verifiable fact** (e.g., a system update, a hard financial closing date) that justifies the deadline? You must trust your constraints to make the target trust them.

10. **The Final Sequence:** Review the critical steps for immediate compliance. Put them in order: **Loss Frame, Scarcity Threat, Immediate Justification (Present Premium), and Consistency Frame**. How would you use this sequence in the last 60 seconds of a negotiation to eliminate all remaining hesitation?

OVERALL CONCLUSION
THE ARCHITECTURE OF TOTAL INFLUENCE

We have finished the system. This collection of five books was a focused study on the mechanics of total influence. We moved from the foundational strategy of the mind to the final, rapid execution of a decision. The core lesson is clear: influence is not an accident of personality. It is a precise, learned architecture built on verifiable psychological facts.

If you internalize this system, you stop relying on hope. You start relying on predictable science. You gain the ability to guide any social interaction, securing deep loyalty and immediate compliance, regardless of the setting.

Here, we review the five pillars of this system. We integrate them into one cohesive model for consistent, repeatable success in social and professional life.

I. Book 1: Covert Persuasion: Psychological Leverage

The Core Principle: Reality is Negotiable.

The system begins by recognizing that people do not act on objective facts. They act on their own **subjective reality**, which is built from their perception of the facts. This personal version of truth dictates behavior. Covert persuasion is the intentional structuring of information to manage that subjective reality.

Key Levers of Control:

- **Exploiting Bias:** We leveraged **cognitive biases**, the systematic, predictable errors in human judgment, to create the path of least cognitive resistance. By subtly increasing pressure, you force the target's brain to use fast shortcuts, bypassing slow, rational thought.

- **Framing and Anchoring:** We used the **Anchoring Effect** to set the highest possible value marker early in the conversation. This anchor dictates the entire acceptable range of subsequent outcomes.

- **Consistency is King:** The greatest leverage is securing a small, initial **Commitment**. We learned that commitment is strongest and most lasting when it is **active, public, and effortful**. This makes the target feel **inner responsibility** for the choice, ensuring they stick with it to maintain consistency with their new self-image.

- **Mitigating Resistance:** We used the **Confirmation Bias** to our advantage. Instead of challenging the target's beliefs, we framed the proposal as the necessary, logical step that **confirms their existing self-image** (e.g., responsible, innovative). This reduces the evidence required for acceptance.

Result: You move the target from being a cautious analyst to being a self-justifying participant in a decision they believe they made entirely on their own logic.

II. Book 2: Magnetic Charisma: Non-Verbal Resonance

The Core Principle: Trust is a Physical Signal.

The next step is securing trust. Influence requires competence, but charisma ensures that competence is projected without the need for words. Non-verbal behavior is a powerful, subtle form of social influence that operates **below conscious awareness**.

Key Levers of Control:

- **Controlled Presence:** We focused on **stillness** and **symmetry**. Nervous energy broadcasts anxiety and instantly undermines competence. Controlled composure acts as the antidote to the target's anxiety, making them feel safe.

- **The Halo Effect:** This projected composure is the single positive trait that triggers the **Halo Effect**. The target infers deep competence and trustworthiness from your stability alone.

- **Emotional Transfer:** Charisma spreads energy. We learned to use **Emotional Contagion**, the automatic transfer of emotional states, to mobilize groups. By focusing positive energy on **high self-monitors**, you initiate a **charismatic cascade** that spreads the desired mood quickly.

- **Haptics and Trust: Touch** is the first language of human security. Strategic, appropriate touch (e.g., a controlled handshake) bypasses the slow, verbal rapport process and establishes fundamental trust immediately.

- **Social Cohesion: Identification Humor** is the fastest tool for group bonding. Shared laughter confirms consensus on core values and dramatically reduces uncertainty, creating a resilient **shared identity**.

Result: Your physical presence becomes a stable, desirable psychological resource. The target is non-verbally inclined to trust, like, and follow you before the argument even begins.

III. Book 3: NLP Mind Control: The Science of Framing and Belief

The Core Principle: Language Constructs Reality.

This book replaced vague theory with precise linguistic mechanics. We learned that the choice of words is the most efficient conduit for psychological influence.

Key Levers of Control:

- **Framing is Control:** We used scientifically verified **framing** to dictate perception. Framing the exact same facts as a "loss" versus a "gain" changes the choice itself. This control ensures the target views the proposal through your positive lens.

- **Linguistic Synchrony: Rapport** is achieved by subtly matching the target's vocabulary density, emotional tone, and pace. This **linguistic mirroring** reduces **cognitive friction** and makes the message feel familiar and effortless.

- **Flexible Influence:** We mastered the ability to switch between **Push energy** (assertion, direction) and **Pull energy** (inquiry, collaboration). This flexibility maintains rapport while ensuring compliance when direction is necessary.

- **Resistance Reframing:** When the target objects, you do not argue the fact. You immediately **validate the feeling** and **change the frame's category** (e.g., "risky" becomes "necessary security"). This disarms resistance by invalidating the target's negative context.

- **Concrete Vocabulary:** We eliminated abstract, vague language. **Concrete vocabulary** (specific numbers, dates, and names) maximizes **emotional density** and minimizes the mental work required of the target. This makes the message persuasive and memorable.

Result: Your words become precision instruments. The target receives the message efficiently and accepts the conclusion, believing they reached it through their own logical process.

IV. Book 4: Irresistible Charm: Relationship Dynamics

The Core Principle: Loyalty is a Shared Structure.

Charm is the system that moves influence from a single event to a long-term, self-sustaining relationship. It generates continuous social attraction.

Key Levers of Control:

- **Frequency Over Intimacy:** We accelerated intimacy by prioritizing **disclosure frequency** over depth. Sharing a high volume of low-stakes details quickly builds familiarity without the high risk of emotional instability.
- **Narrativity Sustains Interest:** We used **disclosure narrativity** to frame personal details as engaging, short stories. This storytelling provides **perceived entertainment value**, ensuring the target remains psychologically invested in the interaction.
- **Calibration is Key:** We mastered the **Calibration Test**. This is the process of gently testing the boundary of intimacy and instantly **retreating** if the target signals discomfort or anxiety. This ensures the bond is maintained at the level of **optimal appropriateness.**
- **Cementing Loyalty:** We solidified loyalty by creating **Shared Social Rituals** (e.g., inside jokes). These rituals provide the **active, public, and effortful** commitment markers that secure long-term consistency.

Result: You build a desirable persona that provides consistent psychological reward. The target is not just compliant; they are personally loyal because the relationship is safe, entertaining, and structurally resilient.

V. Book 5: Instant Influence: Urgency and Action

The Core Principle: Collapse the Decision Window.

The final stage is securing immediate, decisive action. This system bypasses rational thought by leveraging fear and scarcity.

Key Levers of Control:

- **Temporal Discounting:** We exploited the human flaw of **Temporal Discounting**. We made the future reward feel present by using sensory language. We made the cost of delay feel immediate, compelling present action.

- **Loss Aversion:** We used the strongest psychological driver: the pain of loss. We framed non-compliance as a guaranteed, immediate, quantifiable loss, triggering the **Fear Of Missing Out (FOMO)**.

- **Scarcity and Reactance:** We engineered **Scarcity** (limited time or quantity) and **Authority** to legitimize the deadline. This threat to the target's freedom triggers **Psychological Reactance**, forcing them to act now to reassert their control over the threatened resource.

- **Locking the Impulse:** Immediately after securing the action, we provided a **Consistency Frame**. This linguistic justification aligns the impulsive action with the target's core values, locking the commitment and eliminating buyer's remorse.

Result: You gain the ability to generate decisive action on demand. Hesitation is eliminated because the perceived psychological cost of delay is too high.

The Complete System

These five pillars form a comprehensive system. They move you from passive interaction to active, intentional influence. You begin by diagnosing the target's mind. You project authority with your body. You structure every word for effect. You build loyalty through shared connection. Then, you finalize the process by collapsing the final moment of decision.

Mastery of this architecture is not about becoming someone else. It is about maximizing your true, consistent capabilities. It ensures that your goals are achieved reliably, ethically, and with the full, justified conviction of the person you are influencing.

PRINT AND KEEP CHECKLIST
THE TOTAL INFLUENCE SYSTEM

This checklist translates the entire five-book system into actionable, step-by-step practices. Use this guide before and during every high-stakes interaction. The goal is to move from analysis to reflex, ensuring your influence is consistent, precise, and immediately effective.

Book 1: Covert Persuasion: Psychological Leverage

Goal: Control the Decision Environment and Secure Consistency

Before the Interaction	During the Interaction	Post-Agreement Lock
1. Diagnose Reality: Identify the target's core belief or existing bias (e.g., "I value caution").	**1. Set the Anchor:** Introduce the highest justifiable value marker or request first (e.g., 20% budget increase, 6-month delay).	**1. Secure Active Commitment:** Get the target to take an immediate, small, **active** step (e.g., sign the first page, send an internal commitment email).
2. Frame for Alignment: Prepare the linguistic framing that **confirms** their belief (e.g., "This action is the most cautious choice").	**2. Exploit Contrast:** Immediately follow the rejected high anchor with your actual, smaller request. This makes the real request seem disproportionately acceptable.	**2. Ensure Public/Effortful:** Make sure the commitment is visible to others or requires minor effort to reinforce **Consistency**.
3. Prepare the Present Premium: Determine a small, immediate reward the target receives for acting *now*, combating **Temporal Discounting**.	**3. Use Social Proof:** Reference the adoption of similar people, especially those the target respects or identifies with.	**3. Reframe Justification:** Provide the target with the language to justify their decision internally (e.g., "You moved fast because you prioritize stability").

Goal: Establish Pre-Emptive Trust and Mobilize Emotion

Controlled Presence (Authority)	Emotional Transfer (Mobilization)	Haptic and Social Connection (Trust)
1. Maintain Stillness: Eliminate all nervous energy leaks (fidgeting, pen clicking). Controlled stillness projects composure and competence.	**1. Diagnose Susceptibility:** Identify high self-monitors (emotional amplifiers) for fast spread and low self-monitors for long-term stability.	**1. Maximize Haptics:** Use a firm, dry, symmetrical handshake, maintaining steady eye contact for three seconds. This taps into the fundamental need for security.
2. Use Open Posture: Stand and sit with symmetrical, open posture. Claim your space physically to non-verbally assert status.	**2. Project Composure:** Maintain a calm, measured vocal pace and low pitch. This triggers the **Halo Effect**, making the target infer trustworthiness from your stability.	**2. Use Identification Humor:** Deploy humor that targets an external norm or shared frustration. Shared laughter confirms consensus on core values and builds cohesion.
3. Control Gaze: Maintain intentional eye contact during key phrases (opening, closing, critical question) to signal sincerity and focus.	**3. Initiate Cascade:** Focus enthusiasm and energy projection on the high self-monitors to spread the desired mood to the group.	**3. Create Shared Rituals:** Elevate a small shared moment (e.g., an inside joke) into a repeatable ritual. This provides the necessary **effortful** marker for group loyalty.

Goal: Achieve Linguistic Precision and Eliminate Friction

Framing and Clarity	Rapport and Style Synchrony	Resistance Mitigation
1. Use Concrete Vocabulary: Replace abstract nouns ("optimization," "synergy") with specific facts, numbers, and dates (e.g., "$5,000," "Tuesday at 3 PM").	**1. Match Vocal/Linguistic Pace:** Subtly align your speaking speed and vocabulary density with the target's style to reduce cognitive friction.	**1. Validate, then Shift:** When resistance occurs (e.g., "too risky"), immediately validate the feeling, then change the frame's category.
2. Use Active Verbs: Ensure sentences use direct verbs. This communicates certainty and eliminates passive ambiguity.	**2. Use Flexible Influence:** Start with **Pull energy** (inquiry, collaboration) to build rapport and gather information. Switch to **Push energy** (assertion, direction) to close the commitment.	**2. Reframe Loss:** Frame non-compliance as a **guaranteed, immediate loss** (e.g., "you lose the discount tomorrow"). This activates the strongest psychological driver.
3. Align Evidence: If targeting a critical processor (Central Route), lead with **message quality** and detailed evidence. If targeting a peripheral processor, use **authority**.	**3. Deploy Communality Buffer:** If asserting competence (especially for female persuaders), blend the command with language of warmth and shared goals (e.g., "our mutual objective") to reduce resistance.	**3. Pre-Empt the Objection:** State the target's most likely objection before they do, then immediately control the framing of the solution.

Goal: Accelerate Intimacy and Cement Loyalty

Accelerating Closeness	Sustaining Interest (Narrative)	Boundary Management (Calibration)
1. Prioritize Frequency: Maximize the number of small, low-stakes disclosures to build rapid familiarity. **Frequency** predicts closeness faster than intimacy.	**1. Use Narrativity:** Frame all personal details as short, structured stories (Setup, Conflict, Resolution) to create **perceived entertainment value.**	**1. Test Gently:** Offer a disclosure that is *slightly* deeper than the previous one to test the boundary of comfort.
2. Avoid Premature Depth: Never share raw, deep vulnerability too soon. If perceived as inappropriate, it instantly **reduces social attraction**.	**2. Vet Values:** Ensure your stories reveal positive, core values (e.g., integrity, hard work). This reinforces the target's **Confirmation Bias.**	**2. Read Reciprocity:** Use the target's verbal and non-verbal response (matching your disclosure) as the final gauge for appropriateness.
3. Virtual Connection: In digital settings, rely entirely on **words, charm, and seduction.** Use strong narrative to compensate for the lack of physical presence.	**3. Frame Shared Struggle:** Use shared narratives to create a "founding myth" (e.g., "The time *we* overcame the impossible deadline"). This cements collective loyalty.	**3. Retreat Immediately:** If the target shows anxiety, withdrawal, or low reciprocation, immediately reduce the depth of future disclosures to preserve trust.

Goal: Collapse the Decision Window for Immediate Compliance

Time Control (Discounting)	Fear Activation (Urgency)	Final Lock (Commitment)
1. Pay Present Premium: Offer an immediate material or psychological gain for acting now (e.g., instant status upgrade, immediate stress relief).	**1. Frame Loss:** Frame non-compliance as a guaranteed, quantifiable loss (e.g., "you lose the $2,000 discount tomorrow").	**1. Legitimate the Deadline:** Ensure the scarcity or deadline is justified by an **external, verifiable fact** (e.g., system lock-in, financial cut-off).
2. Sensory Immersion: Use language that makes the future reward tangible and sensory (e.g., "You will *see* the surplus on your screen") to minimize the **Temporal Discounting** gap.	**2. Engineer Scarcity:** Introduce a legitimate constraint (limited time or quantity) to trigger the **Fear Of Missing Out (FOMO)**.	**2. Provide Consistency Frame:** Immediately after the signature, provide the target with the linguistic justification that aligns the impulse with their core value (e.g., "You acted responsibly to avoid the loss").
3. Combat Status Quo Bias: Reframe non-action as the true risk to stability. Force the target to choose your solution to maintain the current safe reality.	**3. Activate Reactance:** Threaten the target's future freedom to acquire the item at that price to trigger **Psychological Reactance**.	**3. Close the Loop:** Immediately reiterate the **Loss Avoided** and affirm the target's **effort** to prevent buyer's remorse.

OVERALL RESOURCES

Book 1

Introduction

https://en.wikipedia.org/wiki/Cognitive_bias

https://pmc.ncbi.nlm.nih.gov/articles/PMC8378077/

https://threadlinebranding.com/blog/book-review/review-influence-the-psychology-of-persuasion-by-robert-b-cialdini-phd/

https://salvadorbriggman.com/review-of-influence-the-psychology-of-persuasion/

http://www.communicationcache.com/uploads/1/0/8/8/10887248/gender_and_social_influence.pdf

https://influencecompany.com/blog/how-to-be-succesfull-in-communication-between-men-and-women/

https://fiveable.me/persuasion-theory/unit-12/persuasion-gender-differences/study-guide/LXts1mdLnZ14z04j

https://gap.hks.harvard.edu/how-genderrole-salience-influences-attitude-strength-and-persuasive-message-processing

Chapter 1 - resources

https://en.wikipedia.org/wiki/Cognitive_bias

https://pmc.ncbi.nlm.nih.gov/articles/PMC8378077/

https://salvadorbriggman.com/review-of-influence-the-psychology-of-persuasion/

https://gap.hks.harvard.edu/how-genderrole-salience-influences-attitude-strength-and-persuasive-message-processing

Chapter 2 - resources

https://threadlinebranding.com/blog/book-review/review-influence-the-psychology-of-persuasion-by-robert-b-cialdini-phd/

https://salvadorbriggman.com/review-of-influence-the-psychology-of-persuasion/

http://www.communicationcache.com/uploads/1/0/8/8/10887248/gender_and_social_influence.pdf

https://influencecompany.com/blog/how-to-be-succesfull-in-communication-between-men-and-women/

https://fiveable.me/persuasion-theory/unit-12/persuasion-gender-differences/study-guide/LXts1mdLnZ14z04j

https://gap.hks.harvard.edu/how-genderrole-salience-influences-attitude-strength-and-persuasive-message-processing

https://www.investopedia.com/temporal-discounting-7972594

https://www.profit.co/blog/behavioral-economics/time-discounting-employee-rewards/

https://maccelerator.la/en/blog/entrepreneurship/behavioral-psychology-behind-scarcity/

https://psychotricks.com/scarcity-principle/

Chapter 3 - resources

https://salvadorbriggman.com/review-of-influence-the-psychology-of-persuasion/

https://skeptics.stackexchange.com/questions/74/any-scientific-basis-for-neuro-linguistic-programming

https://en.wikipedia.org/wiki/Neuro-linguistic_programming

https://business.columbia.edu/sites/default/files-efs/citation_file_upload/NLP_paper.pdf

https://pmc.ncbi.nlm.nih.gov/articles/PMC8455714/

https://fiveable.me/persuasion-theory/unit-12/persuasion-gender-differences/study-guide/LXts1mdLnZ14z04j

http://www.communicationcache.com/uploads/1/0/8/8/10887248/gender_and_social_influence.pdf

Chapter 4 - resources

https://pmc.ncbi.nlm.nih.gov/articles/PMC8378077/

https://en.wikipedia.org/wiki/Cognitive_bias

https://fiveable.me/persuasion-theory/unit-12/persuasion-gender-differences/study-guide/LXts1mdLnZ14z04j

https://gap.hks.harvard.edu/how-genderrole-salience-influences-attitude-strength-and-persuasive-message-processing

https://influencecompany.com/blog/how-to-be-succesfull-in-communication-between-men-and-women/

http://www.communicationcache.com/uploads/1/0/8/8/10887248/gender_and_social_influence.pdf

Chapter 5 - resources

https://en.wikipedia.org/wiki/Cognitive_bias

https://skeptics.stackexchange.com/questions/74/any-scientific-basis-for-neuro-linguistic-programming

http://www.communicationcache.com/uploads/1/0/8/8/10887248/gender_and_social_influence.pdf

https://gap.hks.harvard.edu/how-genderrole-salience-influences-attitude-strength-and-persuasive-message-processing

https://business.columbia.edu/sites/default/files-efs/citation_file_upload/NLP_paper.pdf

https://pmc.ncbi.nlm.nih.gov/articles/PMC8455714/

https://maccelerator.la/en/blog/entrepreneurship/behavioral-psychology-behind-scarcity/

https://psychotricks.com/scarcity-principle/

Conclusion

https://threadlinebranding.com/blog/book-review/review-influence-the-psychology-of-persuasion-by-robert-b-cialdini-phd/

https://salvadorbriggman.com/review-of-influence-the-psychology-of-persuasion/

https://maccelerator.la/en/blog/entrepreneurship/behavioral-psychology-behind-scarcity/

https://psychotricks.com/scarcity-principle/

https://fiveable.me/persuasion-theory/unit-12/persuasion-gender-differences/study-guide/LXts1mdLnZ14z04j

http://www.communicationcache.com/uploads/1/0/8/8/10887248/gender_and_social_influence.pdf

https://influencecompany.com/blog/how-to-be-succesfull-in-communication-between-men-and-women/

https://www.investopedia.com/temporal-discounting-7972594

https://pmc.ncbi.nlm.nih.gov/articles/PMC8378077/

https://skeptics.stackexchange.com/questions/74/any-scientific-basis-for-neuro-linguistic-programming

https://gap.hks.harvard.edu/how-genderrole-salience-influences-attitude-strength-and-persuasive-message-processing

Reflection Questions

https://pmc.ncbi.nlm.nih.gov/articles/PMC8378077/

https://salvadorbriggman.com/review-of-influence-the-psychology-of-persuasion/

https://threadlinebranding.com/blog/book-review/review-influence-the-psychology-of-persuasion-by-robert-b-cialdini-phd/

https://maccelerator.la/en/blog/entrepreneurship/behavioral-psychology-behind-scarcity/

https://psychotricks.com/scarcity-principle/

https://skeptics.stackexchange.com/questions/74/any-scientific-basis-for-neuro-linguistic-programming

http://www.communicationcache.com/uploads/1/0/8/8/10887248/gender_and_social_influence.pdf

https://business.columbia.edu/sites/default/files-efs/citation_file_upload/NLP_paper.pdf

Book 2

Introduction

https://pmc.ncbi.nlm.nih.gov/articles/PMC2763368/

https://www.ebsco.com/research-starters/health-and-medicine/nonverbal-communication-and-social-cognition

https://pmc.ncbi.nlm.nih.gov/articles/PMC8378077/

https://faculty.wharton.upenn.edu/wp-content/uploads/2018/12/Barsade_Coutifaris_Pillemer-Emotional-contagion-in-organizational-life.pdf)

https://pmc.ncbi.nlm.nih.gov/articles/PMC10656777/

https://www.mdpi.com/2076-328X/15/1/15 (

https://www.researchgate.net/publication/225596088_The_Social_Function_of_Humor_in_Interpersonal_Relationships)

https://pmc.ncbi.nlm.nih.gov/articles/PMC8455714/

Chapter 1 - resources

https://pmc.ncbi.nlm.nih.gov/articles/PMC2763368/

https://www.ebsco.com/research-starters/health-and-medicine/nonverbal-communication-and-social-cognition

https://pmc.ncbi.nlm.nih.gov/articles/PMC8378077/

https://en.wikipedia.org/wiki/Cognitive_bias

https://gap.hks.harvard.edu/how-genderrole-salience-influences-attitude-strength-and-persuasive-message-processing

Chapter 2 - resources

https://faculty.wharton.upenn.edu/wp-content/uploads/2018/12/Barsadc_Coutifaris_Pillemer-Emotional-contagion-in-organizational-life.pdf)

https://pmc.ncbi.nlm.nih.gov/articles/PMC10656777/

https://www.mdpi.com/2076-328X/15/1/15 (

https://www.researchgate.net/publication/225596088_The_Social_Function_of_Humor_in_Interpersonal_Relationships)

https://pmc.ncbi.nlm.nih.gov/articles/PMC8378077/

https://www.ebsco.com/research-starters/health-and-medicine/nonverbal-communication-and-social-cognition

Chapter 3 - resources

https://www.ebsco.com/research-starters/health-and-medicine/nonverbal-communication-and-social-cognition

https://pmc.ncbi.nlm.nih.gov/articles/PMC2763368/

https://pmc.ncbi.nlm.nih.gov/articles/PMC8378077/

https://pmc.ncbi.nlm.nih.gov/articles/PMC5348110/

https://pdxscholar.library.pdx.edu/cgi/viewcontent.cgi?article=1888&context=open_access_etds

Chapter 4 - resources

https://www.ebsco.com/research-starters/health-and-medicine/nonverbal-communication-and-social-cognition

https://pmc.ncbi.nlm.nih.gov/articles/PMC2763368/

https://pmc.ncbi.nlm.nih.gov/articles/PMC8378077/

https://en.wikipedia.org/wiki/Cognitive_bias

https://gap.hks.harvard.edu/how-genderrole-salience-influences-attitude-strength-and-persuasive-message-processing

Chapter 5- resources

https://www.mdpi.com/2076-328X/15/1/15 (

https://www.researchgate.net/publication/225596088_The_Social_Function_of_Humor_in_Interpersonal_Relationships) (

https://faculty.wharton.upenn.edu/wp-content/uploads/2018/12/Barsade_Coutifaris_Pillemer-Emotional-contagion-in-organizational-life.pdf)

https://pmc.ncbi.nlm.nih.gov/articles/PMC10656777/

https://pmc.ncbi.nlm.nih.gov/articles/PMC2763368/

http://www.communicationcache.com/uploads/1/0/8/8/10887248/gender_and_social_influence.pdf

Conclusion

https://www.ebsco.com/research-starters/health-and-medicine/nonverbal-communication-and-social-cognition

https://pmc.ncbi.nlm.nih.gov/articles/PMC2763368/

https://pmc.ncbi.nlm.nih.gov/articles/PMC8378077/ (

https://faculty.wharton.upenn.edu/wp-content/uploads/2018/12/Barsade_Coutifaris_Pillemer-Emotional-contagion-in-organizational-life.pdf)

https://pmc.ncbi.nlm.nih.gov/articles/PMC10656777/

https://www.mdpi.com/2076-328X/15/1/15

https://pmc.ncbi.nlm.nih.gov/articles/PMC5348110/

https://influencecompany.com/blog/how-to-be-succesfull-in-communication-between-men-and-women/

http://www.communicationcache.com/uploads/1/0/8/8/10887248/gender_and_social_influence.pdf

https://gap.hks.harvard.edu/how-genderrole-salience-influences-attitude-strength-and-persuasive-message-processing

Reflection Questions

https://faculty.wharton.upenn.edu/wp-content/uploads/2018/12/Barsade_Coutifaris_Pillemer-Emotional-contagion-in-organizational-life.pdf)

https://pmc.ncbi.nlm.nih.gov/articles/PMC10656777/

https://www.ebsco.com/research-starters/health-and-medicine/nonverbal-communication-and-social-cognition

https://pmc.ncbi.nlm.nih.gov/articles/PMC5348110/

https://www.mdpi.com/2076-328X/15/1/15

https://pmc.ncbi.nlm.nih.gov/articles/PMC2763368/

Book 3

Introduction

https://en.wikipedia.org/wiki/Cognitive_bias

https://business.columbia.edu/sites/default/files-efs/citation_file_upload/NLP_paper.pdf

https://en.wikipedia.org/wiki/Neuro-linguistic_programming

https://skeptics.stackexchange.com/questions/74/any-scientific-basis-for-neuro-linguistic-programming

https://arxiv.org/abs/2308.00107

https://pmc.ncbi.nlm.nih.gov/articles/PMC8455714/

https://influencecompany.com/blog/how-to-be_succesfull-in-communication-between-men-and-women/

https://fiveable.me/persuasion-theory/unit-12/persuasion-gender-differences/study-guide/LXts1mdLnZ14z04j

Chapter 1 - resources

https://en.wikipedia.org/wiki/Cognitive_bias

https://skeptics.stackexchange.com/questions/74/any-scientific-basis-for-neuro-linguistic-programming

https://psychotricks.com/scarcity-principle/

https://salvadorbriggman.com/review-of-influence-the-psychology_of_persuasion/

https://gap.hks.harvard.edu/how-genderrole-salience-influences-attitude-strength-and-persuasive-message-processing

Chapter 2 - resources

https://business.columbia.edu/sites/default/files-efs/citation_file_upload/NLP_paper.pdf

https://pmc.ncbi.nlm.nih.gov/articles/PMC8455714/

https://influencecompany.com/blog/how-to-be_succesfull-in-communication-between-men-and-women/

https://www.mdpi.com/2076-328X/15/1/15 (

https://www.researchgate.net/publication/225596088_The_Social_Function_of_Humor_in_Interpersonal_Relationships)

Chapter 3- resources

https://en.wikipedia.org/wiki/Cognitive_bias

https://skeptics.stackexchange.com/questions/74/any-scientific-basis-for-neuro-linguistic-programming

https://psychotricks.com/scarcity-principle/

https://maccelerator.la/en/blog/entrepreneurship/behavioral-psychology-behind-scarcity/

https://arxiv.org/abs/2308.00107

https://business.columbia.edu/sites/default/files-efs/citation_file_upload/NLP_paper.pdf

https://pmc.ncbi.nlm.nih.gov/articles/PMC8455714/

http://www.communicationcache.com/uploads/1/0/8/8/10887248/gender_and_social_influence.pdf

Chapter 4 - resources

https://business.columbia.edu/sites/default/files-efs/citation_file_upload/NLP_paper.pdf

https://pmc.ncbi.nlm.nih.gov/articles/PMC8455714/

https://en.wikipedia.org/wiki/Cognitive_bias

https://www.investopedia.com/temporal-discounting-7972594

https://www.profit.co/blog/behavioral-economics/time-discounting-employee-rewards/

https://www.mdpi.com/2076-328X/15/1/15

https://www.researchgate.net/publication/225596088_The_Social_Function_of_Humor_in_Interpersonal_Relationships

https://pdxscholar.library.pdx.edu/cgi/viewcontent.cgi?article=1888&context=open_access_etds

https://psychotricks.com/scarcity-principle/

https://pmc.ncbi.nlm.nih.gov/articles/PMC8378077/

https://www.ebsco.com/research-starters/health-and-medicine/nonverbal-communication-and-social-cognition

Chapter 5- resources

https://fiveable.me/persuasion-theory/unit-12/persuasion-gender-differences/study-guide/LXts1mdLnZ14z04j

https://influencecompany.com/blog/how-to-be_succesfull-in-communication-between-men-and-women/

https://gap.hks.harvard.edu/how-genderrole-salience-influences-attitude-strength-and-persuasive-message-processing

http://www.communicationcache.com/uploads/1/0/8/8/10887248/gender_and_social_influence.pdf

https://pmc.ncbi.nlm.nih.gov/articles/PMC8455714/

https://skeptics.stackexchange.com/questions/74/any-scientific-basis-for-neuro-linguistic-programming

Conclusion

https://maccelerator.la/en/blog/entrepreneurship/behavioral-psychology-behind-scarcity/

https://salvadorbriggman.com/review-of-influence-the-psychology_of_persuasion/

https://en.wikipedia.org/wiki/Cognitive_bias

https://business.columbia.edu/sites/default/files-efs/citation_file_upload/NLP_paper.pdf

https://influencecompany.com/blog/how-to-be_succesfull-in-communication-between-men-and-women/

https://arxiv.org/abs/2308.00107

https://pmc.ncbi.nlm.nih.gov/articles/PMC8455714/

https://fiveable.me/persuasion-theory/unit-12/persuasion-gender-differences/study-guide/LXts1mdLnZ14z04j

https://gap.hks.harvard.edu/how-genderrole-salience-influences-attitude-strength-and-persuasive-message-processing

https://faculty.wharton.upenn.edu/wp-content/uploads/2018/12/Barsade_Coutifaris_Pillemer-Emotional-contagion-in-organizational-life.pdf

https://pmc.ncbi.nlm.nih.gov/articles/PMC10656777/

Reflection Questions

https://psychotricks.com/scarcity-principle/

https://salvadorbriggman.com/review-of-influence-the-psychology_of_persuasion/

https://en.wikipedia.org/wiki/Cognitive_bias

https://business.columbia.edu/sites/default/files-efs/citation_file_upload/NLP_paper.pdf

https://influencecompany.com/blog/how-to-be_succesfull-in-communication-between-men-and-women/

https://gap.hks.harvard.edu/how-genderrole-salience-influences-attitude-strength-and-persuasive-message-processing

https://fiveable.me/persuasion-theory/unit-12/persuasion-gender-differences/study-guide/LXts1mdLnZ14z04j

https://pmc.ncbi.nlm.nih.gov/articles/PMC8455714/

https://skeptics.stackexchange.com/questions/74/any-scientific-basis-for-neuro-linguistic-programming

https://pmc.ncbi.nlm.nih.gov/articles/PMC2763368/

Book 4

Introduction

https://pmc.ncbi.nlm.nih.gov/articles/PMC5348110/

https://arxiv.org/abs/2308.00107

https://pdxscholar.library.pdx.edu/cgi/viewcontent.cgi?article=1888&context=open_access_etds

https://www.ebsco.com/research-starters/health-and-medicine/nonverbal-communication-and-social-cognition

https://pmc.ncbi.nlm.nih.gov/articles/PMC10656777/

https://salvadorbriggman.com/review-of-influence-the-psychology_of_persuasion/

https://www.mdpi.com/2076-328X/15/1/15 (

https://www.researchgate.net/publication/225596088_The_Social_Function_of_Humor_in_Interpersonal_Relationships)

https://pmc.ncbi.nlm.nih.gov/articles/PMC8378077/

Chapter 1 - resources

https://pmc.ncbi.nlm.nih.gov/articles/PMC5348110/

https://arxiv.org/abs/2308.00107

https://pmc.ncbi.nlm.nih.gov/articles/PMC10656777/

https://pdxscholar.library.pdx.edu/cgi/viewcontent.cgi?article=1888&context=open_access_etds

https://salvadorbriggman.com/review-of-influence-the-psychology_of_persuasion/

https://threadlinebranding.com/blog/book-review/review-influence-the-psychology_of_persuasion-by-robert-b-cialdini-phd/

Chapter 2 - resources

https://salvadorbriggman.com/review-of-influence-the-psychology_of_persuasion/

https://www.mdpi.com/2076-328X/15/1/15 (

https://www.researchgate.net/publication/225596088_The_Social_Function_of_Humor_in_Interpersonal_Relationships)

https://pdxscholar.library.pdx.edu/cgi/viewcontent.cgi?article=1888&context=open_access_etds

https://pmc.ncbi.nlm.nih.gov/articles/PMC8455714/

https://pmc.ncbi.nlm.nih.gov/articles/PMC5348110/

Chapter 3 - resources

https://pmc.ncbi.nlm.nih.gov/articles/PMC5348110/

https://pdxscholar.library.pdx.edu/cgi/viewcontent.cgi?article=1888&context=open_access_etds

https://pmc.ncbi.nlm.nih.gov/articles/PMC8378077/

https://pmc.ncbi.nlm.nih.gov/articles/PMC2763368/

https://maccelerator.la/en/blog/entrepreneurship/behavioral-psychology-behind-scarcity/

Chapter 4 - resources

https://arxiv.org/abs/2308.00107

https://pmc.ncbi.nlm.nih.gov/articles/PMC10656777/

https://pdxscholar.library.pdx.edu/cgi/viewcontent.cgi?article=1888&context=open_access_etds

https://pmc.ncbi.nlm.nih.gov/articles/PMC8455714/

https://psychotricks.com/scarcity-principle/

https://www.investopedia.com/temporal-discounting-7972594

https://www.mdpi.com/2076-328X/15/1/15

https://salvadorbriggman.com/review-of-influence-the-psychology_of_persuasion/

https://en.wikipedia.org/wiki/Cognitive_bias

https://pmc.ncbi.nlm.nih.gov/articles/PMC5348110/

Chapter 5 - resources

https://www.mdpi.com/2076-328X/15/1/15 (

https://www.researchgate.net/publication/225596088_The_Social_Function_of_Humor_in_Interpersonal_Relationships)

https://pdxscholar.library.pdx.edu/cgi/viewcontent.cgi?article=1888&context=open_access_etds

https://salvadorbriggman.com/review-of-influence-the-psychology_of_persuasion/ (

https://faculty.wharton.upenn.edu/wp-content/uploads/2018/12/Barsade_Coutifaris_Pillemer-Emotional-contagion-in-organizational-life.pdf)

https://pmc.ncbi.nlm.nih.gov/articles/PMC8378077/

Conclusion

https://pmc.ncbi.nlm.nih.gov/articles/PMC5348110/

https://arxiv.org/abs/2308.00107

https://salvadorbriggman.com/review-of-influence-the-psychology_of_persuasion/

https://www.mdpi.com/2076-328X/15/1/15 (

https://www.researchgate.net/publication/225596088_The_Social_Function_of_Humor_in_Interpersonal_Relationships)

https://www.ebsco.com/research-starters/health-and-medicine/nonverbal-communication-and-social-cognition

https://pmc.ncbi.nlm.nih.gov/articles/PMC8378077/

https://influencecompany.com/blog/how-to-be-succesfull-in-communication-between-men-and-women/

http://www.communicationcache.com/uploads/1/0/8/8/10887248/gender_and_social_influence.pdf

Reflection Questions

https://pmc.ncbi.nlm.nih.gov/articles/PMC5348110/

https://arxiv.org/abs/2308.00107

https://salvadorbriggman.com/review-of-influence-the-psychology_of_persuasion/

https://www.mdpi.com/2076-328X/15/1/15 (

https://www.researchgate.net/publication/225596088_The_Social_Function_of_Humor_in_Interpersonal_Relationships)

https://pmc.ncbi.nlm.nih.gov/articles/PMC8378077/

https://influencecompany.com/blog/how-to-be-succesfull-in-communication-between-men-and-women/

https://fiveable.me/persuasion-theory/unit-12/persuasion-gender-differences/study-guide/LXts1mdLnZ14z04j

Book 5

Introduction

https://www.investopedia.com/temporal-discounting-7972594

https://www.profit.co/blog/behavioral-economics/time-discounting-employee-rewards/

https://psychotricks.com/scarcity-principle/

https://maccelerator.la/en/blog/entrepreneurship/behavioral-psychology-behind-scarcity/

https://salvadorbriggman.com/review-of-influence-the-psychology_of_persuasion/

Chapter 1 - resources

https://www.investopedia.com/temporal-discounting-7972594

https://www.profit.co/blog/behavioral-economics/time-discounting-employee-rewards/

https://salvadorbriggman.com/review-of-influence-the-psychology_of_persuasion/

Chapter 2 - resources

https://psychotricks.com/scarcity-principle/

https://maccelerator.la/en/blog/entrepreneurship/behavioral-psychology-behind-scarcity/

https://salvadorbriggman.com/review-of-influence-the-psychology_of_persuasion/

Chapter 3 - resources

https://www.investopedia.com/temporal-discounting-7972594

https://www.profit.co/blog/behavioral-economics/time-discounting-employee-rewards/

Chapter 4- resources

https://www.investopedia.com/temporal-discounting-7972594

https://www.profit.co/blog/behavioral-economics/time-discounting-employee-rewards/

Chapter 5 - resources

https://psychotricks.com/scarcity-principle/

https://maccelerator.la/en/blog/entrepreneurship/behavioral-psychology-behind-scarcity/

Conclusion

https://www.investopedia.com/temporal-discounting-7972594

https://psychotricks.com/scarcity-principle/

https://maccelerator.la/en/blog/entrepreneurship/behavioral-psychology-behind-scarcity/

https://salvadorbriggman.com/review-of-influence-the-psychology_of_persuasion/

Reflection Questions

https://www.investopedia.com/temporal-discounting-7972594

https://psychotricks.com/scarcity-principle/

https://maccelerator.la/en/blog/entrepreneurship/behavioral-psychology-behind-scarcity/

Overall Conclusion and Print and Keep Checklist - Resources

https://en.wikipedia.org/wiki/Cognitive_bias

https://salvadorbriggman.com/review-of-influence-the-psychology_of_persuasion/

https://pmc.ncbi.nlm.nih.gov/articles/PMC2763368/

https://pmc.ncbi.nlm.nih.gov/articles/PMC8378077/ (

https://faculty.wharton.upenn.edu/wp-content/uploads/2018/12/Barsade_Coutifaris_Pillemer-Emotional-contagion-in-organizational-life.pdf)

https://pmc.ncbi.nlm.nih.gov/articles/PMC10656777/

https://www.ebsco.com/research-starters/health-and-medicine/nonverbal-communication-and-social-cognition

https://www.mdpi.com/2076-328X/15/1/15 (

https://www.researchgate.net/publication/225596088_The_Social_Function_of_Humor_in_Interpersonal_Relationships)

https://skeptics.stackexchange.com/questions/74/any-scientific-basis-for-neuro-linguistic-programming

https://business.columbia.edu/sites/default/files-efs/citation_file_upload/NLP_paper.pdf

https://pmc.ncbi.nlm.nih.gov/articles/PMC8455714/

https://fiveable.me/persuasion-theory/unit-12/persuasion-gender-differences/study-guide/LXts1mdLnZ14z04j

http://www.communicationcache.com/uploads/1/0/8/8/10887248/gender_and_social_influence.pdf

https://influencecompany.com/blog/how-to-be-succesfull-in-communication-between-men-and-women/

https://pmc.ncbi.nlm.nih.gov/articles/PMC5348110/

https://www.investopedia.com/temporal-discounting-7972594

https://www.profit.co/blog/behavioral-economics/time-discounting-employee-rewards/

https://psychotricks.com/scarcity-principle/

https://maccelerator.la/en/blog/entrepreneurship/behavioral-psychology-behind-scarcity/

https://gap.hks.harvard.edu/how-genderrole-salience-influences-attitude-strength-and-persuasive-message-processing